**VARIETIES
OF
PERCEPTUAL
LEARNING**

**McGraw-Hill Series
in Psychology**

Consulting Editors
Norman Garmezy
Harry F. Harlow
Lyle V. Jones
Harold W. Stevenson

VARIETIES
OF
PERCEPTUAL
LEARNING

William Epstein
Professor of Psychology
University of Kansas

Mc Graw-Hill Book Company
New York   St. Louis
San Francisco   Toronto
London   Sydney

**VARIETIES
OF
PERCEPTUAL
LEARNING**

Preface

Among my earliest readings in the psychology of perception were Koffka's discussion of "why the world appears as it does," J. J. Gibson's *Perception of the Visual World*, and several chapters in a collection called *Human Behavior from the Transactional Point of View*. These efforts were undertaken while I was a first-year graduate student in a course in perception given by Hans Wallach. I completed the course, enthusiastic about the study of perception but considerably puzzled by the theoretical divergences which prevailed. Since then I have been at work to reduce the dissonance which resulted from exposure to such disparate but highly persuasive arguments. This book on perceptual learning stems from this larger effort.

The best indication I can give the reader concerning the expectations he may reasonably entertain about this book is to state my original objectives. There were three goals I had hoped to attain: (1) a critical review of the diverse literature pertaining to the question of perceptual learning, (2) a delineation of important unresolved questions related to perceptual learning, (3) a determination of the possibilities for deriving empirically based descriptive generalizations about perceptual learning. I believe that the book has succeeded in the first two objectives. The reader may expect to be informed about the status of the field, or if he is already well versed, he may expect to find an organized exposition of material which helps him to focus on questions of special interest. The book should be useful to readers at varying levels of sophistication, although probably for different purposes. The student who has had only an introductory course in perception will find that the book allows him to develop a more detailed understanding of several important problems of perception. The mature student of perception should find the book useful as a source of research leads, as well as a guide to the literature.

I can tender no promissory notes regarding the third objective. As the book progressed, I grew increasingly discouraged about the possibility of deriving descriptive generalizations which would cut across the variety of phenomena and would stay close to the experimental data. Therefore, the concluding chapter, which originally was intended to serve an integrative function, is chiefly a general summary, rather than a synthesis of the preceding chapters.

Instructors who may wish to assign portions of the book to students who do not have the desired prior course work should consider what assistance the student may derive from the Glossary, which follows the last chapter.

Permission has been granted by many publishers to reproduce illustrations or passages, and the author gratefully acknowledges these permissions. In each case the original source has been cited with the material reproduced.

William Epstein

CONTENTS

Chapter one
Varieties of perceptual
learning

The term "perceptual learning" refers to the broad range of modifications of perception which have been attributed to learning. These diverse effects have in common an independence from experimenter-produced variations of optical stimulation. They are changes in perception which occur in response to unchanging optical stimulation. This statement must be qualified to exclude certain kinds of perceptual changes which have been observed: Alterations of perception which are recognized as products of altered physico-chemical states in the eye or the central projection area are not considered instances of perceptual learning. On these grounds the fluctuating changes noted when retinal images are stabilized (Pritchard, 1961), the figural aftereffects of constant inspection (e.g., Köhler & Wallach, 1944), and the classic adaptation phenomena of color vision (Woodworth & Schlosberg, 1954, Ch. 13) may be excluded. These changes are more appropriately attributed to the satiation or depletion of isolable peripheral or central areas of the visual system, rather than to more general processes of learning. On the other hand, the complex adaptation to artificially produced transformations of the total optic array (I. Kohler, 1951; I. Kohler, 1962) is a striking case of perceptual learning.

Also excluded are the cases in which, in the absence of intentional experimental intervention, there occurs a continuous perceptual alternation between two or more alternative percepts. This is the case with the reversible-perspective figures, e.g., Necker's cube and Schroeder's staircase, and the ambiguous figure-ground patterns, e.g., Rubin's face-vase composite, which yield regular alternations despite the unchanging conditions of stimulation. These perceptual changes

1

are frequently attributed to the influence of certain presumably unlearned principles of organization such as *Prägnanz* or the minimum principle (Hochberg, 1964). Another well-known example of alternation is binocular rivalry under conditions of stereoscopic perception. The term "perceptual learning" will be applied mainly to cases where perception undergoes a progressive sequence of change culminating in stability or to instances of discrete stable change. However, the term will also be used for instances in which the rate or probability of change is influenced by special types of prior training (e.g., Adams, 1954; Solley & Santos, 1958).

This monograph presents an evaluation of the current status of research on perceptual learning. The ultimate objective is to contribute to an integration of the diverse approaches to the question.

Preliminary classification of studies of perceptual learning

At the outset we may distinguish several types of experiments which have been conducted to explore perceptual learning. The experiments differ considerably in the precision with which the independent variables were controlled and also in the degree of response restriction which was imposed.

The effects of long-established, extraexperimental past experience   One important theoretical formulation maintains that perception is governed by the assumptive context of the current visual stimulation. As a result of experience, the perceiver develops assumptions concerning the relationship between stimulation and the external world, or source of stimulation. These learned assumptions determine the perceiver's response to optical stimulation. Thus, different percepts may be correlated with the same optical stimulation, depending on the assumptive context in which it is placed. Similarly, perceptual alternatives, which may be acceptable responses on purely optical analyses, nonetheless may be rare, presumably because the preferred response is supported by the assumptive context.

Many experiments have been conducted to examine this formulation. These experiments are characterized by remote control of the independent variable. On the basis of his knowledge about the everyday experience of the average subject (S), the investigator infers that a particular independent variable is operative in the experimental situation, although the variable has not been directly introduced. For example, the experimenter may present a disk of light on two occasions, labeling the disk first "ping-pong ball" and then "bowling ball." Presumably, S's real-life commerce with these objects will lead to variations in the physical size which S attributes to the disk of light. The experimenter (E) may then examine the effects on perceived distance of the presumed variations of assumed physical size.

The effects of controlled past experience, experimental training or practice   Experiments in this category are preferable to the studies in the first category in at least one respect: the independent variables are directly controlled by E, thereby permitting more precise assessment of the effects. Five types of training have been studied:

1

Certain considerations of Hebb's theory (1949) have led to a series of experiments which have used an "enrichment" technique. The general objective of these studies has been to determine whether enrichment of the exposure history of a S will have positive transfer effects on subsequent tests of discrimination. Most of the published work has been concerned with visual form discrimination following enrichment and nonenrichment exposure treatment. The experimental (enrichment) group receives extended and continuous, nondifferentially reinforced exposures of the to-be-discriminated forms. The control group does not see the forms prior to the test. The objective of the experiment is to determine whether the prior exposure of the visual forms has a facilitating effect on visual-discrimination learning.

2

In the most straightforward procedure the training is a series of practice trials with a task related to the criterial task. In one experiment, S was required to make repeated judgments of size and distance under variable conditions of physical size and distance. The general question under investigation was whether perception can be made more accurate or reliable by practice. Some of the parameters which have been studied are the effects of knowledge of performance, amount of practice, and sequence of conditions.

3

A third type of training, inspired by a stimulus-response (S-R) analysis of perception, has been used in studies which have sought to demonstrate that the discriminability of stimuli may be enhanced by training. The training consists of learning to associate verbal or motor responses with the visual forms later to be discriminated. According to the hypothesis of acquired distinctiveness such training should affect the perceptual distinctiveness of the forms.

4

The fourth type of training reflects the view that perceptual learning, in common with other learning, is motivated. According to this view perceptual learning is regulated, at least in part, by the affective consequences associated with the percepts in question. The experimental paradigm employed to exhibit this relationship involves the experimental association of specific affective events, reward and punishment, with various percepts. The following is an illustration:

Profile A of the Schafer-Murphy ambiguous figure is presented alone, always followed by shock. Profile B is presented alone, followed by a neutral event. At the conclusion of this training period the ambiguous composite is exposed tachistoscopically. The composite, which contains both A and B, is usually seen either as A or B. "Both" responses are relatively infrequent. The responses to the composite are examined for evidence of the influence of prior training. Will the experimentally established affective history of each alternative influence the likelihood that the alternative will be perceived as figure?

5

The last type of training is rarely employed and could in fact be classified separately. The S is instructed to execute specified purposeful, goal-oriented acts. The objective of the experiment is to determine whether these acts lead to a modification of perception. This technique has been used in situations where S's initial percepts are nonveridical. The activity is expected to modify perception in the direction of greater correspondence with the objective situation. An example may be selected from the studies of the distorted room. Under the usual conditions of observation, S perceives a normal rectangular room instead of the distorted projective equivalent. What happens to the perceived shape of the room if S executes certain acts which provide information concerning its objective shape? Will the illusory appearance of normalcy prevail, or will the room appear distorted in agreement with its objective character? This specific example will be especially interesting to the reader who has passively viewed a distorted room after learning the details of its construction. This knowledge in no way diminishes its appearance of normal rectangularity.

Investigations of perceptual conflict   Many perceptual properties are overdetermined. More information is available than is necessary for specifying the perceptual property. The perception of depth is a well-recognized example. This fact has been used to study perceptual learning. Experimental situations are designed which place different depth-cue systems in conflict. The conflicting cues provide dissonant information about the distal source. The objective is to determine whether the conflict will result in an alteration of the normal relationship between the cue system and perception. In one study, the exaggerated retinal disparity produced when a form is viewed in a telestereoscope was brought into conflict with the depth information provided by rotation of the form (kinetic depth effect). The result was a rapid modification of the customary relation between disparity and perceived depth. A subsequent transfer task, e.g., S's viewing the rotating form directly, also revealed the learned modification of the disparity-depth relationship (Wallach, Moore, & Davidson, 1963).

Studies of adaptation to optically produced transformations of the entire stimulus array   These adaptation studies may be distinguished from the classic investigations (e.g., Bartlett, 1965) on several grounds. The classic studies impose a condition of durative, nonchanging exposure to an isolated lower-order stimulus, e.g., a monochromatic light. The studies which will be reviewed have imposed a constant transformation on the optical stimulation, but they have not sought to produce conditions of localized invariant stimulation. In addition to this difference, many of the studies differ from the classic investigations in three other ways: Durations of exposure have been studied which have greatly exceeded the typical exposure period of the classic experiments. The stimulus fields have been more complex. In contrast to the older studies, the studies which will be examined have usually exposed S to transformations of the total visual field. Finally, unlike the earlier studies, the Ss are frequently permitted to move about freely during the exposure period; in some cases, S continues his normal routine.

The following is a simplified description of one experimental procedure (I. Kohler, 1951). The S is fitted with goggles containing prisms or special lenses which produce known optical distortions. Perceptual tests are conducted at the beginning of this period and at successive intervals.

Finally the goggles are removed, and perceptual tests are continued. The first series of tests charts the course of adaptation to the optically produced distortions. The second series of tests examines the nature and strength of the after-effects of the previous treatment. These experiments are considered by their authors to be important in two ways: they reveal fundamental principles of perceptual learning; secondly, the process of adaptation is thought to be analogous to the original development of perception.

Developmental studies   Two types can be included under this heading: First there are the investigations of perception as a function of age. Illustrative of this class of study are investigations of the perceptual illusions and of the perceptual constancies in various age groups. Presumably changes in susceptibility to illusions or changes in the degree of constancy which is exhibited are forms of learning. The second type of study is rare despite its great potential contribution to our understanding of the underlying learning processes. In these studies, perceptually naïve subjects are exposed to controlled variations of stimulation. The objective is to determine whether S's response to a cue system will be conditioned by his previous history of stimulation. The following is an example: One group of chicks is reared from birth with all illumination coming from below. A second group is reared with all illumination coming from above. Will the two groups respond differently when confronted with objects exposed under various conditions of illumination (distribution of light and shade)?

Some general considerations
regarding perceptual learning

In succeeding chapters much of the research alluded to above will be described and evaluated. In the present section, a number of general matters will be discussed which bear importantly on research and theory in this area.

What is perception?

The term "perception" has a long history in philosophy (Hamlyn, 1961) and psychology (Boring, 1942). And yet there remains disagreement concerning the term's proper application (Ittelson, 1962; Postman, 1963). This disagreement has relevance in the present context, because criticism of experiments on perceptual learning frequently takes the form of skepticism regarding the identity of the dependent variable under investigation. In one sense this question may seem pointless. The dependent variable is S's overt discriminatory response. This is true for all investigators, regardless of their theoretical orientation. Still the question is meaningful. This is the case because for most students of perception the observable discriminatory response is of interest only as it serves as a basis for inferences about correlated perceptual processes. Therefore, the question arises concerning the validity of a particular response: do variations of the overt response reflect variables of the perceptual system, or are the variations attributable to variables of the response system, e.g., response availability, judgmental bias?

This skeptical attitude has been forcefully expressed by several writers (Allport, 1955; Hochberg, 1956; Prentice, 1956; Wallach, 1949; Zuckerman & Rock, 1957). As a resolution of the problem of identification, these critics have usually provided a list of criterial attributes, or distinctive properties of perception, which distinguish perceptual processes from related nonperceptual processes. This approach will be discussed in the context of an evaluation of two commonly proposed criteria: immediacy and stimulus-dependence.

Immediacy   It has been suggested often that a criterial attribute of the perceptual event is immediacy. "We shall use the term perception only for the immediate form of behavior. . . . Perception . . . immediately follows or accompanies energistic impingements upon the sense organs. . . . Perception . . . is to be distinguished in all cases from behavior that has less close temporal connections with external events" (Bartley, 1958, p. 22).

There are a number of general difficulties in applying this criterion. However, before these difficulties are considered, brief mention will be made of an ambiguity of application which is peculiar to the phenomenological viewpoint with which the criterion of immediacy is frequently associated. No special difficulties arise if immediacy refers to the overt *response* which is mediated by the perceptual experience.

However, from the phenomenological viewpoint, it is the private *experience* and not the overt response to which the term "perception" properly applies. Therefore, it follows that all criteria for specifying perception, including immediacy, must refer to unobservable experience. If this is granted, then it is difficult to know how the experimenter can determine the immediacy of the event, since the latency of the perceptual experience and the latency of the indicator-response may not be coordinate.

The application of the criterion of immediacy is complicated further when it is considered in the context of experimental methodology. Consider a typical experiment which seeks to determine the point of subjective size equality by the method of adjustment (e.g., Rock & Ebenholtz, 1959). A standard and a variable are presented, separated by an angle of 180°. The subject is asked to adjust the size of the variable to the same size as the standard. The typical subject will look back and forth between the standard and variable several times before he decides on a particular setting of the variable. Does this setting reflect pure perception, perception plus judgment, or perhaps judgmental processes only? A reading of the literature reveals that most investigators, including those who are oriented phenomenologically, would choose between the first two alternatives. However, the criterion of immediacy has not been met on at least two counts: First, we noted that S's terminal setting is actually an integration of several perceptions spread over time. Therefore, the performance contains a memorial component. Secondly, it could be argued that the criterion would not be satisfied even if a single momentary glance had been sufficient for the setting. A reservation would remain because the 180° lateral separation of the standard and the variable made it impossible for the subject to view the standard and variable simultaneously.

The conditions of our hypothetical experiment are typical. There are very few perceptual tasks which can be executed without a series of comparison responses. Even if S is presented with a pair of *identical* objects, he will not react immediately. Most Ss enter the laboratory with a set for accuracy, which leads them to respond carefully. The best that E can do is to make his instructions unambiguous and to include a postexperimental interview which will give him information about S's procedure in making his match.

The second aspect of the problem can be resolved simply by guaranteeing that the standard and variable are viewed simultaneously. In fact, F. H. Allport (1955) seems to have elevated this recommendation to the status of a methodological canon. His view would seem to be that simultaneous observation of standard and variable is a necessary condition for experimentation on perceptual phenomena. This is a useful precautionary rule. Many interpretative disputes doubtless would be eliminated by its observance. However, application of this methodological rule sometimes is precluded by the very nature of the phenomenon under investigation. These are the cases when the standard and variable will interact to contaminate the effect. A good example of this can be seen in Wallach's experiments (1948) on achromatic color and brightness constancy.

Finally, the criterion of immediacy needs to be accommodated to the empirical situation. Even so primitive a perceptual attribute as contour requires time for development. The experiments on visual masking (Alpern, 1952; Kolers & Rosner, 1960; Werner, 1935) show that contour formation and the perception of surface are inhibited when the required developmental period is disrupted. Other studies (Ittelson, 1960) suggest that a similar conclusion is justified for more complex perceptual events as well.[1]

Dependence on stimulation ". . . one set of implicit criteria of the perceptual nature of [the] response . . . [is] that the *presence of the stimulus, and its excitation of neural processes, are necessary (but perhaps not sufficient) for at least certain aspects of that response*" (Hochberg, 1956, p. 403). The experimenter should be able to account for the

---

[1] We might note, in passing, another general difficulty with the distinctive-properties approach: It is not unusual to discover that another writer considers a feature, diametrically opposed, to be the distinctive attribute. Thus, Brown (1961), in his discussion of the concept "perception," proposes that appeals to perception are superfluous in studies ". . . in which subjects respond *immediately* and *overtly* to the presentation of stimulus objects" (p. 268). Brown continues to assert that the concept may be useful when the ". . . overt identifying responses do not occur until some time after a stimulus has been withdrawn" (p. 324). Such lack of consensus guarantees that the distinctive-properties approach will fail to resolve the ambiguities surrounding the term "perception."

systematic variance of the subject's response (experience?) on the basis of his knowledge of the stimulus. Thus, Hochberg argues, the subject's response to a Rorschach inkblot which is presented under the usual conditions of administration is not perceptual. Only a small portion of the response variance could be accounted for by an exclusive consideration of the physical properties of the blot, i.e., shape, size, color.

Although the Rorschach example is clear, the criterion of stimulus-dependence becomes vague as it is inspected more closely. The vagueness is due to the ambiguous use of the term "stimulus." On the one hand, if the term is neutral, meaning only antecedent conditions, then the statement is necessarily true but not very useful. Since all responses, judgmental, interpretative, as well as perceptual, depend on antecedent conditions, this dependence could not be used to distinguish between perceptual and other systems. On the other hand, if by the term "stimulus" is meant optical stimulation, then the criterion represents disguised theoretical pleading. To assert that the only responses which may be called "perceptual" are those which are in perfect psychophysical correspondence with optical stimulation is to legislate arbitrarily what has been an empirical issue in the psychology of perception. The criterion also implies an exhaustive search for stimulus-response correlations as a prerequisite for the correct application of the term "perception." Since this search is yet to be concluded for any psychological phenomena, we are enjoined from using the term.

The foregoing analyses could be extended to include other criteria, e.g., external reference, which have been proposed. The general conclusion which emerges is that the distinctive-properties approach is not very useful. In the following paragraphs the concept of perception will be discussed with the main emphasis on the *procedures* which *E* has available for determining whether perceptual processes are implicated.

Perception is an intervening construct that refers to inferred processes that intervene between the measurable stimulus conditions and the measurable overt response. The status of the concept "perception" is the same as that of the concept "learning." Two points should be noted regarding this formulation:

1

The concept "perception" is not identical with the overt discriminatory responses, verbal or motor, which are used to infer
the properties of perception. This is also the case for the concept "learning." Thus, if under appropriately controlled conditions a S in a paired-associates learning experiment provides
the prescribed response, E infers that S has learned the association. The occurrence of the correct response is not the learning
but is only the manifestation of some inferred underlying modification. This intervening modification is what is denoted by the
term "learning." That learning needs to be distinguished from
correct responding is indicated by the opinion that a correct
guess is not considered to be evidence that the prescribed association has been learned. More generally, there is wide acceptance of the necessity for distinguishing between learning
and performance. An analogous distinction between perceiving
and responding is also necessary.

2

Procedures can be devised for distinguishing those variations of
the overt response which are attributable to perceptual processes from those response variations produced by nonperceptual determinants.

It follows from the foregoing assertions that valid questions may be raised about the interpretation of data. Does
the experimental design permit us to attribute the observed
changes to the perceptual system, or are other interpretations equally plausible? Three procedures are available for
resolving this question. They will be discussed in the order
of their importance.

Converging operations   "Converging operations may be
thought of as any set of two or more experimental operations
which allow the selection or elimination of alternative hypotheses or concepts which could explain an experimental
result. They are called converging operations because they
are not perfectly correlated and thus can converge on a
single concept" (Garner, Hake, & Eriksen, 1956, pp. 150–
151). The frequent argument concerning the nature of the
processes responsible for observed effects, i.e., whether
these processes are perceptual, may be viewed as a contest
between alternative hypotheses to account for the data. As
such, diacritical experiments could be conducted to assess
the probabilities which may confidently be assigned to each
hypothesis. The use of converging operations introduces this
test of alternative hypotheses as part of every experiment in

which alternatives may be reasonably entertained. As noted earlier, this is the case in many studies of perceptual learning.

The following two illustrations will demonstrate the use of converging operations. A recent study (Long, Reid, & Henneman, 1960a) has shown that the presentation of a set of alternative responses, one of which is the prescribed response, prior to a test of tachistoscopic recognition will facilitate identification of the test word. This observation may be interpreted in two ways: (1) Prior presentation of alternatives enhances the perceptual discriminability of the test words. (2) Prior presentation of alternatives does not affect perceptual discriminability; identification is facilitated, because the probability of emission of the prescribed response (response availability) has been enhanced.

These two alternative hypotheses may be examined by designing an experiment which incorporates a set of converging operations. (A similar experiment has actually been conducted by Long et al., 1960a.) The operations are manipulations of the temporal order of the presentation of alternatives and the test word. Under condition B, the alternatives are presented *before* the test exposure. Under condition A, the alternatives are presented *after* the test exposure but prior to the identification response. Under a control condition no alternatives are presented. Hypothesis 1 predicts an interaction between the set factor (alternatives present or absent) and the temporal factor. Hypothesis 2 predicts that the influence of the set factor will be independent of the temporal factor. The interaction effect allows E to decide between the two hypotheses. If the interaction is significant in such a way that the effect of set is significantly greater under condition B than under condition A, then hypothesis 1, implicating perceptual discriminability, is supported. If there is no difference between condition B and condition A, then hypothesis 2 is sufficient to account for the observed effects.[2]

[2] The experiments of Long et al. (1960a) showed that set can indeed augment perceptual discrimination but only under special conditions. When only two alternatives were presented and the stimulus patterns contained discriminable elements, the presentation of alternatives both before and after the test exposure produced more correct identifications than presentation of alternatives only after. The interested reader should also see the subsequent experiments in this series (Long et al., 1960b; Reid, Henneman, & Long, 1960).

The second illustration concerns the perception of size. An experiment is conducted to determine the effects of knowledge on the perceived size of objects at various distances from S. The results show greater invariance of perceived size (more constancy) for objects which are familiar and identifiable, e.g., a cigarette package, than for nonrepresentative equivalents, e.g., a blank rectangle. Can we conclude that knowledge or past experience affects the perceived size of objects? To answer this question conclusively it would be desirable to have included another condition of judgment. This condition, which has been studied originally by Bolles and Bailey (1956), requires S to make nonvisual estimates of the sizes of the objects, based only on verbal descriptions of the objects. Results obtained under this nonvisual condition which were comparable to those obtained under the visual condition would suggest that a perceptual interpretation of the visual estimates is not necessary. In fact, Bolles and Bailey (1956) did find that insofar as familiar objects are concerned, size constancy ". . . is just as high without any mediation from the visual system as it is with the visual system available" (p. 225).

Unique perceptual contingencies   In some instances, it is possible to determine the nature of the intervening processes by observing certain secondary responses the occurrence of which is generally believed to be contingent on the perceptual nature of the primary response.

The following are three illustrative uses of this procedure: In an experiment on the effect of memory on depth perception, Wallach, O'Connell, and Neisser (1953) showed that an appearance of internal depth was imparted to a static plane shadow form if the static exposure was preceded by an exposure of the same form undergoing continuous oscillation. The preliminary oscillation produced certain specifiable transformations of the shadow pattern which resulted in a perception of tridimensionality. Wallach et al. (1953) were concerned with determining whether the subsequently presented static form actually *looked* tridimensional or whether the tridimensional appearance of the rotating form merely encouraged S to *say* that the static shadow was tridimensional. To enable them to make this determination, Wallach et al. (1953) had their Ss continue to view the static form after the initial report was given. Continuous observation resulted in spontaneous perceptual reversals of perspective and appropriate changes in the perceived sizes of the parts. Wallach et al. (1953) concluded that memory had indeed affected perception, not solely response probability or judgment.

What is the justification for using the occurrence of reversals as evidence for the perceptual nature of the original response? The justification is twofold: First, the occurrence of spontaneous reversals is known to occur with other ambiguous plane perspective figures that are perceived in depth. Reversals have not been observed when S is merely informed of the possibility of their occurrence for a pattern that does not spontaneously elicit an initial depth perception. Second, the report of reversals includes specifications of change that could not have been directly transferred from the experience provided by the rotating exposure. These specifications are uniquely appropriate to the alternative tridimensional perceptual configurations that are correlated with the plane perspective pattern. The introduction of this "additional information" (Hochberg, 1956) by Ss who are not practiced in, or cognizant of, the details of the laws of perspective is unlikely unless these additional specifications are present in direct perception.

The second illustration concerns the perception of color. Suppose S is hypnotized and instructed that a white sheet of paper is red. If S reports that the white paper appears red, is he merely complying with the hypnotic suggestion, or is he actually seeing red? An experiment by Hibler (1940) suggests a procedure for answering the above question. Hibler investigated the afterimages which follow hypnotically hallucinated colors. If Ss spontaneously report appropriately colored afterimages after "fixating" on the suggested color, then we may infer that hypnotically hallucinated colors resemble actual colors. This is to say that the colors are perceived. On the other hand, failure to obtain appropriate negative afterimages suggests that the initially induced color report may reflect only compliance at the response level.[3]

[3] Hibler (1940) found that if the S is induced hypnotically to "see" one color as another, the afterimages reported in the trance may be the complement of either the induced or the actual color. From this and other observations, Hibler concluded that hypnotic induction does not produce any central or sensory change. The effects that are observed should be attributed to ". . . mere verbal agreement, and cooperation, with the experimenter."

The effectiveness of the procedure would be enhanced by including a condition of actual stimulation by the color which is hypnotically induced. We may also note the desirability of using Ss who are not aware of the afterimage phenomenon or who are ignorant of the specific relationship between the color of the inspection target and the color of the afterimage. For such Ss, a report of an appropriately colored afterimage would have the character of "additional information." An instructive discussion of the relationship between hypnotically hallucinated colors and their negative afterimages is provided by Barber (1964).

A final example will be presented regarding the effects of reinforcement on figure-ground perception. Suppose we wish to know whether rewarding figure-responses to the left side of an ambiguous composite actually produced the prescribed perceptual organization. Perhaps S has learned a response bias. This question could, of course, be settled by the procedure of converging operations. However, let us illustrate the use of the method of contingent responses for the same purpose. It is well known that the appearance of a figure-ground pattern is affected drastically by the figure-ground organization imposed upon it. Two series of unambiguous figures are prepared representing variations, along a dimension of similarity, of the two figural possibilities in the ambiguous composite. If the figural responses to the composite reflect perceptual organization, then stimulus generalization should occur for the series of "figure" variations, and not for the series which contains variations of the presumed "ground."

The subject's introspection   Hochberg suggests that identifying the underlying process, e.g., perceptual or judgmental, would be facilitated ". . . if subjects were asked whether their reports concerned objects 'really seen' as present, rather than inferred or imagined" (1956, p. 401). Prentice (1956) and other phenomenologically oriented writers (Zuckerman & Rock, 1957) make the same suggestion. An implicit premise of this proposal is that the experimenter and the subject speak the same language. This premise is questionable on several grounds (Bergmann & Spence, 1944). Let us recall that the structural analysis of experience attempted by Wundt and Titchener required subjects who were highly trained in introspection. Despite this precaution, the analyses were frequently questioned, and intersubject agreement often was not obtained.

The semantic difficulty mentioned above is important; however, assuming it can be resolved there remain other difficulties. Suppose the use of the term "perception" is restricted to situations in which the subject answers affirmatively to a question of the following sort: "Did you *really see* the smaller square as more distant than the larger one?" or "Did the four of spades *really look* purple?" If a subject set a comparison corresponding to the smaller square farther than a comparison corresponding to the larger square and then replied negatively to the inquiry, his original response would be termed "judgmental." Similarly for the subject who replied negatively after setting a variable color wheel to produce purple. Plainly there is something unsatisfactory about this claim. The comparison between the two sets of data, motor discriminatory responses and introspective reports, is certainly confounded by many uncontrolled variables. Furthermore, no rules are proposed for resolving the diverse discrepancies which may arise from these comparisons. The value of the inquiry could be enhanced by demanding more than a simple statement of affirmation or negation. The subject's report would be significant if it contained a specification of the distal source which would be unlikely in the absence of special information.

This is to argue that the results of an inquiry are equivocal unless the number of plausible alternative responses is high. Contrasting examples may help clarify this point. Suppose we wish to determine, by inquiry, whether a subject who made a red match upon presentation of a green standard actually perceived red. To our inquiry the subject responds, "No, I did not really see red. I saw green." Since "green" is only one of many color names the subject has available, its probability of emission in the absence of specific contemporary determinants is relatively low. Therefore, we presume that its occurrence in the inquiry is correlated with direct knowledge of the distal source, i.e., is mediated by perception, whereas the early datum—red—is the product of nonperceptual factors.

Contrast the above situation with the following case: A subject is shown the horizontal-vertical illusion (e.g., Finger & Spelt, 1947). In accordance with expectations, his adjust-

ment of a comparison device indicates that he has overestimated the length of the vertical line relative to the horizontal. Next, the subject is asked whether the vertical line really
looked longer than the horizontal line. To this he responds,
"No. The two lines looked equal." This set of events is
analogous to our hypothetical study of color perception. Yet
our proposal is that no conclusion can safely be drawn in the
case of the vertical-horizontal illusion. Any conclusion must
be qualified by the recognition that, even in the absence of
the illusory pattern, the theoretical probability of "looked
equal" as a response to our question is 0.33. Indeed, the
empirical probability may be higher on the premise that the
subject will tend to change from his previous response if he
construes the inquiry as a challenge. The high probability of
"spontaneous" emission of the "looked equal" response
prohibits us from attributing its occurrence to perceptual
mediation.

This concludes our discussion of the available approaches
for distinguishing between perceptual processes and related
nonperceptual processes. Although these procedures have
been discussed separately, more than one procedure may be
usefully incorporated in the design of an experiment. Unfortunately, the procedures have not been used with the
frequency that they warrant. As a consequence there will be
many instances when the interpretation of experimental data
can be debated. Whenever appropriate the possibilities for
modifying the experiment to include one of the procedural
controls will be indicated.

The generality of the
principles of learning

Unlike the case of the term "perception" there is little
controversy over the definition of the term "learning." The
term "learning" is used when there is evidence of a relatively
lasting change in performance resulting from prior experience. Changes which can be attributed exclusively to matura-
tion or to alterations of local physiological states are not
considered as examples of learning.

Although there is little disagreement about the proper
application of the term, there is considerable disagreement
concerning the nature and conditions of learning. Not all
aspects of this latter question are of direct relevance to the

subject of this book. For example, the controversy between the advocates of all-or-none and incremental conceptualizations of learning is not important at the present stage of analysis in the field of perceptual learning. On the other hand, the questions which arise concerning the motivational conditions of learning will sometimes enter prominently into discussions of perceptual learning.

Another question, of a more general character, will also receive consideration: There is considerable disagreement regarding the appropriateness of generalizing from observations made on one type of learning, e.g., rote verbal learning, to other descriptively different forms of learning, e.g., problem solving. In the context of our consideration of perceptual learning the question is whether the principles which govern the learning of percepts are the same as those which regulate other forms of learning. This question has usually been settled on theoretical grounds. Although for very different reasons, the majority view is that the same principles operate in perceptual learning as in other types of learning. For the Gestalt psychologists (Koffka, 1935; W. Köhler, 1947) this commonality is maintained on the ground that the principles of learning are corollaries of the principles of perception (Hilgard, 1956). For those with S-R orientation the opinion is grounded on the conviction that the principles of perception are corollaries of the principles of learning (Postman, 1955). Despite this tendency to have recourse to theoretical predispositions in order to decide this question, the question can best be resolved empirically. Investigations of perceptual learning can be designed to determine whether a recognized variable of rote learning or operant conditioning is also a controlling variable of perceptual learning. Unfortunately, systematic investigations of this sort are infrequent.

References

Adams, P. A. The effect of past experience on the perspective reversal of a tridimensional figure. *Amer. J. Psychol.*, 1954, **67**, 708–710.

Allport, F. H. *Theories of perception and the concept of structure.* New York: Wiley, 1955.

Alpern, M. Metacontrast: historical introduction. *Amer. J. Optom.*, 1952, **29**, 631–646.

Barber, T. X. Hypnotically hallucinated colors and their negative afterimages. *Amer. J. Psychol.*, 1964, **77**, 313–318.

Bartlett, N. R. Dark adaptation and light adaptation. In C. H. Graham (Ed.), *Vision and visual perception.* New York: Wiley, 1965. Ch. 8.

Bartley, S. H. *Principles of perception.* New York: Harper & Row, 1958.

Bergmann, G., & Spence, K. W. The logic of psychological measurement. *Psychol. Rev.,* 1944, **51**, 1–24.

Bolles, K. L., & Bailey, D. B. Importance of object recognition in size constancy. *J. Exp. Psychol.,* 1956, **51**, 222–225.

Boring, E. G. *Sensation and perception in history of experimental psychology.* New York: Appleton-Century-Crofts, 1942.

Brown, J. S. *The motivation of behavior.* New York: McGraw-Hill, 1961.

Finger, F. W., & Spelt, D. K. The illustration of the horizontal-vertical illusion. *J. Exp. Psychol.,* 1947, **37**, 243–250.

Garner, W. R., Hake, H. W., & Eriksen, C. W. Operationism and the concept of perception. *Psychol. Rev.,* 1956, **63**, 149–159.

Hamlyn, D. W. *Sensation and perception: a history of the philosophy of perception.* New York: Humanities, 1961.

Hebb, D. O. *Organization of behavior: a neuropsychological theory.* New York: Wiley, 1949.

Hibler, F. W. An experimental investigation of negative afterimages of hallucinated colors in hypnosis. *J. Exp. Psychol.,* 1940, **27**, 45–57.

Hilgard, E. R. *Theories of learning.* New York: Appleton-Century-Crofts, 1956.

Hochberg, J. E. Perception: toward the recovery of a definition. *Psychol. Rev.,* 1956, **63**, 400–405.

Hochberg, J. *Perception.* Englewood Cliffs, N.J.: Prentice-Hall, 1964.

Ittelson, W. H. *Visual space perception.* New York: Springer, 1960.

Ittelson, W. H. Perception and transactional psychology. In S. Koch (Ed.), *Psychology: a study of a science.* Vol. 4. New York: McGraw-Hill, 1962.

Koffka, K. *Principles of Gestalt psychology.* New York: Harcourt, Brace & World, 1935.

Kohler, I. *Ueber Aufbau und Wandlungen der Wahrnehmungswelt.* Vienna: R. M. Rohrer, 1951.

Kohler, I. Experiments with goggles. *Scient. Amer.,* 1962, **206**, 62–84.

Köhler, W. *Gestalt psychology.* New York: Liveright, 1947.

Köhler, W., & Wallach, H. Figural aftereffects. *Proc. Amer. Phil. Soc.,* 1944, **88**, 269–357.

Kolers, P. A., & Rosner, B. S. On visual masking (metacontrast): dichoptic observation. *Amer. J. Psychol.,* 1960, **73**, 2–21.

Long, E. R., Reid, L. S., & Henneman, R. H. An experimental analysis of set: variables influencing the identification of ambiguous visual stimulus-objects. *Amer. J. Psychol.,* 1960, **73**, 553–562. (a)

Long, E. R., Reid, L. S., & Henneman, R. H. An experimental analysis of set: the role of sense modality. *Amer. J. Psychol.*, 1960, **73**, 563–567. (b)

Postman, L. Association theory and perceptual learning. *Psychol. Rev.*, 1955, **62**, 438–446.

Postman, L. Perception and learning. In S. Koch (Ed.), *Psychology: a study of a science.* Vol. 5. New York: McGraw-Hill, 1963.

Prentice, W. C. H. "Functionalism" in perception. *Psychol. Rev.*, 1956, **63**, 29–38.

Pritchard, R. M. Stabilized images on the retina. *Scient. Amer.*, 1961, **204**, 72–78.

Reid, L. S., Henneman, R. H., & Long, E. R. An experimental analysis of set: the effect of categorical restriction. *Amer. J. Psychol.*, 1960, **73**, 568–572.

Rock, I., & Ebenholtz, S. The relational determination of perceived size. *Psychol. Rev.*, 1959, **66**, 387–401.

Solley, C. M., & Santos, J. Perceptual learning with partial verbal reinforcement. *Percept. Mot. Skills*, 1958, **8**, 183–193.

Wallach, H. Brightness constancy and the nature of achromatic colors. *J. Exp. Psychol.*, 1948, **38**, 310–324.

Wallach, H. Some considerations concerning the relation between perception and cognition. *J. Pers.*, 1949, **18**, 6–13.

Wallach, H., Moore, M. E., & Davidson, L. Modification of stereoscopic depth-perception. *Amer. J. Psychol.*, 1963, **76**, 191–204.

Wallach, H., O'Connell, D. N., & Neisser, U. The memory effect on visual perception of three-dimensional form. *J. Exp. Psychol.*, 1953, **45**, 360–368.

Werner, H. Studies on contour: qualitative analysis. *Amer. J. Psychol.*, 1935, **47**, 40–64.

Woodworth, R. S., & Schlosberg, H. *Experimental psychology.* New York: Holt, 1954.

Zuckerman, C. B., & Rock, I. A reappraisal of the role of past experience and innate organizing processes in visual perception. *Psychol. Bull.*, 1957, **54**, 269–296.

Chapter two
The assumptive context:
I The perception of
size and distance

The notion that perception depends on past experience has a long history in philosophy and prescientific psychology. At the time that psychology as a laboratory science was born, the empiristic position seemed very secure in the authority of Helmholtz, one of the greatest scientists of the day. Although Helmholtz was opposed by notable contemporaries and although the empiristic position has been severely criticized by the Gestalt psychologists (Koffka, 1935; Köhler, 1947) and others (Pratt, 1950; Zuckerman & Rock, 1957), the view has maintained a strong hold on psychology, especially in the United States.

In his treatise *Physiological Optics*, Helmholtz (1866, transl., 1925) included an entire volume dealing with the "perceptions of vision." In introducing this topic Helmholtz proposed a rule of perceptual functioning which he considered to be fundamental: ". . . such objects are always imagined as being present in the field of vision as would have to be there in order to produce the same impression on the nervous mechanism, the eyes being used under ordinary normal conditions" (Helmholtz, 1866, transl., 1925, vol. III, p. 2). Although quoted rarely, Helmholtz's Rule has had a pervasive influence on explanatory efforts in the field of perception. This has been especially true for the problems of space perception. The analogy between certain perceptual relationships and certain geometrical relationships has encouraged the conceptualization of the perceptual system as if under the governance of an invisible geometer.

One group of investigators do explicitly recognize Helmholtz's influence, although they deny that their views are identical with those of Helmholtz (Kilpatrick, 1952, pp. 89–

21

90). The term "transactionalism" has been used to identify this contemporary neoempiristic position. The following statement expresses the view of transactionalism:[4]

■ Any present perceptual experience consists of a total complex of significances. . . . Through the course of experiencing, certain significances are found by the perceiver to have high probabilities of being related to each other and other aspects of the situation. . . . These probabilities, high or low, are in turn weighted in terms of the relevance of the unique situation in which they have occurred. . . . All this is accomplished through a largely unconscious process and results in a set of assumptions or weighted averages of previous experiences, which are brought to the present occasion, and play a principal role in determining how the occasion is experienced. . . . The assumptive world of any particular individual at any particular time determines his perceptions, that is, provides him with predictions of probable significances (Ittelson, 1960, p. 31).

Allegiance or opposition to the transactional viewpoint has stimulated much of the work on perceptual learning to be reported in this chapter and Chapter 3. The research will be presented according to a classification in terms of the perceptual properties under investigation, e.g., size and distance, shape and slant.

The perception of
size and distance

That the perception of size and the perception of distance are frequently interdependent has long been recognized. Early formulations of the relationship may be noted in the various accounts of the moon illusion beginning with Ptolemy (150 A.D.). Ptolemy argued that the distance to the horizon appears greater than the distance to the zenith, since the former space is filled and the latter is empty. Therefore, the horizon moon appears farther away and consequently larger. Ptolemy's account has been the subject of considerable de-

[4] Readers who are familiar with Helson's adaptation-level theory (1958, 1964) will note certain similarities between the transactionalist viewpoint and Helson's approach, particularly in Helson's emphasis on the pooling, interaction, integration, and weighting of stimuli. For a variety of reasons, Helson's theory has not been included in the discussions that follow. The reader who wishes to explore the potentialities of adaptation-level theory should begin with Helson's own writings (e.g., Helson, 1964, Chs. 2, 3, 5).

bate (cf. Helmholtz, 1866, transl., 1925, vol. III, pp. 360–362). It has been vigorously rejected (Boring, 1942) and most recently revived (Kaufman & Rock, 1962). Regardless of the correctness of Ptolemy's explanation of the moon illusion, his account, which formulated a relationship among perceived size, perceived distance, and visual angle (retinal image size), is a clear precursor of current thinking.

In contemporary form, the size-distance relationship has been stated in the size-distance invariance hypothesis: a given visual angle determines a unique ratio of apparent size to apparent distance (cf. Epstein, Park, & Casey, 1961). There are only two degrees of freedom in this relationship. Given the values of any two of the variables the value of the remaining variable is fixed. Thus, if visual angle and apparent size are determined, the value of apparent distance is fixed. It will be noted that apparent size and apparent distance are psychological variables the values of which may or may not correspond with the values of their corresponding physical variables, i.e., physical size and physical distance. For example, a playing card may have a larger apparent size than a calling card even though the playing card has been especially designed so that it is the same physical size as the calling card. In this example, apparent size is determined by the assumptions which the perceiver has learned regarding the relative physical sizes of the cards. This example also illustrates an important aspect of the size-distance hypothesis. The hypothesis does not specify how apparent size and apparent distance are produced. The interaction predicted by the hypothesis is expected regardless of the conditions which determine apparent size and distance.

The experiments reported in this section are concerned mainly with examining the interaction when apparent size or distance is determined by those assumptions which S may be presumed to have developed in the course of everyday commerce with the objects serving as standards. Almost exclusively, these have been studies of the effect of size assumptions on the interaction between visual angle and apparent distance. The effect of distance assumptions on the interaction of visual angle and apparent size has not been examined. This is probably due to the fact that, in general, distance is highly variable and, therefore, assumptions about distance are not likely to develop. For example, cigarette packages vary little in size, which leads to the establishment of a specific assumed size. On the other hand, the distance at which a cigarette package has been viewed will vary greatly, thus discouraging the development of a specific assumed distance for cigarette packages.

The perception of distance

The earliest studies (Hastorf, 1950; Ittelson, 1951a; Ittelson, 1951b), as well as several later experiments, were conducted with an apparatus termed by Ames (1946) the "thereness-thatness apparatus," because it was used to demonstrate that the "thereness" (apparent distance) of the standard was determined by its "thatness" (representative nature). The S is exposed to two adjacent parallel alleys. (This arrangement has been produced optically or by actual physical arrangement.) One alley contains the standard. In several of the experiments reported in this section, the standards have been viewed in surrounding darkness with only monocular aperture vision and stationary head. These conditions of observation are intended to have the effect of eliminating all sources of information about the distance of the standard, thereby allowing E to exhibit the effects of the assumptive context of the standard.

The second alley is the comparison field. It is well illuminated and highly structured, so as to provide reliable information about the distances of objects located in the alley. Frequently, the side of the alley is lined with equisized, equispaced rods, and the floor of the alley is covered with a regular pattern. The comparison object(s) exposed in this alley may be viewed binocularly either successively or simultaneously with the monocularly viewed contents of the standard alley. The distance of the comparison object may be continuously varied by the subject to comply with the requirements of the task which the investigator has formulated. In most studies, S has been asked to set the comparison at the distance at which the standard appears. The setting of the comparison is then taken as the measure of the perceived distance of the standard. Therefore, variations of perceived or apparent distance which are reported in studies that use the "thereness-thatness table" refer to variations in the mean settings of the comparison object.

Another condition common to many experiments has been the instructional variable. Instructions in experiments on size and distance perception have been varied in three main ways: *Phenomenal instructions* ask S to direct his attention to the appearance of the targets in unmediated experience, i.e., refraining from judgment and disregarding considerations of veridicality. *Objective instructions* require S to make a match which will correspond perfectly to the physical dimensions of the standard, regardless of how it may look to him. *Analytic or projective instructions* instruct S to make a retinal or visual angle match, to take into account the relationship between distance and visual angle and report the projective dimensions of the standards. It is a well-documented fact that the instructional variable is a highly significant source of variance (Carlson, 1962; Epstein, 1963b; Landauer & Rodger, 1964). Unless otherwise indicated, in the experiments described in this section phenomenal instructions have been administered.

Ittelson's experiments   Ittelson (1951a) was the first to give an explicit statement of what has since been called the "Known Size—Apparent Distance Hypothesis" (Epstein, 1961): "Size operates as a cue to distance in the following manner. A perceptual integration is reached between the physiological stimulus-size and the assumed-size related to . . . [a] particularly characterized stimulus-pattern. The object is localized by O at the point at which an object of physical size equal to the assumed-size would have to be placed in order to produce the given retinal size" (Ittelson, 1951a, p. 66).

The experiment which Ittelson designed to demonstrate this relationship required S to provide equidistance settings of various standards in the thereness-thatness apparatus under the conditions described above. The first series of standards consisted of three pairs: small playing card (1¹¹⁄₁₆ by 2⅝ inches) and large playing card (3⅜ by 5¼ inches); small, irregularly contoured inkblot and large inkblot; small diamond shape and large diamond shape. Each standard was presented individually, all at the same distance of 9 feet. The second series consisted of three playing cards (normal-sized, double-sized, half-sized), one typewritten business letter which was the same size as the double-sized card, and one matchbox which was the same size as the half-sized playing card. Each member of the second series was presented at a distance of 7.5 feet. Different Ss judged each series; however, all the standards in the particular series were judged by the same S.

The results are summarized in Table 1. Consider first the mean apparent distances for the three playing cards of series 2. These results are interpreted to mean that variations of visual angle produce corresponding variations of perceived distance when assumed size is constant. A comparison between the letter and the double-sized card and between the matchbox and the half-sized card allows us to determine the effects of variations of assumed size without accompanying variations of visual angle. For example, the assumed size of the letter is greater than the assumed size of the playing card, although, under the conditions of the experiment, both subtend the same visual angle. Table 1 shows that variations of assumed size produced variations of perceived distance; e.g., the letter was judged to be farther away than the double-sized card.

The results for series 1 are interpreted similarly by Ittelson (1951a). It is less clear, however, how the assumed-size hypothesis can be applied to the inkblot and diamond standards. These objects are unlikely to be associated with any specific size. Unlike with the playing card, letter, and matchbox there has been no opportunity for prior learning of specific size assumptions. Yet the results for the blots and diamonds are comparable to those for the representational standards. One explanation of these findings is suggested by the work of Gogel, Hartman, and Harker (1957) and Epstein (1961) to be considered later.

Table 1
The effect of size on apparent distance*

Series 1 standards	Mean distance, ft	SD	Series 2 standards	Mean distance, ft	SD
Small card	11.88	1.77	Normal card	7.46	0.51
Large card	6.19	0.81	Double-sized	4.61	0.49
Small blot	10.72	2.27	Half-sized	14.99	2.51
Large blot	5.83	1.17	Letter	8.58	1.01
Small diamond	7.93	2.38	Matchbox	8.96	1.73
Large diamond	4.59	1.67			

* Adapted from Ittelson, 1951a, pp. 63–64.

Ittelson (1951b) has performed an analogous study of the apparent radial motion which is correlated with the continuous symmetrical expansions and contractions of the visual angle of a stationary target. This phenomenon was earlier reported by Wheatstone (1852) and subsequently investigated by Hillebrand (1894), who found that an illuminated diaphragm, viewed without distance cues, appeared to approach when its size was continuously increased and to recede when its size was continuously decreased. Ittelson (1951b) studied the perceived movement of the objects in series 2 (Table 1) when these objects were made to undergo continuous changes of visual angle. The apparent distance of movement was shown to depend on the assumed size of the object.

Hastorf's experiment   Hastorf (1950) has conducted a similar study of the relationships among perceived distance, visual angle, and assumed size. Aside from several differences in measurement procedure the main difference between the Hastorf study and Ittelson's (1951a) concerns the procedure for manipulating assumed size. Ittelson varied assumed size by choosing as standards representational objects which normally differ in physical size. Hastorf used as standards two nonrepresentational familiar geometric forms—a circle and a rectangle. In order to impart different assumed sizes to these forms Hastorf labeled the forms differently on different trials. Thus, by labeling the circle "ping-pong ball" on one trial and "billiard ball" on another trial, Hastorf intended to impart a small and a large assumed size, respectively, to the circle. A similar effect was sought by naming the rectangle "envelope" (large-assumed-size meaning) or "calling card" (small-assumed-size meaning).

Each S judged the distance of each of the four standards by manipulating the *size* of the stationary standard until it appeared at the same distance as one of the rods lining the comparison alley. If perceived distance is determined by assumed size, then the size settings of the forms should be larger when a large assumed size is attributed to the form than when a small assumed size is attributed to the form. Table 2 shows that this was the case.

At this point it will be useful to distinguish two types of situations studied by Ittelson and Hastorf. In the one, the

Table 2
Mean size settings of standards*

Standard	Mean	SD	P
Rectangle (calling card)	5.0†	1.1 ⎞	
Rectangle (envelope)	6.5†	1.6 ⎠	<.01
Circle (ping-pong ball)	4.6‡	0.8 ⎞	
Circle (billiard ball)	6.0‡	1.9 ⎠	<.01

* Adapted from Hastorf, 1950, p. 210.
† Height in centimeters.
‡ Diameter in centimeters.

visual angle is varied while assumed size is invariant and perceived distance is the dependent variable. In the other, assumed size is varied while visual angle is invariant; again, perceived distance is the dependent variable. Despite their interdependence the two cases will be considered separately.

The influence of variations of
visual angle on perceived
distance when assumed
size is invariant

The interpretation which Ittelson placed on his data has been questioned on two grounds: one criticism has been that the hypothesis of known size is unnecessary, since the results can be accounted for more parsimoniously in terms of the effect of relative size; the second major criticism is that the effect observed by Ittelson concerns perceived relative distance instead of perceived absolute distance. A series of experiments by Hochberg and Hochberg (1952, 1953), Gogel et al. (1957), and Epstein (1961) appear to support the relative size—relative distance interpretation.

Ittelson has been vigorously criticized by Hochberg and Hochberg (1952), who have argued that Ittelson and others have failed to distinguish between familiar size on the one hand and the *relative* size of the stimuli on the other (i.e., change or difference in size of objects of similar shapes). For this reason, Hochberg and Hochberg (1952) designed an experiment in which familiar size and relative size were separated. Two figures were drawn on a two-dimensional reversible-screen drawing. One panel contained a drawing of a man, and on the other panel a boy of the same size and approximate contour was represented. The question is whether the panel with the boy appears to be nearer more often than the panel containing the man. This is to be expected if familiar size is determining apparent localization. The results showed that familiar size was ineffective in this situation.

In a second experiment, the effectiveness of *relative* size was tested. The same procedure was followed with one difference: whereas the first experiment held relative size constant while familiar size was varied, the second experiment held familiar size constant while varying relative size. The two panels contained drawings of the same boy, but one was a reduced version of the other. Here, relative size would lead to localizing the panel containing the larger boy nearer than the other panel. The results were in agreement with this expectation. These findings led the writers to suggest that there may be a stimulus-bound correlation between retinal size and perceived distance which would make the introduction of unconscious assumptions (about known size) unnecessary.

Further experimental evidence in support of this emphasis on relative size is presented by Hochberg and McAlister (1955). Four cards, each bearing one small figure and one large figure 8 inches apart, were presented singly, each for 100 seconds. Card 1 bore a large circle and a small circle; card 2, a large square and a small square; card 3, a large circle and a small square; and card 4, a large square and a small circle. Thirty-three sound signals randomly spaced were given during the presentation, and S was instructed to indicate the mode of appearance of the figure which was seen *immediately preceding the signal*. In terms of relative size, it would be expected that cards 1 and 2 should yield more three-dimensional responses than cards 3 or 4. This was the case.

In a second experiment the writers inquired whether the direction of the three-dimensional responses is in accordance with what would be predicted in terms of relative size. "In terms of the cue of relative size, the larger figure should appear nearer than the small one in Cards 1 and 2. They did. If this were due to the operation of familiar size, we would expect similar results to hold with respect to Cards 3 and 4"

(Hochberg & McAlister, 1955, p. 296). This did not happen.

Ittelson (1953) has replied to the above criticisms by citing several instances in which relative size is not involved. These are cases when only a *single* object is present in the field. Ittelson argues that if a single, familiar object viewed monocularly in a dark room is replaced by another of the same physical size but of different assumed size, the apparent distance of the second will be different from the first. In support of this contention Ittelson cites Ames's "watch-card-magazine" experiment (Ames, 1946–1947) and Hastorf's similar investigations (1950).

In addition Ittelson (1953) maintains that if a single, familiar object is viewed monocularly in a dark room, it is perceived immediately and unequivocally at some definite distance which can be correctly predicted on the basis of the familiar size of the object. Finally, the claim is made that the size-distance perceptions related to a given stimulus can be changed by immediately prior experiences that change the size that is attributed to the stimulus. As an illustration, Ittelson cites the experiments which demonstrate the influence of size assumptions on perceived radial motion (see Kilpatrick & Ittelson, 1951).

The latter two assertions are incompatible with an explanation based on the relative-size cue. However, subsequent investigations have failed to confirm their validity and also have provided further support for the relative-size thesis. The experiments reported by Gogel et al. (1957) show that the retinal size of a familiar object is totally inadequate as a cue for the *absolute* apparent distance of that object. The investigations reported by Epstein (1961) confirm the findings of Gogel et al. and also demonstrate that experiences which modify S's assumptions concerning object size do not modify his perceptual experiences. The problem for Gogel et al. was to ". . . investigate whether the retinal subtense of a familiar object can act as a determiner of the apparent absolute distance of that object from the observer" (1957, p. 1). This study employed a nonvisual method of measuring perceived distance of the object. S was asked to throw a dart to the perceived distance without seeing the results of the throw. Since successive throws might involve relative distance judgment, only the response to the *initial* exposure of the object was considered in measuring the perceived absolute distance of that object. The stimulus object was a normal-sized or double-sized playing card, located at a distance of 10 or 20 feet in a reduced-cue situation.

The distance responses for the stimuli initially presented did not confirm the expectations which follow from the Known Size–Apparent Distance Hypothesis. Not only did the results fail to agree with any precise predictions of apparent localization, e.g., that the double-sized card at a physical distance of 20 feet should be localized at 10 feet, but also the less stringent prediction, e.g., that the double-sized card should appear to be nearer than the normal card, was not confirmed. Under these conditions, perceived distance was totally unrelated to retinal size.

When a similar analysis was performed for all four reduced-cue situations collectively (i.e., the *same* Ss in all four situations), partial support was obtained for the Known Size–Apparent Distance Hypothesis in its less precise formulation. The implication of this finding is clear. The secondary analysis shows only that *relative*-distance perception, as some function of *relative* retinal subtense, can occur for successively presented stimuli.

The first of three experiments reported by Epstein (1961) was essentially a replication of Ittelson's (1951a) experiment with several modifications:

1

A control group of twenty Ss judged the apparent distance of playing cards and blank rectangles of cardboard of identical dimensions under conditions which were very similar to Ittelson's situation in all essential respects. An experimental group of twenty Ss made the same judgments. However, prior to the judgmental task, Ss in this group participated in a card game which was designed to modify their assumptions concerning the normal size of cards and the constancy of the physical size of cards.

2

At the conclusion of the distance settings, all Ss were required to judge the apparent size of the stimuli.

3

A great number of card sizes were employed.

The results of this experiment did not support the known-size hypothesis. The main findings were as follows:

1
Despite the modifying treatment experienced by the experimental group, there was no difference between the distance judgments of the control and experimental groups.
2
There was no difference in the distance judgments for the playing cards (stimuli of known size) and the blank cards of identical size (nonrepresentative stimuli).
3
None of the distance judgments met the precise quantitative requirements of the known-size thesis; e.g., while the quarter-sized card appeared to be more distantly located than the normal-sized card, it was *not* set at four times the distance of the normal-sized card.
4
The stimuli of different physical size were also judged to be of different size; i.e., the smaller stimuli were judged to be farther and smaller, and conversely for the larger cards.

Experiment II demonstrated that similar apparent-distance effects would obtain when only relative retinal size is operative (known size and assumed constancy of physical size absent). Finally, Exp. III demonstrated that, in the absence of the relative-size cue, no systematic size-distance effects are obtained. The results of Exps. II and III bolster the position adopted by Hochberg and Hochberg and by Gogel.

In this connection the results reported by Gogel and Harker (1955) may also be cited. Gogel and Harker obtained judgments of apparent distance for two playing cards of different sizes under reduced-cue and near-complete-cue conditions. They found that the relative apparent depth of the two cards was a function of the lateral separation between the two cards. They concluded that ". . . the effectiveness of size cues to relative depth increased as the lateral separation of the differently sized cards was increased" (Gogel & Harker, 1955, p. 315). There is no reason to expect such results if the original depth effects were based on the operation of an assumed-size factor.

An experiment by Baird (1963, Exp. II) concludes our consideration of the influence of visual angle variations when assumed size is constant. Separate groups of Ss provided verbal estimates of the distance of 6-, 12-, and 24-inch rectangular strips of light presented individually at a distance of 25 feet and viewed under reduced-cue conditions. Prior to the judgment, S was informed that the measured size of the strip was the same as a 1-foot ruler. The predictions from the Known Size—Apparent Distance Hypothesis are that the apparent distance of the 12-inch strip would be 25 feet; of the 24-inch strip, 12.5 feet; and of the 6-inch strip, 50 feet. The mean distance estimates obtained for the three groups were 12-inch strip, 24 feet (SD = 7.3 feet); 24-inch strip, 14.3 feet (SD = 5.6 feet); and 6-inch strip, 48.2 feet (SD = 42.6 feet). A Kruskal-Wallis test showed overall significance for the variance between the distance estimates. Further analysis showed that only the 6- versus 12-inch comparison was not significant.

Baird's experiment does not seem open to the relative-size—relative-distance interpretation, since each S judged only one standard presented without accompanying visual comparators. Baird (1963) concludes that ". . . these results support the thesis that known size (Ittelson, 1951a; Ittelson, 1953) or assumed size (Hastorf, 1950; Smith, 1952) is a cue to distance and are contrary to conclusions drawn from studies in which it was found that such cues were not effectively used in distance perception (Epstein, 1961; Gogel et al., 1957; Hochberg & Hochberg, 1952; Hochberg & McAlister, 1955)" (Baird, 1963, pp. 159–160).

The influence of variations of
assumed size on perceived
distance when visual
angle is invariant

The evidence concerning this relationship was provided mainly by Hastorf (1950) and by portions of Ittelson's studies (1951a, 1951b). In this section additional evidence reported by Epstein (1963a, 1965) and Baird (1963, Exp. I) will be described.

The standards in Epstein's experiment (1963a) were three photographs of identical size. One was a normally sized (diameter = 2.4 centimeters) photograph of a quarter (Q). The second standard was a photograph of a dime (D) enlarged to the size of a quarter. The third was a photograph of a half dollar (H) reduced to the size of a quarter. Each of these photographs was pasted on a disk cut from cardboard for mounting. Under the experimental conditions the standards were indistinguishable from actual coins. Thus, Ss were exposed to three standards which normally vary in physical size and thus presumably in assumed size. Visual angle, however, was invariant, since the standards were actually the same size and were located at the same distance (135 centimeters from S).

The thereness-thatness table was used. The distance comparison was a cigarette pack whose distance from S could be continuously varied. The size comparison was a projected circle of light whose diameter was continuously variable. The projection screen was located in the comparison alley at the mean perceived distance of the standard. Each S judged only one of the standards, and each standard was presented individually. First the distance and the size of the standard were judged under monocular, reduced conditions. Then the judgments were repeated under binocular, full-cue conditions.

The mean apparent distances and sizes are shown in Tables 3 and 4. Table 3 shows that under conditions of restricted, monocular observation apparent distance varied ($F = 17.59$, $P < .001$) as a function of assumed size. All the individual comparisons, H-D, H-Q, and Q-D, were significant by a Duncan's test. The means for the condition of binocular full-cue viewing did not vary significantly; each mean approximated closely the objective distance of 135 centimeters.

Table 4 shows that apparent size varied ($F = 12.78$, $P < .001$) as a function of assumed size for the condition of monocular, reduced observation. Each mean differed significantly from each other mean. The mean judgments of size for the full-cue condition were almost identical for the three standards; each mean approximated closely the physical diameter of 2.4 centimeters.

Tables 3 and 4 show that there were considerable differences in variability between the measures for monocular and

Table 3
Apparent distance of standard stimuli with
monocular and binocular observation*

Standard	Monocular observation		Binocular observation	
	Mean	SD	Mean	SD
Dime	112.74	23.9	135.70	2.57
Quarter	132.73	17.5	135.44	1.88
Half dollar	164.19	29.7	135.40	1.92

* From Epstein, 1963a, p. 260. (In centimeters; physical distance = 135 cm)

binocular observation. For apparent distance, the SDs are in a ratio of more than 10 to 1, and for apparent size the ratios vary from 8 to 2. These differences in variability are not unexpected. The relatively small SDs for apparent distance and size under conditions of unimpeded binocular vision reflect the fact that many cues for distance were available and, therefore, all Ss gave judgments which were nearly veridical. However, the elimination of distance cues, under the condition of monocular observation, created a situation of indeterminate distance, i.e., apparent distance unspecified by the cues which are normally available. Within the range of possible apparent distances, the localization of the standard is determined by the factor of assumed size. Since this factor depends on *remembered* size, it will vary somewhat among Ss (and perhaps for the same S on different occasions) (McKennel, 1959; McKennel, 1960). This variability in assumed size presumably can produce variability in apparent distance. The variability in apparent distance is not, however, in itself of importance. The significant consideration concerns the relationship between the variations in assumed size (apparent-size judgments) and variations in apparent distance.

Next, the relationship between the apparent distance and apparent size of each of the three standards under monocular observation was assessed. For this purpose the Spearman rank correlation coefficient (corrected for ties) was used. This analysis revealed the positive correlation between apparent size and apparent distance for each standard which was theoretically expected. *Rho* was .77 (P < .01), .56 (P < .05), and .76 (P < .01) for the dime, quarter, and half dollar, respectively.

In Figure 1 the mean judgments of apparent distance can

Table 4
Apparent size of standard stimuli under monocular and binocular observation*

Standard	Monocular observation		Binocular observation	
	Mean	SD	Mean	SD
Dime	1.96	0.34	2.47	0.18
Quarter	2.55	0.33	2.52	0.04
Half dollar	2.93	0.73	2.47	0.16

* From Epstein, 1963a, p. 260. (In centimeters; physical size = 2.4 cm)

be compared with the values which are required if apparent distance is, in fact, determined by the assumed size of the standard. In this experiment the apparent-size judgments can be taken to represent the assumed sizes of the standards. With this in mind, the requirements of the assumed-size hypothesis can be determined by the following simple formula:

$$ad = \frac{as}{ps}\, pd$$

where ad = theoretically required apparent distance; as = apparent (judged) size; ps = physical size; pd = physical distance.

Solving this formula for the appropriate values yielded the theoretical values of apparent distance of 110.70, 141.75, and 164.70 centimeters for the dime, quarter, and half dollar, respectively. These values have been plotted in Fig-

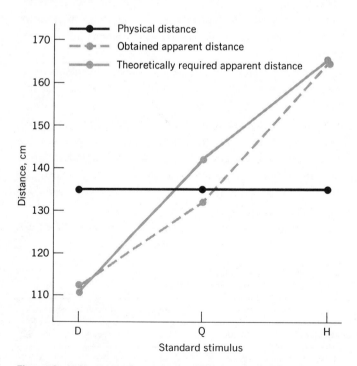

Figure 1. Judgments of apparent distance compared with physical distances and the theoretically predicted values. (For derivation of predicted values, see text.)

ure 1 along with the values which were actually obtained. Inspection of these two curves reveals a striking degree of agreement. For the dime the difference between the obtained and theoretical values was 2.04 centimeters (1.80 percent), while the discrepancy for the half dollar was 0.51 centimeters (0.03 percent). The deviation for the quarter was somewhat greater. The difference of 9.02 centimeters (6.03 percent) represents a slight underestimation (2.27 centimeters) of distance instead of the overestimation (6.75 centimeters) which is required theoretically.

One reservation must be imposed on the conclusion implied by the results of the preceding analysis. Although the analyses based on grouped data confirmed impressively the assumed-size hypothesis, equally strong confirmation was not present in the individual data. The discrepancies in the individual size-distance pairings may be illustrated by referring to the results of one S under condition Q. This S ranked first in distance setting, i.e., he judged the quarter to be nearer than any other S in the group, but he ranked eleventh (largest) in size setting. Applying the formula which was presented earlier to this S's data revealed a deviation of 56.60 centimeters (35.5 percent) from the theoretical requirements. Thus, for this S, and for all other Ss also, the precise quantitative linkage between apparent size and apparent distance was not observed.

The overall picture presented by the preceding analysis represents an impressive confirmation of the hypothesis about the relationship between assumed size and apparent distance. The apparent distance of the standard was shown to vary systematically with the identified characteristics of the object. Furthermore, apparent size also was shown to vary with the identity of the standard. The direct proportionality between apparent size and apparent distance which is indicated by the fairly high positive correlations between size and distance, and also by the curves in Figure 1, provides compelling additional support for the hypothesis.

Epstein's (1963a) experiment has been criticized by Gogel (1964) along, by now, familiar lines. The cigarette pack, which served as the distance-comparison object, and the standard coin both are known objects. There is a modal visual-angle relationship which obtains when the two, cigarette pack and coin, are equidistant from S. The settings of the cigarette pack in Epstein's study (1963a) do not necessarily reflect the perceived absolute distance of the standard. The identical settings could result from S's effort to duplicate the modal angular relationship which obtains when the objects are indeed equidistant. To accomplish this the pack would have to be set nearer than the objective distance when the standard was the "dime" and farther than the objective equidistance for the "quarter." The Ss did precisely that.

The variations in size judgments can be similarly explained. The explanation is based on the plausible presumption that in the absence of distance cues two objects which appear equidistant will appear the same size when they subtend the same visual angle (e.g., Epstein, Park, & Casey, 1961; Holway & Boring, 1941). Recall that the size-comparison disk was set at a distance equal to the mean apparent distance of the standard. Since the physical size and distance of the standards were invariant and the physical distance of the comparison disk for a given match was not free to vary, only the physical size of the comparison could be adjusted to produce the desired visual-angle match. The size setting would have to vary proportionally with the distance of the comparison. This would be sufficient to account for the size variations reported by Epstein (1963a) without invoking "assumed size" as an explanation.

To check the validity of the above reinterpretation Epstein (1965) repeated the original assumed-size study employing nonvisual (tactual) measures of the visual impressions of the size and distance of the "coins." If visual relationships were responsible for the original results, then the elimination of these relationships, in the new study, should lead to different results.

Except for the procedure for obtaining judgments, the 1965 study was a repetition of the 1963 study. The coins, under the reduced conditions, were presented without any accompanying visual objects. The distance comparison was a coiled rope which could be pulled by E through S's hand. For the distance judgments E pulled the rope through S's hand until S tightened his grip and said, "Stop." S was instructed to stop the passage of the rope when the length which had passed through his hand equaled the apparent distance of the coin. The size comparison consisted of a series of raised disks which varied in diameter from 1.43 to

3.33 centimeters in steps of 0.125 centimeter. S matched his visual impressions of size by selecting the raised comparison disk which was subjectively equal to the standard.

The results of the tactual judgments conformed to those obtained for the visual judgments. Since this study did not involve visual comparisons, it is reasonable to conclude that the interpretation considered earlier cannot apply to the present study.

Another experiment to examine the dependence of apparent distance on assumed size was reported by Baird (1963, Exp. I). Baird's Ss judged the apparent size and distance of a 12-inch-high equilateral triangle presented for reduced monocular vision at a distance of 25 feet. Prior to judging the triangle S was shown a rectangular strip of light which was 6, 12, or 24 inches long at a distance of 25 feet and was told it was the size of a 12-inch ruler. S was then shown the 12-inch triangle and told it was at the same distance as the previously seen rectangular strip. In this manner Baird intended to impart different assumed sizes to the same triangle: for the normal-sized-ruler condition the assumed size of the triangle should have been 12 inches; for the large-ruler condition, 6 inches; and for the small-ruler group, 24 inches. These variations of assumed size should in turn affect the perceived distance of the triangle: large assumed size should produce smallest perceived distance; small assumed size should produce largest perceived distance; normal assumed size should result in an intermediate distance. Table 5 shows the mean judgments of size (these are presumed to be directly proportional to assumed size) and distance under two instructional conditions, analytic and

Table 5
Size and distance estimates of a 12-inch
triangle presented at a distance of 25 feet*

	Analytic instructions		Objective instructions	
Size training	Mean size, in.	Mean distance, ft	Mean size, in.	Mean distance, ft
Normal ruler	8.2	12.0	9.3	19.7
Large ruler	7.3	13.5	6.3	9.1
Small ruler	8.6	11.6	18.2	23.3
No ruler	7.8	10.3	7.5	10.1

* Based on Baird, 1963, Exp. I.

objective. Size judgments were made by adjusting a comparison triangle, and distance judgments were made verbally.

We will consider only the estimates obtained under objective instructions. Although not all the individual comparisons among the four means were significant, there was a general trend for the mean size judgments to vary according to the assumed-size hypothesis. (The main effect of training was significant.) The mean distance estimates also varied in accordance with the assumed-size hypothesis. A correlation of .47 ($P < .05$) was obtained between size and distance estimates of the standard.

Although the data are uncomplicated, the interpretation of the distance estimates is complicated by the fact that comparison triangles of varying sizes, i.e., representing various size estimates, were present while S judged the distance of the standard triangle. For example, comparison triangles with mean altitudes of 18.2 and 6.3 inches were present for the small-ruler and large-ruler conditions, respectively. The differences between the standard-comparison size ratios 12 to 18.2 and 12 to 6.3 are sufficient to account for the different distance estimates obtained under these conditions. The Known Size—Apparent Distance Hypothesis is not needed to account for the variations that occur in the distance estimates.

The relative-size cue to
relative perceived distance

A persistent criticism of the experiments on the known-size hypothesis has been that they failed to demonstrate an effect of known size independent of relative size. The implication is that judgments of relative distance are in psychophysical correspondence with relative visual angle and, therefore, no recourse to intervening assumptions is necessary. This implication can be questioned. The fact is that relative visual angle does *not* uniquely specify its distal source. Figure 2, representing the retinal subtenses of three squares, may be produced by three squares of identical size at different distances from S. However, the same retinal situation may result from the presence of three equidistant squares which differ in size in the same proportion as the visual-angle differences. Thus, relative size is optically equivocal, admit-

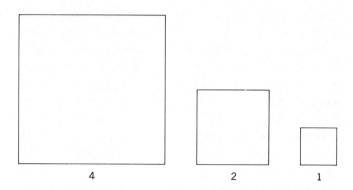

4   2   1

Figure 2. Relative-size cue.

ting of at least two perceptual alternatives. Yet the perceptual response is highly predictable.

This analysis suggests that on some basis the perception of a depth difference is favored over perception of a size difference. One explanation of the effect of relative size has been alluded to by Ittelson (1960): "For a given ratio of visual angles, assuming the ratio of physical sizes determines the ratio of distances. If the assumed sizes are equal, the object subtending the larger visual angle appears nearer and the one subtending the smaller appears farther" (p. 69). The proposal is that the effect of relative size is mediated by the subjective assumption of identity. Ames (1946) has expressed this proposal succinctly: "You presume identity of size . . . from similarity, and use the appearance of difference [in size] as an indication of distance" (p. 46). If Ittelson and Ames are right, the relative-size cue is itself based on the assumptive context, and reinterpreting data in terms of relative size does not eliminate the reliance on assumptions as explanatory variables.

The evidence on the Ames-Ittelson hypothesis is sparse and leaves room for debate. We may note at first that the hypothesis requires only an assumption of identity of size, not that the assumed size be veridical. Thus, the finding of relative-size effects for nonrepresentational targets (Carr, 1935; Epstein, 1964; Epstein & Franklin, 1965; Gogel, 1954) does not contradict the hypothesis. Only two experiments (Epstein & Baratz, 1964) are known which examined this effect directly.

In Exp. I, Epstein and Baratz examined the Ames-Ittelson hypothesis by observing the effect of experimentally trained size assumptions on subsequent relative-distance judgments. In the training stage of Exp. I, S performed an oddity task the purpose of which was to establish prescribed size-color associations such that S would develop a tendency to assume the size of a target from observation of its color. The size-color conjunctions learned by the three experimental groups are shown in Table 6. A control group had no size-color training.

Immediately following the training task S made relative-distance judgments of twenty pairs of standard squares. Table 7 shows a sample of these pairs. The pairs were viewed under reduced conditions on the thereness-thatness table. S reported their relative distance by adjusting the distance of two different irregularly contoured nonsense forms in the comparison alley.

Table 7 shows that three classes of pairings were presented:

1
Both standards from the same *trained*-size category but different in physical size when presented
2
Each standard from a different trained-size category but identical in physical size when presented
3
The standards from different trained-size categories and also of different physical size

Classes 2 and 3 are of special interest, since on these trials the assumptional hypothesis and a pure relative-visual-angle hypothesis make incompatible predictions (see right-hand columns of Table 7). Table 8 shows the results for the eight trials listed in Table 7. In every case the outcome was pre-

Table 6
Size-color conjunctions learned by the experimental Ss

Color of training square	Size of square during training, in.		
	Subgroup 1	Subgroup 2	Subgroup 3
Blue, yellow	4	2	1
Red, brown	2	1	4
Orange, green	1	4	2

Table 7
Schematic description of a sample of
trials and the theoretical expectations

Class	Left square Size trained*	Left square Size presented	Right square Size trained	Right square Size presented	Predictions† Assumptional	Predictions† Visual angle
1	L	L	L	I	R F	R F
1	I	S	I	L	RN	RN
2	L	L	I	L	RN	E
2	L	I	I	I	RN	E
2	L	S	I	S	RN	E
3	L	L	I	I	E	R F
3	S	S	I	I	E	RN
3	L	L	S	I	RN	LN

* L = large; I = intermediate; S = small.
† RF = right square farther; RN = right square nearer; LN = left square nearer; E = squares equidistant.

dictable solely on the basis of visual-angle relationships. The same was true for the remaining twelve trials. No evidence was obtained to suggest that size assumptions play a role in this situation.

Experiment II (Epstein & Baratz, 1964) followed the same rationale as Exp. I. The main difference, however, was the procedure for manipulating size assumptions. In Exp. II this was accomplished by using known objects as standards. The nine standards were photographs of a dime (D), quarter (Q), and half dollar (H), each reproduced in its own normal size and in the sizes of the two other coins. A sample of the twenty-three pairs of standards the relative distance of which was judged is shown in Table 9.

Table 8
Mean apparent distances of standards
for the trials described in Table 7

Class	Experimental Ss (N = 30) Left square	Experimental Ss (N = 30) Right square	Experimental Ss (N = 30) Apparent radial separation	Control Ss (N = 12) Left square	Control Ss (N = 12) Right square	Control Ss (N = 12) Apparent radial separation
1	133	153	20	114	161	47
1	185	128	57	197	127	70
2	136	137	1	122	128	6
2	154	153	1	156	156	0
2	183	183	0	183	189	6
3	131	159	28	116	159	43
3	185	157	28	189	149	40
3	130	156	26	122	160	38

The trials can be classified as in Exp. I. The trials in classes 2 and 3 are tests of the assumptional and visual-angle hypotheses.

The results shown in Table 9 are as unequivocal as those obtained in Exp. I. However, whereas Exp. I failed to provide evidence for the influence of assumptions, the results for all seven critical trials in classes 2 and 3 of Table 9 support the assumptional hypothesis. This was also true for the remaining seven trials in classes 2 and 3.

A supplementary analysis provided additional support for the assumptional interpretation. If the difference in the perceived distance between standards is mediated by assumptive factors, then the magnitude of the difference should be determined similarly. As an illustration, pairing 2b may be compared with pairing 2a (see Table 9). In both cases the assumptional hypothesis predicts separation, while visual-angle considerations suggest equidistance. However, on closer consideration, it will be apparent that the assumptional view also demands that the difference in perceived distance for pairing 2b be greater than for pairing 2a. This follows, in the most general way, from the fact that the discrepancy between assumed and actual physical sizes is greater for pairing 2b. Table 10 shows a sample of the twelve comparisons which were made. In order to make these comparisons more convincing we have compared trials which presented the same *visual-angle relationships*. Table 10

Table 9
Sample of pairings presented in Exp. II:
theoretically required and obtained relative distance

		Predictions		Obtained apparent distance		
Class	Pairing	Assump-tional	Visual angle	Left	Right	t
1a	DS vs. DI	DI nearer	Same	176.21	125.62	10.56*
1b	DI vs. DL	DL nearer	Same	148 18	119.56	7.22*
2a	DS vs. QS	D nearer	Equidistant	150.53	193.84	7.95*
2b	DS vs. HS	D nearer	Equidistant	151.12	213.34	9.48*
2c	DI vs. QI	D nearer	Equidistant	127.96	158.15	5.90*
2d	DI vs. HI	D nearer	Equidistant	130.59	177.40	6.14*
3a	QI vs. DS	Equidistant	Q nearer	147.71	154.03	0.35
3b	HL vs. QI	Equidistant	H nearer	152.43	157.68	1.18
3c	HL vs. DI	D nearer	H nearer	159.56	133.21	3.39*

* P < .01.
NOTE: Letters a, b, c, and d in class designations are used to distinguish pairings within the same class. D = dime, Q = quarter, H = half dollar, S = dime-sized, I = quarter-sized, L = half dollar-sized; thus DS vs. DI = dime-sized dime versus quarter-sized dime.

shows that the results for all the comparisons confirmed the requirements of the assumptional hypothesis. The same was true for the remaining seven comparisons.

Especially convincing are two special cases not included in Table 10. These are comparisons between pairing QI versus QL and pairing DI versus HL, and between pairing HS versus HI and pairing DS versus HI. In these cases the assumptional hypothesis predicts a difference in the *direction* of apparent separation despite the identical retinal stimulation. The standards subtending the *larger* visual angles should appear nearer when both the members of the pair have the same identity. In contrast the standard subtending the *smaller* visual angle should appear nearer when the members of the pair are different coins. These expectations were satisfied in both cases.

The two experiments produced conflicting results. Experiment I showed that perceived relative distance could be predicted solely in terms of relative visual angle, while in Exp. II, the knowledge of the relative visual angle was an insufficient basis for prediction. Subjective size assumptions plainly governed S's response to the visual-angle relationships in Exp. II.[5] These results lend qualified support to the

---

[5] An interpretation of the difference between the results of these two experiments is suggested by Taylor (1965, pp. 10–11) in the context of a behavioristic analysis of perceived size and distance. Taylor suggests that the critical difference between the procedures of Exps. I and II is that the latter used objects that had a long history of manipulation, while the colored squares used in Exp. I were never handled. It is Taylor's contention that the ". . . motor responses that are adapted to the dimensions of the goal, such as placing the fingers . . . at such a distance apart that the object can be easily grasped" are important determinants of the perception of size. Because the opportunity to manipulate the colored squares was not present, the size associations were less effective.

Table 10
Predicted and obtained apparent radial separations for comparisons between pairings

Predicted radial separations for selected comparisons	Obtained radial separations			
	Pairing	Separation	Pairing	Separation
1a > 3a	1a	51.09	3a	6.32
1b > 3b	1b	28.62	3b	5.25
2b > 2a	2b	62.22	2a	43.31
2b > 2c	2b	62.22	2c	30.19
2d > 2c	2d	46.81	2c	30.19

NOTE: Letters a, b, c, and d are used to distinguish pairings within the same class.

Ames-Ittelson hypothesis. This complicates the attempt to eliminate assumptive variables from the explanation of the known-size experiments by referring to the effect of relative size.

Known size, relative size, and
the assumptive context

The original proposition under examination asserted that known size can determine absolute distance. The review which has been presented shows that much of the evidence advanced to support this proposition may be challenged. With the exception of Epstein's study (1965) the findings may be explained in terms of relative-size effects on relative distance. The argument of those who criticized the known-size hypothesis was not only that a relationship between known size and perceived absolute distance was not demonstrated but also that relative visual angle and perceived relative distance are in psychophysical correspondence, thus eliminating the need for assumptive variables. However, the experiments of Epstein and Baratz (1964) showed that assumptive variables may be involved in the relative-size cue.

The following conclusions are suggested: In the absence of reliable determinants of relative distance, perceived relative distance is determined by an interaction of perceived relative size and relative visual angle. Perceived relative size is determined by assumptions introduced by S. If the objects are nonrepresentational, e.g., squares, then S will assume that all objects which are similar in some specifiable property, e.g., shape, are also similar in size. This assumption will then determine perceived relative size. If the objects are familiar representative objects, then the relative sizes normally associated with the objects will determine their perceived relative size. In both cases the perceived relative sizes will interact with relative visual angle to determine perceived relative distance. The familiar-size and relative-size cues do not differ in the nature of the psychological interaction which underlies their effect. Nor do the two cues differ because one involves assumptions while the other does not. Both involve subjective assumptions. They differ only in the character of the assumption which determines perceived relative size. For the relative-size cue the assumption is less differentiated, e.g., "All things which are alike in one property are alike in all other properties." The known-size cue involves identification and specific experience with the objects. Gogel (1964) has expressed a similar view:

■ Familiar size and similarity of shape are merely different methods of determining values of perceived size (S'). . . . Therefore, the familiar size cue and the relative-size cue are never in opposition. It is the perceived sizes of the objects regardless of the manner in which these perceived sizes are produced which together with the retinal sizes results in a perceived depth. The concept that the relative values of S'/θ for the several objects determine the resulting perceived depth between the objects subsumes both the relative and familiar size cues into one system (p. 221).

In both cases when $S'_A/\theta_A > S'_B/\theta_B$, target A appears more distant than target B; when $S'_A/\theta_A = S'_B/\theta_B$ the targets appear equidistant; and when $S'_A/\theta_A < S'_B/\theta_B$ target A appears less distant than target B.

The perception of size

The effect of size assumptions on perceived size has been studied only rarely. The main investigations have been those of Slack (1956) and Fillenbaum, Schiffman, and Butcher (1965). Additional findings provided as by-products of other studies (Baird, 1963; Epstein, 1961; Epstein, 1963a; Epstein, 1965; Ittelson, 1951a) will also be presented. Also the interpretive question implied by the results of Bolles and Bailey (1956) and Churchill (1962) will be considered.

Slack (1956) investigated the effect of familiar size upon apparent size. The experiment was done under full-cue conditions and objective-size-matching instructions. The Ss judged three chairs of varying sizes: smaller than usual, normal, and larger than usual. In addition they judged three sticks, each the same height as one of the chairs. The following expectations were derived from the hypothesis that perceived size is influenced by the ". . . experience-determined range of characteristic heights" (Slack, 1956, p. 195): The large chair should be judged smaller than a stick of its size, the small chair should be judged larger than a stick of its size, and the normal-sized chair should be judged equal to a stick of its size. "The Ss would tend to regress their apparent-size judgments toward the assumed or familiar size; familiar size would operate to make objects smaller than expected seem larger and objects larger than expected seem smaller even in the presence of many other non-object-determined cues" (Slack, 1956, p. 195).

The mean judgments of height for three different viewing distances are presented in Table 11. This table shows that the results were in the expected direction. Analysis of variance yielded a significant interaction between the familiar-size variable (chairs versus sticks) and the physical-size variable. Individual comparisons for the six pairs of means obtained for the large and small standards were all significant (one-tail t, $P < .05$).

An experiment by Fillenbaum et al. (1965) repeated Slack's study in an expanded design which included additional control objects. These were abstract constructions in three sizes. These constructions were arrangements of horizontal and vertical stakes which were comparable to the chairs in complexity. Otherwise the conditions of size judgments were comparable to those of Slack's experiment. Unlike Slack's results, however, Fillenbaum et al. failed to find a tendency for size judgments to vary as a function of familiar size. Furthermore, verbal distance estimates which were obtained following the size judgments gave no evidence that the size-distance relationship is affected by the presence of an "off-size" version of the familiar standard.

Fillenbaum et al. (1965) failed to replicate Slack's results (1956). An examination of the two experiments does not suggest any reasons for the disagreement. Even if we disregard the results of Fillenbaum et al., there are some puzzling aspects in Slack's data. Although Slack's results are generally in agreement with the hypothesis of familiar size,

Table 11
Apparent height of chairs and sticks
at three distances averaged over Ss*

Standard	20-yd mean	30-yd mean	40-yd mean
58-in. chair	58.60	59.30	58.07
58-in. stick	60.88	62.41	63.91
34½-in. chair	39.83	41.76	42.18
34½-in. stick	37.63	39.87	41.59
25½-in. chair	32.29	33.54	34.54
25½-in. stick	30.44	30.54	31.50

* Adapted from Slack, p. 196. (In inches)

an inspection of Table 11 reveals discrepancies. Two of these merit comment: There was a significant main effect of distance (F = 7.9, df = 187/2, P < .01) which may be described as a tendency for increasing size overestimation as a function of increasing distance. This finding is not unusual in studies of size perception (Carlson, 1962; Epstein, 1963b; Epstein et al., 1961). However, we would expect this tendency to be less marked for objects of known constant physical size, i.e., the chairs, than for nonrepresentative objects, which customarily appear in a wide range of sizes. This much is implied by the transactional analysis of size constancy (Ittelson, 1951c). Yet the absence of a significant interaction between the distance variable and the familiar-size variable indicates that size overestimation as a function of distance was independent of the characteristics of the standard. The absence of an interaction is apparent by inspection of Table 11.

A second finding warranting comment concerns the judgments of the normal-size chair and its equivalent stick. Table 11 shows that the chairs were judged to be larger than the sticks at each distance, although only the differences for the 30- and 40-yard distances proved significant. These differences are not compatible with the assumptional hypothesis.

Putting aside the questions raised by the overestimation data and the data for the judgments of the normal chair and stick, there remains a more fundamental question: do the mean heights in Table 11 reflect a regression of perceived size, or do they merely reflect a tendency to provide a match for each standard chair which would be a reasonable compromise between the remembered average chair size and the perceived size?

The results of Bolles and Bailey (1956) and Churchill (1962) lend credence to this question. The Ss in the Bolles-Bailey study made two sets of verbal size judgments of a sample of familiar objects such as pencils, books, automobiles, and articles of clothing found in and around one of the investigator's home. First, S made nonvisual judgments; with his eyes closed S was asked to guess the size of the object. Then S repeated the estimate with his eyes open. The correlations of the judgments with the measured sizes of the objects was .994 for the visual estimates and .988

for the nonvisual estimates. Furthermore, only a small proportion of the cases showed any improvement with the addition of visual information provided by the visual presentation. In those cases where such improvement was observed, there was evidence that the improvement resulted from the more precise identification of the object made possible by visual inspection. These findings have been confirmed with a variety of measurement procedures by McKennell (1960) and Churchill (1962). These investigators also found that Ss display a high degree of accuracy in their nonvisual estimates of the size of familiar objects.

The next series of results to be described were obtained under conditions of reduced observation. Ittelson (1951c) presented three playing cards, normal-sized, half-sized, and double-sized, in total darkness, each presented individually at the same distance from S. These cards were perceived as all of normal size but at different distances. Another set of standards, wrist watch, playing card, and magazine cover, each identical in size with one of the cards, was perceived as different in size and at the same distance. These results are readily interpretable in terms of the influence of familiar size on perceived size.

The influence of familiar size on perceived size also seems evident in the results obtained by Epstein (1963a, 1965). Epstein's (1963a) results, presented in Table 4, show that the "coins" which were identical in size and at the same distance were not perceived to be identical in size. The "dime" was underestimated, the "half dollar" was overestimated, and the "quarter" was perceived veridically. Comparable results were obtained in the subsequent revision of this experiment (Epstein, 1965). Thus, the judgments covaried with the assumed familiar size of the standard.

The only discordant results are those obtained by Epstein (1961). In this experiment Ss judged the size of playing cards presented under reduced viewing conditions. The same playing card was presented in five sizes: normal size, quarter size, half size, double size, and triple size. Each card was presented individually at the same distance. Perceived size was found to vary with the physical size of the card, thus contradicting Ittelson's findings (1951c). In addition, the perceived sizes of the cards did not differ from the perceived sizes of a set of blank rectangles of identical dimensions.

This latter finding is not consistent with Slack's hypothesis (1956) or his findings.

Although evidence is available that known size can influence judgments of size, other experiments are required to clarify certain aspects of the question. An experiment is required to delimit the nature of the effect. We have seen that familiarity with the size of an object is sufficient for accurate size estimates in the absence of the object. The introduction of the object for visual inspection does not improve the judgments. These facts suggest the possibility that known size may affect the S's report of size without necessarily affecting perceived size. An experiment which would assess this possibility would be useful. Also useful would be an investigation of the influence of attitudes of judgment. Variations in instructions may well be responsible for several of the inconsistencies between the data reported by different investigators.

References

Ames, A., Jr. *Nature and origin of perception: preliminary laboratory manual for use with demonstrations disclosing phenomena which increase our understanding of the nature of perception.* Hanover, N.H.: Institute for Associated Research, 1946–1947.
Baird, J. C. Retinal and assumed size cues as determinants of size and distance perception. *J. Exp. Psychol.,* 1963, **66,** 155–162.
Bolles, K. L., & Bailey, D. B. Importance of object recognition in size constancy. *J. Exp. Psychol.,* 1956, **51,** 222–225.
Boring, E. G. *Sensation and perception in the history of experimental psychology.* New York: Appleton-Century-Crofts, 1942.
Carlson, V. R. Size-constancy judgments and perceptual compromise. *J. Exp. Psychol.,* 1962, **63,** 68–73.
Carr, H. A. *An introduction to space perception.* New York: Longmans, 1935.
Churchill, A. V. Supplementary report: effect of mode of response on judgment of familiar size. *J. Exp. Psychol.,* 1962, **64,** 198–199.
Epstein, W. The known size apparent distance hypothesis. *Amer. J. Psychol.,* 1961, **74,** 333–346.
Epstein, W. The influence of assumed size on apparent distance. *Amer. J. Psychol.,* 1963, **76,** 257–265. (a)
Epstein, W. Attitudes of judgment and the size-distance invariance hypothesis. *J. exp. Psychol.,* 1963, **66,** 78–83. (b)
Epstein, W. Effective difference in influence of relative size on

perceived relative distance. *Percept. Mot. Skills*, 1964, **18**, 383–384.

Epstein, W. Nonrelational judgments of size and distance. *Amer. J. Psychol.*, 1965, **78**, 120–123.

Epstein, W., & Baratz, S. S. Relative size in isolation as a stimulus for relative perceived distance. *J. Exp. Psychol.*, 1964, **67**, 507–513.

Epstein, W., & Franklin, S. Some conditions of the effect of relative size on perceived relative distance. *Amer. J. Psychol.*, 1965, **78**, 466–470.

Epstein, W., Park, J., & Casey, A. The current status of the size-distance hypotheses. *Psychol. Bull.*, 1961, **58**, 491–514.

Fillenbaum, S., Schiffman, R., & Butcher, J. Perception of off-size versions of a familiar object under conditions of rich information. *J. Exp. Psychol.*, 1965, **69**, 298–303.

Gogel, W. C. Perception of the relative distance position of objects as a function of other objects in the field. *J. Exp. Psychol.*, 1954, **47**, 335–342.

Gogel, W. C. Size cue to visually perceived distance. *Psychol. Bull.*, 1964, **62**, 217–235.

Gogel, W. C., & Harker, G. S. The effectiveness of size cues to relative distance as a function of lateral visual separation. *J. Exp. Psychol.*, 1955, **50**, 309–315.

Gogel, W. C., Hartman, B. O., & Harker, G. S. The retinal size of a familiar object as a determiner of apparent distance. *Psychol. Monogr.*, 1957, **71**, No. 13 (Whole No. 442).

Hastorf, A. H. The influence of suggestion on the relationship between stimulus size and perceived distance. *J. Psychol.*, 1950, **29**, 195–217.

Helmholtz, H. von. *Physiological optics.* (Transl. by J. P. C. Southall.) Vol. III. Optical Society of America, 1925.

Helson, H. Adaptation level theory. In S. Koch (Ed.) *Psychology: a study of a science.* Vol. 1. New York: McGraw-Hill, 1958.

Helson, H. *Adaptation-level theory: an experimental and systematic approach to behavior.* New York: Harper & Row, 1964.

Hillebrand, F. Das Verhaltnis von Accomodation und Konvergenz zur Tiefenlokalisation. *Z. Psychol. Physiol.*, 1894, **7**, 77–151.

Hochberg, C. B., & Hochberg, J. E. Familiar size and the perception of depth. *J. Psychol.*, 1952, **34**, 107–114.

Hochberg, C. B., & Hochberg, J. E. Familiar size and subception in perceived depth. *J. Psychol.*, 1953, **36**, 341–345.

Hochberg, C. B., & McAlister, E. Relative size vs. familiar size in the perception of represented depth. *Amer. J. Psychol.*, 1955, **68**, 294–296.

Holway, A. H., & Boring, E. G. Determinants of apparent visual size with distance variant. *Amer. J. Psychol.*, 1941, **54**, 21–37.

Ittelson, W. H. Size as a cue to distance: static localization. *Amer. J. Psychol.*, 1951, **64**, 54–67. (a)

Ittelson, W. H. Size as a cue to distance: radial motion. *Amer. J. Psychol.*, 1951, **64**, 188–202. (b)

Ittelson, W. H. The constancies in perceptual theory. *Psychol. Rev.*, 1951, **58**, 285–294. (c)

Ittelson, W. H. Familiar size and the perception of depth. *J. Psychol.*, 1953, **35**, 235–240.

Ittelson, W. H. *Visual space perception*. New York: Springer, 1960.

Kaufman, L., & Rock, I. The moon illusion. *Scient. Amer.*, 1962, **207** (1), 120–130.

Kilpatrick, F. P. (Ed.) *Human behavior from the transactional point of view*. Hanover, N.H.: Institute for Associated Research, 1952.

Kilpatrick, F. P., & Ittelson, W. H. Three demonstrations involving the visual perception of movement. *J. Exp. Psychol.*, 1951, **42**, 394–402.

Koffka, K. *Principles of Gestalt psychology*. New York: Harcourt, Brace & World, 1935.

Köhler, W. *Gestalt psychology*. New York: Liveright, 1947.

Landauer, A. A., & Rodger, R. S. Effect of "apparent" instructions on brightness judgments. *J. Exp. Psychol.*, 1964, **68**, 80–84.

McKennel, A. C. Single stimuli judgments based on a standard of familiar size. *Percept. Mot. Skills*, 1959, **9**, 119–126.

McKennel, A. C. Visual size and familiar size: individual differences. *Brit. J. Psychol.*, 1960, **51**, 27–35.

Pratt, C. C. The role of past experience in visual perception. *J. Psychol.*, 1950, **30**, 85–107.

Slack, C. W. Familiar size as a cue to size in the presence of conflicting cues. *J. Exp. Psychol.*, 1956, **52**, 194–198.

Smith, W. M. Past experience and the perception of visual size. *Amer. J. Psychol.*, 1952, **62**, 389–403.

Taylor, J. G. The behavioral basis of perceived size and distance. *Canad. J. Psychol.*, 1965, **19**, 1–14.

Wheatstone, C. On some remarkable and hitherto unobserved phenomena of binocular vision. *Phil. Mag. Ser.*, 1852, **4** (3), Part II, 504–523.

Zuckerman, C. B., & Rock, I. A reappraisal of the roles of past experience and innate organizing processes in visual perception. *Psychol. Bull.*, 1957, **54**, 269–296.

Chapter three
The assumptive context:
II The perception of
shape, slant, and motion

The perception of
shape and slant

The problem of size perception arose because perceived size is independent of retinal size. The solution to the problem was achieved by postulating a combination of variables as the basis for size perception. The manner in which these variables combined to produce perceived size was expressed in the generalized size-distance invariance hypothesis. The history of the problem of shape perception is characterized by a parallel development. This should not be surprising, since the factors involved in both cases may be defined by the same variables. The terms which distinguish the variables in the two analyses are useful mainly because they are convenient and because they refer to differences which exist in unanalyzed perception. For example, the term "slant" could be replaced by "relative distance of points on a surface," but this would complicate the designation of the variable value. In any event, this example illustrates the substitutability of the variables, e.g., slant and distance, which constitute the analysis of shape-slant and size-distance perception.

The relationships among perceived shape, perceived slant, and projective retinal shape have been expressed in a form analogous to the size-distance invariance hypothesis: "A retinal projection of a given form determines a unique relation of apparent shape to apparent slant" (Beck & Gibson, 1955, p. 126). The experimental evidence concerning the shape-slant invariance hypothesis has been reviewed by Epstein and Park (1963). The present section will consider the interaction of perceived shape, perceived slant, and projective shape when either of the first two variables is determined by subjective assumptions. In point of fact, all the studies which will be discussed have dealt with the effects of shape assumptions on perceived slant. The influence of slant assumptions on perceived shape has not been examined.[6] The probable reason for this neglect is that slant is a highly variable property; e.g., the slants of manipulable objects may vary on each successive presentation. For most objects there probably is little tendency toward, or environmental support for, the development of a stable slant assumption. This is not true for all objects, e.g., tables and bookcases, and conceivably studies of the influence of slant assumptions could be conducted with such objects as standards.

A corollary simply derived from the shape-slant invariance hypothesis is that a specific perceived shape should determine a unique relation of apparent slant to projective shape. If a target of fixed perceived shape undergoes projective transformation, concomitant changes in apparent slant depth should be obtained. As was the case for the size-distance invariance hypothesis, the interaction is expected regardless of the conditions which determine the perceived shape of the target, e.g., when perceived shape is determined by assumptive variables.

The perceived slant depth
of moving targets

The rotating trapezoidal window   A number of striking phenomena, originally reported by Ames (1951), are frequently attributed to the influence of shape assumptions. The Ss viewed a trapezoid (length, 19½ inches; height of long side, 23⅝ inches; height of short side, 12½ inches) enclosing white-mullioned plane surfaces with painted shadows to represent a three-dimensional window. The trapezoid was rotated on a vertical shaft at a speed between 3 and 6 rpm. The display was viewed from distances of 10 and 20 feet under full-cue conditions or reduced conditions with similar results.

In the present discussion our concern will be with the perceived motion (change in slant depth) and perceived

[6] Excluded are the studies of the effect of induced perceived slant on perceived shape (e.g., Beck & Gibson, 1955; Epstein, Bontrager, & Park, 1962).

shape of the rotating trapezoid. The rotating window appears to *oscillate* through an angle of 100°. The perceived reversal of the direction of movement occurs when the window passes through S's frontoparallel plane. As the window approaches the frontoparallel plane, it appears to slow up, then to stop altogether, and then to reverse its direction of movement. At the same time apparent alterations of shape and size occur. As the trapezoidal window rotates, it appears as a rectangular window which is continually changing in both shape and size. These highly reliable effects contrast sharply with the perceptual effects which are obtained when a rectangular form without painted window cues is rotated. In Ames's study the rectangular display was perceived as a rotating invariant shape.

Ames's explanation (1951) of these phenomena has two essential premises, one factual and the other hypothetical:

1
The lengths of the parallel edges of the trapezoidal window are in a proportion such that, except at very short viewing distances, the larger side will always subtend a larger visual angle than the smaller side.
2
Because of past experience S has ". . . learned to interpret the particularly characterized retinal images that exist when he looks at doors, windows, etc., as rectangular forms. Moreover, he learned to interpret the particular degree of trapezoidal distortion of his retinal images in terms of the positioning of the rectangular form to his particular viewing point" (Ames, 1951, p. 14).

The role which is assigned to these factors may be clarified by the following illustration: Suppose the initial position of the trapezoid is at 80° from S's frontoparallel plane with the left, shorter side more distant. Since S identifies the trapezoid as a window, he assumes it to be rectangular and construes the difference between the visual angles subtended by the two vertical sides to be the result of the slant depth of the window. The window is perceived as slanted away from S on the left. As the window rotates slowly toward the frontoparallel plane, projective alterations occur. The difference between the retinal sizes of the sides diminishes, and the solid horizontal visual angle expands. The retinal-size difference between the sides continues to diminish as the rotation continues. However, because the smaller side can never subtend a larger angle than the large side, the trapezoid appears slanted on the left, with its smaller side more distant, even when the reverse is actually the case. When the trapezoid passes through the frontoparallel plane, the horizontal visual angle at once begins to shrink. A decreasing horizontal visual angle associated with a rectangular form perceived as slanted can only result from increasing the slant in the same direction as the perceived slant. This is the reason for the apparent reversal in the direction of motion which occurs when the objective rotation brings the window through the frontoparallel plane. The net result is perceived oscillation.

Ames's interpretation (1951) has been challenged by Pastore (1952), Day and Power (1963, 1965), Graham (1963), and Allport and Pettigrew (1957). Pastore (1952) agrees that the oscillatory effect depends on the disparity between perceived slant and actual slant. However, he doubts that this disparity is due to the two factors described above. He was able to obtain the oscillatory effect with a wide range of forms. These included forms for which subjective assumptions would lead to other outcomes, e.g., diamond, circle, and forms of which assumptions are unlikely, e.g., a highly irregularly contoured form. Pastore advances what he considers to be an alternative to Ames's interpretation. However, close inspection of Pastore's thesis shows it to be the same as Ames's with only one exception: Ames attributes the disparity between perceived slant and actual slant to the influence of assumed rectangularity. Pastore rejects this aspect of the explanation. In its place, he proposes that ". . . the basis for the tilt of the perceived surface lies in the asymmetrical retinal projection of a given figure and the central processes which are innervated by the retinal projection. Such central processes may attain a more appropriate equilibrium when a given figure is perceived in other than its true orientation" (Pastore, 1952, p. 323).

This hypothesis is too vague to be useful. In rejecting Pastore's interpretive efforts there is no intention to disregard his findings. If the oscillatory effect is a general one, obtained with a great variety of figures, then the possibility is open that a general explanation can be formulated which does not include assumptive variables. Pastore's findings need to be checked. The oscillatory effects are not consistent with observations made by others (Epstein, 1965; J. J. Gibson & E. J. Gibson, 1957; Langdon, 1951; Langdon, 1953; Wallach, O'Connel, & Neisser, 1953) of the effects of rotation on perceived depth.

Graham (1963) has also presented a reinterpretation of the perceived movement of the trapezoidal window. Like Pastore (1952), he denies that the effects depend on experience with trapezoids or windows. Instead Graham accounts for the effects solely in terms of stimulus conditions. Graham points out that the rotating trapezoid provides two types of cues: (1) the differential angular velocities existing between selected points on the surface of the trapezoid and (2) linear perspective. The cue of motion parallax is ambiguous, since the differential angular velocities of points on the surface of the trapezoid are identical for clockwise and counterclockwise movement. The S cannot determine whether the points on the window are approaching him in one of the near quadrants or moving away from him in the far quadrant, because the sign and quantity of differential angular velocity are identical in the two quadrants.

How does S handle this ambiguity? "The answer is that he resolves the ambiguity of movement parallax cues by depending on perspective cues. The short end of the window is always seen as farther from the S than the long end; and the ambiguous parallax cues are interpreted as in harmony with perspective cues" (Graham, 1963, p. 2002). From these considerations Graham proceeds to account for the perceived movement of the window. Two remarks regarding Graham's account are in order:

1
Like Ames and Pastore, Graham contends that the existence of a discrepancy between objective and perceived slant is an essential prerequisite for the illusory apparent motion.
2
Graham assumes that linear perspective, in this case relative size of the vertical edges, is an unambiguous determinant of relative distance, but as was noted in Chapter 2, this premise has been questioned.

Day and Power (1963, 1965) have reported a series of experiments whose results created difficulties for the explanations considered thus far. In Exp. I, Day and Power

showed that while trapezoidal shapes yielded significant perceived reversals, so did elliptical and irregularly contoured
shapes. In addition, varying the surface characteristics of the
trapezoid so that varying degrees of "windowness" were
produced did not affect the frequency of perceived reversals.
These results are incompatible with Ames's interpretation
but might be handled by Pastore's and Graham's accounts.
However, the results of Exps. II and III of Day and Power
(1965) seem to be incompatible with all three accounts. Day
and Power obtained judgments of the apparent slant of the
stationary surfaces prior to the rotating exposure. According
to the explanations of Ames, Pastore, and Graham non-
veridical perception of the slant of the surfaces is an essential condition of the perceived oscillatory movement. The
results did not support this contention. For example, both a
trapezoid and an ellipse yielded perceived oscillation, although only the stationary slant of the trapezoid was misperceived; the slant of the ellipse was judged accurately.

As an alternative to the interpretations of Ames, Pastore,
and Graham, it was suggested by Day and Power (1965) that
the effect depends entirely on the ambiguity of motion parallax. This is sufficient to account for the perceived reversals
of movement direction. The fact that the reversals occur
exclusively when the surface is frontoparallel or sagittal
needs to be explained. Day and Power suggested that these
positions are favored because a reversal at these points
requires the minimum shifts in apparent orientation. At all
other positions ". . . reversals would not be expected since
these would necessarily result in abrupt changes in apparent
orientation" (Day and Power, 1965, p. 125). Why minimum
shifts are favored over abrupt changes was left unexplained.

Allport and Pettigrew (1957) also questioned Ames's interpretation. Their reservations stemmed from the results of
a study of cultural influences on the perception of the
trapezoidal window. The expectation of cross-cultural variability was based on the premise that the degree of illusori-
ness would be a function of the amount of experience with
windows. Members of a culture whose dwellings do not incorporate windows or who have a definite disinclination for
fabricating rectangular objects should be less subject to the
illusory effects than members of North American society.

Such results would implicate the role of "object connotation" (Allport and Pettigrew, 1957), e.g., windowness, in the perception of the trapezoidal window. Presumably Ames's interpretation would be contraindicated if no cultural variability were observed.

These speculations were examined by comparing the responses of two groups of children. One was a group of urban South African children. The other was a group of Zulu children who lived in rural Zulu areas. The Zulu culture ". . . is virtually devoid . . . of windows, . . . of angles, straight lines, and other experiential cues that would presumably 'cause' the illusion if it were wholly a product of experience" (Allport and Pettigrew, 1957, p. 106). The Ss reported the perceived motion of a rectangular window and a trapezoidal window viewed monocularly and binocularly from distances of 10 and 20 feet. The findings differed according to the conditions of observation. When the trapezoidal window was viewed monocularly from a distance of 20 feet (conditions which Ames found to be optimal), the proportion of rural Zulus reporting illusory motion was not smaller than the proportion of whites or urban Zulus who reported oscillation. In the remaining conditions the proportion of urbanized Ss was greater than the proportion of rural Zulus. The greatest difference was obtained for binocular vision and the 10-foot viewing distance (these conditions are least favorable for obtaining the effect).

After completing the perceptual judgments, S was asked to state his preference for one of two geometrical drawings presented to him in pairs (a circle and a square or trapezoid). Circle-preferring children (mainly rural Zulus) did not differ from angle-preferring children (e.g., urban Zulus) in their responses to the rotating trapezoid under monocular observation. Presumably, circle-preferring rural Zulus would be less inclined to make the assumption of rectangularity than the angle-preferring Ss and should have been, on this account, less susceptible to the illusory effects.

The results may be summarized as follows: when suboptimal conditions prevail, e.g., binocular viewing at short distance, object connotation is an important determinant; however, identification, or object connotation, is not necessary under optimal conditions, e.g., monocular viewing from 20 feet. Allport and Pettigrew (1957) conclude that Ames's interpretation is contradicted by the results for the optimal conditions.

Slack (1959) has taken exception to the conclusion of Allport and Pettigrew. Slack maintains that the results ". . . are perfectly consistent with the strong empiristic position which gives little or no weight to nativistic factors" (p. 131). Slack argues that the crucial variable of experience is the relative frequency of experience with rectangular objects as compared with experience with trapezoidal objects. A S who had experienced trapezoidality more frequently than rectangularity would, on an empiristic view, be expected to respond differently from a S with reversed relative frequency of experience. However, under optimal conditions, differences in frequency of rectangularity should not be expected to affect the appearance of the trapezoidal window if trapezoidality is equally rare for both groups. The fact that one group favors circle, e.g., the rural Zulus, is inconsequential, since the important variable is rectangularity versus trapezoidality. On the other hand, when suboptimal conditions prevail, the additional experience of the urban children with rectangularity should counteract the effect of the cues to trapezoidality, thereby facilitating the illusion. For the rural Zulus, with little experience with rectangularity, the autochthonous "give-away" cues should operate to produce the perception of trapezoidality and rotation.[7]

The literature we have been considering has raised serious questions about the Ames interpretation of the effects obtained with the rotating trapezoid. Four types of evidence have been advanced by critics of Ames's analysis:

1

The occurrence of perceived oscillation is independent of the windowlike characteristics of the trapezoid (Day & Power, 1963; Pastore, 1952).

---

[7] Cross-cultural studies are far from being ideally suited for the purpose of testing assumptive hypotheses. If we consider that the man-made environment is only a fraction of the total environment, it is obvious that the comparative exposure histories of two cultural groups cannot be assessed in the manner implied by Allport and Pettigrew. However, the cross-cultural studies may be useful as a basis for generating questions that will then be tested experimentally. Turnbull's naturalistic reports (1961) of size constancy in the Pygmy people of Africa illustrates the value of this approach.

2

The oscillatory effect occurs for shapes other than trapezoids including irregular shapes (Day & Power, 1963; Pastore, 1952).

3

The apparent orientation of the surface does not determine the occurrence of oscillation. Instead the opposite is claimed to be true. "Apparent orientation is held to be a consequence of, rather than a necessary condition for, apparent reversals" (Day & Power, 1965, p. 124).

4

The frequency of apparent reversals is independent of differences in relevant exposure histories of the observers (Allport & Pettigrew, 1957).

When viewed in the total evidential context Ames's account is unconvincing. The postulation of assumptive determinants seems unnecessary, since the effects can be accounted for in other terms. Nor is the Ames account sufficient as a general explanation of the occurrence of perceived oscillation with the variety of forms which have been studied. We are forced to the conclusion that the results of the rotating trapezoid experiments cannot be confidently introduced to support the known-shape–apparent-slant hypothesis.

The perceived slant depth
of stationary targets

The effect of known shape on perceived slant has also been investigated with stationary targets. Epstein (1962) had Ss report the perceived slant of four types of standards under reduced conditions of observation: (1) objectively slanted textureless rectangle, (2) frontoparallel projections of the slanted rectangle presented in S's frontoparallel plane, (3) a playing card identical in size to the textureless rectangle slanted to the same degree, (4) frontoparallel projective representations of the playing card presented in S's frontoparallel plane.

The known-shape hypothesis leads to the prediction that the slanted playing cards should appear slanted. The perceived slant should vary systematically with the variations of objective slant. If known shape is crucial for perceived slant, then the slanted rectangles should not appear slanted, since they are nonrepresentational. However, the projective cards should also appear slanted. The perceived slant of each projective representation should be comparable to the perceived slant of the objectively slanted playing card which it represents. The results showed that perceived slant did vary in the expected manner for both the slanted playing cards and their frontoparallel projective representations. However, contrary to expectations, the perceived slant of the projective standards was always greater than the perceived slant of the objective slanted cards.

The above results provide some support for the known-shape hypothesis. The results for the rectangles, however, suggest that specific object connotations may be unnecessary. The variable of rectangle versus playing card was not a significant source of variation. Results comparable to those obtained for the playing cards were also obtained for the rectangles. A hypothesis which would account for the results for all four types of standards would be the following: a convergence of contours in isolation will determine a reliable perception of slant depth if there is a high probability that the contours of the distal shape are regular and physically invariant. This is an assumptive hypothesis; however, it is more general, including the case of a representative identifiable object as one instance. Some additional support for the hypothesis may be gleaned from the studies which show that the effect of motion on perceived depth is more reliable for regularly contoured forms (e.g., Gibson & Gibson, 1957).

Do shape assumptions influence perceived slant?   The evidence which has been summarized in the preceding pages permits only a tentative answer to this question. The experiments are few in number, and the data which they have produced are subject to different interpretations. Perhaps some progress would be made if known or assumed shape could be isolated in an experimental setting where no other cues for slant depth were available. This cannot be achieved for forms which are members of the modal class of form, e.g., circles, rectangles. Displacement of these forms produces characteristic transformations which are highly correlated with physical slants. These transformations may serve as direct cues for slant independently of the identification of the object. Therefore, identifiable representative forms which are randomly contoured are to be preferred. If it were possible to manipulate shape assumptions with this type of form, then conditions would be present for a more convincing test of the known-shape hypothesis. In the absence of more evidence the verdict must be: "Not proved."

The perception of movement

The role of the assumptive context has been examined for many types of movement phenomena. The main approach has been to determine whether objects which characteristically connote movement are perceived differently from objects which are not normally associated with movement. Another approach has been to compare the apparent movement of objects which have differing movement connotations. The dependent variables have been the apparent speed, distance traversed, direction, and quality of movement. The question has been examined for induced movement (notably by Krolik, 1935), stroboscopic motion, autokinetic motion, and real motion.

Basic explanations of these movement phenomena continue to be the subject of controversy. For example, despite its long history of investigation, there is no generally accepted account of stroboscopic motion. The contending explanations range from Wertheimer's (1912) classic cortical short-circuit theory to a neoempiristic account in terms of a ". . . very strongly weighted unconscious translation of ordinal events into 'movement' " (Toch & Ittelson, 1956, p. 199). The purpose of this discussion will not be to choose between these or similar alternatives. The objective will be to evaluate the evidence that assumptions, and particularly the movement connotations of meaningful objects, affect perceived movement. Evidence of this sort does *not* have necessary implications for a nativistic or empiristic account of these phenomena.

The effect of movement connotation on stroboscopic motion

Stroboscopic motion, or the phi phenomenon, refers to the apparent movement of successively exposed stationary objects. Thus if two stationary lights are alternately flashed at some optimal rate of succession, the S will report one light traversing a path between the locations of the two flashing lights. Graham (1951) lists the following as variables which affect phi: length of pause between stimuli, duration of stimulus exposure, distance between stimuli, stimulus form, relative differences in intensity, wavelength distributions, and instructions. Our present concern will be the effect of movement connotations; however, the listing of other variables makes clear that the danger of experimental confounding is present whenever movement connotation is varied by using meaningful representations of objects.

Investigations of the phi phenomenon using meaningful figures were first reported by DeSilva (1926). DeSilva and subsequently Blug (1932) both reported that movement connotations affected the threshold and direction of apparent movement. The studies were conducted with few Ss and a surprising lack of attention to structural factors which favor apparent movement. For this reason these studies will be bypassed in favor of more recent work. The experiments of Jones and Bruner (1954), Toch and Ittelson (1956), Krampen and Toch (1960), and Toch (1963) will be considered.

Jones and Bruner (1954) were the first contemporary psychologists to reexamine the role of movement connotation. Of their four experiments, the last is most interesting and will be dealt with in greatest detail. The first experiment involved successive exposures of a "stick man" in three different lateral positions, changing places with a nonsense form which was displaced on successive exposures an equal distance in the opposite direction. The S was asked to report the relative speed and distance of movement of the two objects. After the first trial 85 percent of the Ss reported that the man appeared to move faster and also traversed a greater distance. This effect disappeared by the fifth trial. The second experiment showed that the omission of the middle stage in the exposure series disrupts the perceived quality of movement, e.g., smooth versus jerky movement, less for meaningful objects in a meaningful context than for a nonmeaningful situation. Analogous findings were obtained in Exp. III, although in this study there was the possibility that variations of the meaning variable were confounded by structural variations.

Most appropriate for an examination of the role of movement connotation is Exp. IV of Jones and Bruner. This experiment studied the direction of perceived motion when alternative directions are possible. A prototypal situation has been described by Ternus (in Ellis, 1938): (1) O O, (2) OO, (3) O O. This exposure series is perceived in one of two ways:

1
The left and right circles move so as to exchange places.
2
In phase 2 the left and right circles meet, as if in collision, then return to their original positions.

Jones and Bruner (1954) presented Ternus's sequence in two contexts depicting different scenes: a baseball game context and a billiards game context. The essential difference between the movement connotations of the two scenes is that in a baseball game two balls moving in opposite directions will generally continue in an uninterrupted path of movement past each other, while collision and subsequent recoil commonly occur for two balls involved in billiards. Table 12 shows that the frequency with which the alternatives were reported did not differ significantly. However, the distribution of the alternative responses depended on the meaning context of the exposures. "Crossovers" predominated for the baseball context, while "bounces" predominated in the billiard context.

Toch and Ittelson (1956) studied the role of movement connotation in a comparable situation, originally studied by Von Schiller (1933). In successive exposures Von Schiller presented a central figure followed by simultaneous presentation of two figures on either side of the central figure. In the absence of determining factors, e.g., figural similarity or spatial separation, perceived movement takes place about equally in both directions. Toch and Ittelson (1956) studied

Table 12
Responses to ambiguous movement patterns in two contexts*

Context	Crossover	Bounce
Baseball	10	5
Billiard	4	11
Total	14	16

* From Jones & Bruner, 1954, p. 164.

the perceived direction of movement in the Von Schiller situation using meaningful objects which differ in their characteristically experienced direction of movement. Three series were used: a series of three bottles exposed in horizontal order, a series of three solid outline drawings of bombs pointed downward, and a series of three airplanes (nose upward). The bottle series was presumed to be neutral as regards characteristic movement direction and served as a control condition. For the bomb and airplane series ". . . it was postulated that . . . the direction in which the objects represented would move according to past experience would be that in which preferential movement . . . would be seen by observers" (Toch & Ittelson, 1956, p. 205). The results for eight observers were generally in agreement with expectations. However, not all Ss responded in the expected direction.

Krampen and Toch (1960) also studied stroboscopic motion in the Von Schiller paradigm, this time using arrows and arrowlike designs as stimulus figures. Their results were comparable to those of Toch and Ittelson, leading to the general conclusion that ". . . the effects of meaning connotation in determining movement are definite but circumscribed. They are obtained with *most* Ss under *some* conditions and with *some* Ss under *most* (nonoptimal) conditions" (Toch, 1963, p. 623).

The somewhat inconclusive nature of the evidence may be due to several factors. Chief among these are the imprecise control of the S's movement assumption and, secondly, the influence of uncontrolled nonassumptive determinants, e.g., point of fixation. Evidence of the effect of fixation is contained in Toch's study (1963) of the interaction of factors in determining apparent movement direction in the Von Schiller paradigm. Toch's results seem to indicate that the movement connotation of an object influences the direction of apparent movement only when connotation is combined with another determinant, such as direction of fixation. Unfortunately, the design of Toch's experiment (1963) does not allow an unambiguous assessment of the interaction effect. A well-designed factorial experiment would contribute importantly to our knowledge of the role of movement connotation.

The precision with which the variable of movement connotation is controlled is probably limited in experiments in which variations of connotaton are inferred from common experience with familiar objects. Procedures which establish the connotations within the experiment allow more precise control. However, even within the limitations of the type of experiment under consideration more can be done to determine the stability of the movement connotation of the stimuli.

The effect of movement connotation on autokinetic motion

Autokinetic movement refers to the apparent movement of a fixated stationary point exposed in surroundings which are minimally articulated. In most experiments the target has been a point of light presented in a totally darkened room; however, the dark room is not an essential condition (Luchins & Luchins, 1963). Autokinetic movement has been the subject of numerous investigations. The following is a partial list of the determinants of autokinetic movement which have been identified: target size (Edwards, 1954; Luchins, 1954), target brightness (Chapanis, Rouse, & Schachter, 1949), retinal locus (Luchins, 1954), simultaneous auditory stimulation (Miller, Werner, & Wapner, 1958), social pressure (Sherif, 1935). The present section will describe those experiments which were designed to demonstrate an effect of movement connotation on the perceived direction of autokinetic movement.

The experiments conducted by Comalli, Werner, and Wapner (1957) stemmed from their involvement with the "sensory-tonic field theory of perception." In addition earlier studies (Kaden, Wapner, & Werner, 1955; Werner & Wapner, 1954) had shown that the apparent median plane and the apparent horizon were affected by the directional connotations of stationary objects. These theoretical and empirical considerations led Comalli et al. (1957) ". . . to hypothesize that the directional quality of a pictured object should affect autokinetic motion so that the stimulus object apparently moves in the direction of the dynamics" (p. 290). In Exp. I lighted silhouettes of a running horse, a running boy, and an arrow were exposed in a dark room. Each stimulus figure was presented in two orientations: facing right and facing left.

S was instructed to expect the appearance of movement and to report continuously on the direction of movement. Two dependent measures were obtained: (1) perceived direction of initially reported motion, and (2) duration of motion in a particular direction during 30 seconds of reported motion. The results for both measures agreed with the hypothesis. Toch (1962) has independently conducted a similar experiment. Toch's results (1962) are comparable to those obtained by Comalli et al.

Comalli et al. (1957) raised the possibility that the variable of directional connotation was confounded by differences in the retinal distributions of the figures in the two orientations. To eliminate this possible source of confounding, Exp. II was conducted using a single figure invariantly oriented. The figure could be interpreted as one of two representations: a bird flying in one direction or an airplane flying in the opposite direction. The procedure of Exp. I was followed, with the exception that half the Ss were told that they would see a picture of a flying bird and half a picture of a flying airplane. For half the Ss in each of these instructional conditions the airplane was directed left, bird right, and for the other half the orientation was reversed. The results showed the expected interaction of instructions and orientation. The directional connotations produced by the instruction (labeling) determined the direction of the perceived movement. In a third experiment, similar to Exp. II, Comalli et al. (1957) obtained the same effect for movement in the up-down direction.

A different approach to the same question was employed in a later study by Comalli (1960). Werner (1956) has distinguished two "modes of cognition": the geometric-technical and the expressive, or physiognomic. Wapner and Werner (1957) have reported that Ss who differ along this dimension differ in the way they perceive movement. Comalli (1960) tested a group of artists and a group of scientists (chemists) under the conditions of Exp. I of Comalli et al. (1957). "Artists are assumed to be more oriented in terms of the expressive qualities of objects whereas scientists are assumed to be more oriented toward the realistic . . . geometric-technical qualities of objects. . . . Artists should be more greatly affected by physiognomic qualities (directional connotations) than scientists" (Comalli, 1960, p.

100). The main finding was a small but statistically greater susceptibility to the directional connotations among the artists. More generally, the results agreed with those of Comalli et al. (1957) in exhibiting an influence of directional connotations on the direction of autokinetic motion.

The experiments which have been described all agree in showing that the perceived direction of autokinetic movement can be significantly influenced by the directional connotations of the objects. Apparently, the typical direction of movement in preexperimental experience becomes the basis for a learned association between the identification of an object and its movement characteristics. This association is able to determine the perceived direction of movement. The *direction* of autokinetic motion is probably among the more susceptible dependent variables. This is so because, omitting certain figural characteristics, the apparent direction of movement does not seem to be controlled by any known variables. Under these conditions the assumptive context is able to dominate the outcome. Other variables, such as latency of initial report of movement and extent of movement, could be studied to provide supplementary information.

References

Allport, G. W., & Pettigrew, T. F. Cultural influence on the perception of movement: the trapezoidal illusion among Zulus. *J. Abnorm. Soc. Psychol.*, 1957, **55**, 104–113.

Ames, A. Visual perception and the rotating trapezoidal window. *Psychol. Monogr.*, 1951, **65** (7) (Whole No. 324).

Beck, J., & Gibson, J. J. The relation of apparent shape to apparent slant in the perception of objects. *J. Exp. Psychol.*, 1955, **50**, 125–133.

Blug, A. Neue Untersuchungen ueber Scheinbewegung bei tachistoskopischen Beobachtungen. *Z. Psychol.*, 1932, **127**, 290–324.

Chapanis, A., Rouse, R. O., & Schachter, S. The effect of intersensory stimulation on dark adaptation and night vision. *J. Exp. Psychol.*, 1949, **39**, 425–437.

Comalli, P. E., Jr. Studies in physiognomic perception. VI. Differential effects of directional dynamics of pictured objects on real and apparent motion in artists and chemists. *J. Psychol.*, 1960, **49**, 91–109.

Comalli, P. E., Jr., Werner, H., & Wapner, S. Studies in physiognomic perception. III. Effect of directional dynamics and meaning-induced sets on autokinetic motions. *J. Psychol.*, 1957, **42**, 289–299.

Day, R. H., & Power, R. P. Frequency of apparent reversal of rotary motion in depth as a function of shape and pattern. *Austral. J. Psychol.*, 1963, **15**, 162–174.

Day, R. H., & Power, R. P. Apparent reversal (oscillation) of rotary motion in depth: an investigation and a general theory. *Psychol. Rev.*, 1965, **72**, 117–127.

DeSilva, H. R. An experimental investigation of the determinants of apparent visual movement. *Amer. J. Psychol.*, 1926, **37**, 469–501.

Edwards, W. Autokinetic movement of very large stimuli. *J. Exp. Psychol.*, 1954, **48**, 493–495.

Epstein, W. A test of two interpretations of the apparent size effects in a distorted room. *J. Exp. Psychol.*, 1962, **63**, 124–128.

Epstein, W. Perceptual invariance in the kinetic depth effect. *Amer. J. Psychol.*, 1965, **78**, 301–303.

Epstein, W., Bontrager, Helen, & Park, J. The induction of non-veridical slant and the perception of shape. *J. Exp. Psychol.*, 1962, **63**, 472–479.

Epstein, W., & Park, J. Shape constancy: functional relationships and theoretical formulations. *Psychol. Bull.*, 1963, **60**, 265–288.

Gibson, J. J., & Gibson, E. J. Continuous perspective transformations and the perception of rigid motion. *J. Exp. Psychol.*, 1957, **54**, 129–138.

Graham, C. H. Visual perception. In S. S. Stevens (Ed.), *Handbook of experimental psychology.* New York: Wiley, 1951.

Graham, C. H. On some aspects of real and apparent visual movement. *J. Opt. Soc. Amer.*, 1963, **53**, 1019–1025.

Jones, E. E., & Bruner, J. S. Expectancy in apparent visual movement. *Brit. J. Psychol.*, 1954, **45**, 157–165.

Kaden, S. E., Wapner, S., & Werner, H. Studies in physiognomic perception. II. Effect of directional dynamics of pictured objects and of words on the position of the apparent horizon. *J. Psychol.*, 1955, **39**, 61–70.

Krampen, M., & Toch, H. The determinants of perceived movement direction. *J. Psychol.*, 1960, **50**, 271–278.

Krolik, W. Veber Erfahrungswirkungen beim Bewegungssehen. *Psychol. Forsch.*, 1935, **20**, 47–101.

Langdon, J. The perception of changing shape. *Quart. J. Exp. Psychol.*, 1951, 3, 157–165.

Langdon, J. Further studies in the perception of changing shape. *Quart. J. Exp. Psychol.*, 1953, 5, 89–107.

Luchins, A. S. The relation of size of light to the autokinetic effect. *J. Psychol.*, 1954, **38**, 439–452.

Luchins, A. S., & Luchins, E. H. Half views and autokinetic effect. *Psychol. Rec.*, 1963, 13, 415–444.

Miller, A., Werner, H., & Wapner, S. Studies in physiognomic perception. V. Effect of ascending and descending gliding tones on autokinetic motion. *J. Psychol.*, 1958, **46**, 101–105.

Pastore, N. Some remarks on the Ames oscillatory effect. *Psychol. Rev.*, 1952, **59**, 319–323.

Sherif, M. A study of some social factors in perception. *Arch. Psychol.*, N.Y., 1935 (187), 1–60.

Slack, C. W. Critique on the interpretation of cultural differences in the Ames trapezoid. *Amer. J. Psychol.*, 1959, **72**, 127–131.

Ternus, J. The problem of phenomenal identity. In W. D. Ellis (Ed.), *A source book of Gestalt psychology.* London: Routledge, 1938.

Toch, H. The effect of "meaning" on the autokinetic illusion. *Amer. J. Psychol.*, 1962, **75**, 605–611.

Toch, H. Interaction of determinants of perceived movement direction. *Percept. Mot. Skills*, 1963, **16**, 621–628.

Toch, H., & Ittelson, W. H. The role of past experience in apparent movement: a reevaluation. *Brit. J. Psychol.*, 1956, **47**, 195–207.

Turnbull, C. M. Some observations regarding the experiences and behavior of BaMbuti pygmies. *Amer. J. Psychol.*, 1961, **74**, 304–308.

Von Schiller, P. Stroboskopische Alternativversuche. *Psychol. Forsch.*, 1933, **17**, 180–214.

Wallach, H., O'Connel, D. N., & Neisser, U. The memory effect on visual perception of three-dimensional form. *J. Exp. Psychol.*, 1953, **45**, 360–368.

Wapner, S., & Werner, H. *Perceptual development.* Worcester, Mass.: Clark Univer. Press, 1957.

Werner, H. On physiognomic perception. In G. Gikepes (Ed.), *The new landscape.* Chicago: Theobald, 1956.

Werner, H., & Wapner, S. Studies in physiognomic perception: I. Effect of configurational dynamics and meaning-induced sets on the position of apparent median plane. *J. Psychol.*, 1954, **38**, 51–82.

Wertheimer, M. Experimentelle Studien über das Sehen von Bewegung. *Z. Psychol.*, 1912, **61**, 161–265.

Chapter four
The assumptive context:
III The perception of color

The germinal study of the effects of the assumptive context on perceived color was conducted by Duncker (1939), a Gestalt psychologist who made important contributions in the fields of motion perception and problem solving. The phenomenon which Duncker studied had been observed earlier by Hering (1907) and had been assigned a role of considerable importance in his theory of color constancy.

■ The color in which we have oftenest seen an external thing impresses itself indelibly on our memory and becomes a fixed characteristic of the memory image. What the layman calls the real color of a thing is a color which has become firmly attached to the thing in his memory; I might call it the memory color of the thing. All the things which are known to us from past experience, or which we believe to be known to us in respect to color, are seen through the spectacles of the memory colors (Hering, 1907, p. 7; also see Woodworth, 1938, Ch. 14).

Katz (transl., 1935), in his classic treatise, *The World of Colour,* also took note of memory colors; however, he dismissed memory colors as insignificant factors (cf. especially pp. 264–265). Although the discussions found in the work of Hering and Katz are evidence of an interest in memory color, there had been no controlled investigations of the phenomenon. Prior to Duncker's study, the empirical evidence was in the form of demonstrations (e.g., see Adams, 1923; Katz, transl., 1935). Therefore, Duncker's investigation (1939) may be considered as the genuine precursor of the contemporary investigations.[8]

---

[8] In everyday observation, it is unlikely that the existence of memory colors would be recognized. Usually, the color experience stimulated by the light entering the eye and the memory color are in agreement. Therefore, the influence of memory color cannot be noticed. These re-

As stimuli, Duncker used an artificial green leaf and a "donkey" cut out from the same green material. The two objects were presented successively under red illumination. The illumination was such as to make a circular form cut from the same green material appear gray. Duncker expected that if memory color was operative, then the leaf, characteristically green, would appear greener than the donkey, characteristically gray. A color wheel presented under normal illumination, simultaneously with the standard, was used to obtain color matches. Duncker found that the mixtures on the color wheel that were considered equivalent to the color of the standard contained a 29° green sector for the donkey and a 60° green sector for the leaf. The donkey's match was only half as green as the leaf's match. Duncker concluded that an influence of memory color had been demonstrated.

Several features of Duncker's procedure (1939, pp. 262–263) warrant notice:

1
The leaf and donkey were not exposed simultaneously.
2
The illumination was not monochromatic. Therefore, some degree of "sensory support" was provided for the memory color.
3
The experimental arrangement was such as to make S aware that abnormal conditions of illumination prevailed. S did not have to discover the facts of illumination by observation of the standard.
4
The standard and the color wheel could not be perceived simultaneously.

A similar experiment has been reported by Bruner, Postman, and Rodrigues (1951). The stimuli were eight patches cut from gray paper to represent a tomato, tangerine, lemon,

marks should not be construed to mean that memory color is inconsequential in normal viewing. The potency of memory color is suggested by the absence of disturbances in perception when color is eliminated, as is the case in black-and-white photographs. Achromatic photographs do not appear in the least strange, although everything depicted in the photograph has lost its accustomed color. In this connection, it is interesting to note that ". . . in painting and photography, the greatest satisfaction to the observer is likely to result if the memory colors corresponding to familiar objects are matched rather than the actual colors aroused by the original subject" (Burnham, Hanes, & Bartleson, 1963, p. 87).

boiled lobster claw, carrot, banana, neutral oval, and neutral elongated ellipse. A variable color wheel made up of yellow and red segments served as the comparator. Ss viewed the standards under four conditions:

1

Induced color. Each patch was presented on a blue-green background. The entire display was covered by a finely ground glass and was directly illuminated by a beam from above. S was told: "This is a (tangerine, banana . . .). Make the color-wheel the same color as it" (Bruner et al., 1951, p. 218).

2

Induced color (informed). These Ss were informed about the nature of color induction prior to making the settings.

3

Stable color. In place of the induced color, well-saturated orange patches were used.

4

Optimal matching. Extraneous stimulation was eliminated, and S matched the orange patches with the color wheel and patch in simultaneous view. In the previous conditions the color wheel and the standard patch were separated by 80° of visual arc, thus necessitating successive viewing of the standard and comparison.

Bruner, Postman, and Rodrigues predicted an interaction of the memory color variable with conditions of observation. They expected that the effect of memory would diminish as the conditions of observation became less ambiguous. This expectation was confirmed. Under conditions 1 and 2, the standards, which were characteristically red objects, required color-wheel mixtures which were redder than the average mixture, and yellow objects required mixtures which were significantly yellower than the average level. These effects, which were attributed to memory color, were not present under conditions 3 and 4.

The results of this experiment gave evidence of an effect of memory color. The operation of memory color was induced by the labeling procedure, and labeling was a sufficiently powerful inductor to overcome the opposing influence of knowledge about the conditions of exposure (condition 2). The ineffectualness of explicitly provided general information will also be noted in other instances. On the other hand, labeling was ineffective under optimal conditions. This is compatible with Duncker's (1939) analysis of the conditions which are favorable for exhibiting an effect of memory color.

Harper (1953) has criticized the experiment of Bruner, Postman, and Rodrigues. Harper contended that the findings were ambiguous, because ". . . they can be interpreted in terms of perceptual modification or in terms of response generalization" (p. 86). To eliminate this ambiguity Harper introduced a new procedure for examining memory color. The test figures were superimposed on a background, and the color of the background was varied until the figure was no longer detectable. Harper reasoned that ". . . if O is unable to detect a colored figure superimposed on a colored background, then the figure and ground are not merely being *responded* to as the same but are being *perceived* as the same" (p. 87). Six figures were cut from the same sheet of orange paper. Three figures were representative shapes, all of them characteristically red (an apple, a heart, and a lobster). Each of these representative shapes was compared with a nonrepresentative shape of equal area and similar contour (an oval, an isosceles triangle, and the letter Y). The figures were individually exposed in front of a reflecting differential color mixer. The degree of red in the background color mixer was varied, and S was instructed to report when the figure was no longer distinguishable from the background. Prior to exposing each standard, S was told, "There is a reddish apple [heart or lobster]" or, for the nonmeaningful shapes, "There is a yellowish-orange oval [triangle or Y]."

The following reasoning underlies this experiment: If memory color influences the apparent color of the figures, then the meaningful figures which are characteristically red should require a redder background than the nonrepresentative figures. The number of degrees of red in the mixture required for indistinguishability was $71.34°$ for the nonmeaningful figures and $134.90°$ for the meaningful figures. This effect was obtained under conditions which may be ranked with conditions 3 and 4 of the Bruner, Postman, and Rodrigues (1951) experiment, indicating that the effect may not be restricted to ambiguous viewing conditions.

Harper's results (1953) are clear, but questions may still be raised concerning their interpretation. An inspection of Harper's data (table 1, p. 88) shows considerable variability among the redness means both for the meaningful figures (lobster, $156°$; heart, $105°$) and the nonmeaningful figures

(Y, 111°; oval, 36°). Similar variability between the variances can be noted. These observations suggest that certain nonassumptive determinants are operative. Secondly, the assumptive variable was confounded by an instructional variable. The experimental design contains no provision for assessing the influence of instructions.

Other questions are suggested by the results of a study by Fisher, Hull, and Holtz (1956). Experiment I was essentially an improved replication of Harper's study (1953) with similar, but less marked or consistent, results. The smaller differences between the representative shapes and their nonrepresentative correlates may be due to the fact that Fisher et al. did not inform their Ss of the color of the nonmeaningful figures.

Experiment II was designed to study the effects of memory color for representative and nonrepresentative figures which were identical structurally. Figural differences between the meaningful and nonmeaningful figures were eliminated by using the same figure in both conditions. The meaningful and nonmeaningful figures were distinguished by orientation and labeling. In one case the figure was a cross, labeled as a "red cross" symbol, and in the other case the figure was rotated through 45° to represent the letter X. These two figures were interpolated in a series of other figures to prevent S from recognizing that the red cross and X were identical figures. The degree of background redness was not significantly different for these two figures.

In Exp. III Fisher et al. studied the effects of variations of area and complexity of contour. Harper's nonmeaningful figures were used. The main finding was that areal variation was a significant source of variance; the greater the area of the figure, the greater the degree of redness required for indistinguishability. This relationship is consistent with other results obtained in the study of the threshold for visual form (Krauskopf, Duryea, & Bitterman, 1954).

While the results of Fisher et al. (1956) do not confirm Harper's findings (1953), they do not contradict the results of Duncker (1939) and Bruner et al. (1951), since these latter investigators also reported that the influence of memory colors is confined to less informative conditions of viewing. However, in demonstrating an effect of figural factors, e.g., area, Fisher et al. reinforce the impression that these variables need to be taken into account in design of experiments on memory color. What is required is an experiment in which color connotation, instructions, figural properties, and viewing conditions are varied in an orthogonal design.

Delk and Fillenbaum (1965) have provided information about the influence of the instructional variable. Three different instructions were used in an experiment similar to Harper's (1953). One version of the instructions was fashioned after Harper's instructions. The red-associated figures were called "reddish" and the other figures called "yellowish-orange." In the second version, Ss were told the name of each figure, but no mention was made of its color. The third set of instructions mentioned neither the names nor the colors of the figures. The test figures were of three types: red-associated figures, e.g., an apple; abstract neutral figures, e.g., an oval; and characteristically nonred figures, e.g., a bell. Harper's indistinguishability procedure was used to determine the perceived color of the form.

Analysis of variance showed only one significant effect: the three types of figures required significantly different amounts of red in the backgrounds in order to merge with the background. Each of the three red-associated figures required significantly more red than any of the other figures. Differences in instructions had no effect, nor was there a significant interaction between instructions and figures. Delk and Fillenbaum (1965) conclude that ". . . past association of color and form does in some way influence perceived color, since that is the one respect in which the figures did clearly differ" (p. 293).

Assuming that one can agree that the figures differed only in past association (surely this is not true for the shape of a horse and a heart), several aspects of the results are puzzling. The absence of a significant interaction between meaningfulness and instructions is surprising. The instructions should have different effects depending on the past associations of the figures with color. The absence of differences between the nonred and neutral figures also needs to be explained. Contrary to the implications of the memory-color hypothesis, the characteristic colors of the nonred objects apparently did not influence the appearance of these figures.

Bolles, Hulicka, and Hanly (1959) have raised a different

objection to two of the studies we have been considering. They note that the apparatus for making comparisons which was used in the experiments by Duncker (1939) and Bruner et al. (1951) made it literally impossible for S to make an exact match. Unable to achieve an accurate match S will tend to settle for the most reasonable mismatch, i.e., one which conforms to the characteristic color. Bolles et al. set out to show that ". . . if the subject is permitted to make a colour match, then he will do so regardless of possible memory colour influences. Memory colour effects . . . occur only when a psychophysical equation is impossible" (1959, p. 176).

The first experiment followed the procedures used earlier by Baker and Mackintosh (1955). Baker and Mackintosh obtained matches for nonsense forms presented under condition 1 of the Bruner et al. study. The nonsense forms had previously been associated with the color names yellow, orange, and red. The color matches for the forms, in the absence of labels, required decreasing amounts of yellow in accordance with the color name which had been associated with the form. However, the matching conditions in the Baker-Mackintosh study made an exact match impossible. The standards were gray figures against a blue-green background, while the color wheel contained only red and yellow sectors. The main innovation of the Bolles, Hulicka, and Hanly experiment was the introduction of 90° sectors of black and white into the color wheel. This modification makes possible a rather close color match. Under these conditions the influence of previous color associations disappeared.

In a second experiment Bolles et al. studied memory color in a situation similar to Duncker's original study. Five figures were used as stimuli: Duncker's donkey and leaf and three control figures, a rough contoured nonsense form, a smooth contoured nonsense form, and a square. The nonsense forms were included to determine whether the differences obtained by Duncker were due to differences in contour regularity of the leaf and donkey.

The main findings of this experiment were:

1

Duncker's results were confirmed when an exact match was precluded by apparatus limitations.

2

There was no difference between the donkey and the leaf when an exact match could be achieved, and thus the critical analysis of the writers was supported.

3

Contour variations did not significantly affect the judgments of the nonsense forms.

On the basis of these observations Bolles et al. (1959, p. 183) conclude that the memory color effect is an artifact of conditions which prohibit exact equations. The effects do not represent an influence on ". . . phenomenal, immediately given, perception of color." Instead they represent a reasonable cognitive resolution of an impossible task.

An earlier experiment by Bruner and Postman (1949) will conclude the presentation of evidence on memory color. Bruner and Postman were not concerned with the question of memory color. Their concern was to determine how Ss deal with perceptual incongruity. Normal and trick playing cards were exposed tachistoscopically for varying durations until correct recognition occurred. The trick cards were printed with color and suit reversed, e.g., black three of hearts, red two of spades. They found that the recognition threshold for the incongruous trick cards was four times as high as the threshold for normal cards. Our main concern, however, is with the verbal prerecognition responses. These responses revealed a marked tendency to assimilate the color of the trick card to the characteristic color of the card. This took the form either of complete dominance of the memory color or a compromise between the memory color and the actual color. Presumably, these results reflect the influence of memory color. However, the results may also be interpreted entirely in terms of response bias rather than color perception.

The experiments which have been reviewed in this section have not succeeded in providing conclusive evidence of the influence of color connotations on perceived color. The positive findings in the Duncker situation have been shown to be peculiar to conditions which absolutely preclude an exact match. The results reported by Harper (1953) are made inconclusive by the findings of Fisher, Hull, and Holtz (1956). Nor are the positive findings obtained by Delk and Fillenbaum (1965) completely decisive. Plainly, a decision about the influence of assumptions on the perception of color must be deferred until further research is completed.

The experience of the previous investigators has contributed significantly to our knowledge of the design requirements of future experiments:

1

Ideally, the test forms should differ only in their histories of association with specific color. Structural differences, e.g., contour regularity and area, should be held constant, since these differences have an independent effect on perceived color. Adherence to this condition would reduce the population of forms that could be studied. There are two ways of circumventing this limitation. One is to include variations of structure and color connotation as orthogonal factors in a factorial experiment. The independent effects of these two factors and the interaction effect could then be assessed. Experiments of this design are conspicuously absent in the literature of memory color. A second procedure for circumventing the limitation is to establish the color assumptions by experimental training. In this way, the same visual form could be made to connote a variety of colors for different Ss. The introduction of a training procedure will confer another advantage: the E can control the specificity of the color connotation, and the effects of varying specificity can be explored. Parenthetically, we may note that experiments which have not employed training procedures have usually assumed that the memory color corresponds with the natural color of the object, i.e., the color of the surface in normal illumination. This premise is not greatly in error, but neither is it completely accurate. Bartleson (1960) determined the memory colors of ten familiar objects by asking O to choose the color of the object from memory from an array of 931 Munsell color chips. Bartleson found that each of the ten memory colors was significantly different from the natural colors. "Each memory color tended to be more characteristic of the dominant chromatic attribute of the object in question; grass was more green, bricks more red, etc."

The same tendency was noted earlier by Katz (transl., 1935, pp. 163–164). Katz suggested that language habits were responsible for this tendency. Whatever the explanation, it is likely that a procedure which trains color connotation can successfully eliminate this discrepancy. A training procedure has been introduced by Baker and Mackintosh (1955), but unfortunately a methodological artifact tends to make their findings suspect. A variety of training procedures could be explored. There may be training routines which are more effective than conventional paired-associates training.

2

The experimental evidence suggests that varying the instructions and S's knowledge about the conditions of stimulation does not affect the outcome. Still these variables ought to be reexamined, preferably in combination with other variables. Of greatest relevance for an assessment of the generality of memory color are variations of the information available to S concerning the conditions of stimulation, e.g., the color and distribution of illumination.

3

Two procedures have been used to obtain measures of perceived color. Of the two, Harper's method of adjustment to indistinguishability is preferable. Harper's method is not subject to the criticism that Bolles et al. leveled at Duncker's procedure. In addition, the S tested with Harper's method is less likely to discover the purpose of the experiment. The objectives of the experiment are less well concealed with Duncker's procedure, and the risk is greater that S will modify his response to conform to his hypothesis about E's purposes. These two procedures do not exhaust the possibilities. Suppose S was trained to give response 1 upon exposure to a random collection of gray forms and response 2 upon exposure to a random collection of greenish forms. After the discriminatory conditioned responses have been established, two stimuli are presented: (a) an irregularly contoured form cut from green material exposed in red illumination and (b) a leaf shape cut from the same material and presented in the same red illumination. If Duncker's results are valid, S should produce response 1 for stimulus a and response 2 for stimulus b. This testing procedure could be combined with a regime for training color connotations. The result might be an experiment better controlled than those which have been thus far reported.

References

Adams, Grace K. An experimental study of memory color and related phenomena. *Amer. J. Psychol.*, 1923, **34**, 359–407.

Baker, K. E., & Mackintosh, I. The influence of past associations upon attributive color judgments. *J. Exp. Psychol.*, 1955, **49**, 281–286.

Bartleson, C. J. Memory colors of familiar objects. *J. Opt. Soc. Amer.*, 1960, **50**, 73–77.

Bolles, R. C., Hulicka, I. M., & Hanly, B. Color judgment as a function of stimulus conditions and memory color. *Canad. J. Psychol.*, 1959, **13**, 175–185.

Bruner, J. S., & Postman, L. On the perception of incongruity: a paradigm. *J. Pers.*, 1949, **18**, 206–223.

Bruner, J. S., Postman, L., & Rodrigues, J. Expectations and the perception of color. *Amer. J. Psychol.*, 1951, **64**, 216–227.

Burnham, R. W., Hanes, R. M., & Bartleson, C. J. *Color: a guide to basic facts and concepts.* New York: Wiley, 1963.

Delk, J. L., & Fillenbaum, S. Differences in perceived color as a function of characteristic color. *Amer. J. Psychol.*, 1965, **78,** 290–293.

Duncker, K. The influence of past experiences upon perceptual properties. *Amer. J. Psychol.*, 1939, **52,** 255–265.

Fisher, S. C., Hull, C., & Holtz, P. Past experience and perception: memory color. *Amer. J. Psychol.*, 1956, **69,** 546–560.

Harper, R. S. The perceptual modifications of colored figures. *Amer. J. Psychol.*, 1953, **66,** 86–89.

Hering, E. Grundzuge der Lihre vom Lichtsinn. In Graefe-Saemisch (Eds.), *Handb. ges. Augenhik,* 1907.

Katz, D. *The world of colour.* London: Kegan Paul, Trench, Trubner, & Co., 1935.

Krauskopf J., Duryea, R. A., & Bitterman, M. E. Threshold for visual form: further experiments. *Amer. J. Psychol.*, 1954, **67,** 427–440.

Woodworth, R. S. *Experimental psychology.* New York: Holt, 1938.

Chapter five
Controlled practice or training:
I The role of practice
and prior exposure

In a review of the experimental literature dealing with the question of practice and perception, E. J. Gibson (1953) has defined the independent variable which concerns us in this chapter: "Practice, for present purposes, will be defined as any controlled activity of O which involves repeated perception of the test stimuli or ones similar to them. This definition assumes attention on the part of O, but it deliberately omits any requirement of reinforcement, correction, or reward" (Gibson, 1953, p. 403). Although this definition excludes reinforcement as a necessary condition, it does not imply any decision concerning the efficacy of reinforcement. The definition is neutral regarding this question, leaving a decision about the role of reinforcement for empirical determination.

Gibson (1953) and Francés (1962) have surveyed the experimental literature dealing with the effects of practice. The present discussion will be less exhaustive than the reviews presented by these writers. The literature under review will be selected primarily from the more contemporary material. Furthermore, several topics considered by Gibson and Francés will not be treated, e.g., visual acuity, perceptual span, tachistoscopic word recognition, in favor of a more detailed examination of two topics: visual space perception and visual form perception.

The effect of practice on
the judgment of distance

Is the judgment of distance affected by training? The common procedure for studying this question has involved tests

of transfer of training. The critical question has been
". . . whether it is possible to train Ss in judging distances
in such a way that generalizable improvement is obtained"
(Gibson & Bergman, 1954, pp. 473–474). Two transfer
tasks have been used to test the generality of learning. The
test which has been used most often has called for judgments of distance stretches not presented during the training series. The reasoning underlying this test is that performance on a transfer test series, which does not repeat
previously judged distances, could only be affected by the
previous judgments if general ability has been improved. A
second method of testing for transfer effects has been to
obtain size judgments following training in making distance
judgments. Presumably, improvement or decrement in distance estimation should have corresponding effects on size
judgment.

The major studies are those reported by Gibson and
Bergman (1954), Gibson, Bergman, and Purdy (1955), and
Wohlwill (1964). Gibson and Bergman wished to determine if
verbal absolute estimates of distance would be improved by
practice when the possibilities of establishing associations
between specific cues and specific distances were precluded.
Two groups of Ss, an experimental and a control group,
provided two sets of *uncorrected* verbal estimates of eighteen
different distances ranging from 52 to 395 yards. The experimental group received training between the two sets of
distance estimates. The training consisted of *corrected* judgments of ninety different distances ranging from 39 to 435
yards. The control group received no intervening training.
The standards were metal plates attached to wooden stakes.
The experiment was conducted in an outdoor setting. The
terrain was a level stretch of mown grass which served as an
athletic field. Except for the target no other objects were in
view, so that interposition and linear perspective were not
present. The chief available distance cue was the gradient of
optical texture correlated with the mown field. Also operative
were motion parallax and vertical height in the plane.

Our principal concern is with the evidence of modifications
of distance estimation as a function of practice. This question may be approached in three ways: analysis of the constant error (accuracy), analysis of the variable error (consistency), and analysis of errors by trials (course of learn-

ing). Forty-one (95.6 percent) of the forty-five Ss in the experimental group exhibited a reduction in their mean constant error, while only twenty-six (55.3 percent) of the forty-seven control Ss showed a reduction. Also important was the finding that while only two experimental Ss enhanced their error, by shifting in the same direction, seventeen of the control Ss increased their constant error. These results show that training leads to improvement in judgment of distance. Learning curves were plotted showing the median error as a function of blocks of eighteen trials. The curve may be seen in Figure 3, which shows that the pretest median error of 33 percent was halved during the first block of training trials. No further error reduction was obtained, nor did the error rise during the final uncorrected posttest block. Thus the learning appears to be independent of continued correction. For both experimental and control groups a reduction in variability was observed with increasing practice; however, the reduction was greater for the experimental

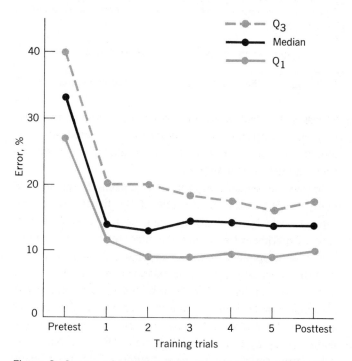

Figure 3. Course of learning as measured by the median error of the experimental group. (*From Gibson & Bergman,* 1954, *p.* 479, *fig.* 3.)

group. Gibson and Bergman (1954) concluded that generalizable improvement can be obtained by training even when no opportunity is provided for learning specific cue-distance associations.

Since the learning of specific cue-response associations could not have been the basis of the transfer effect, the question may be raised concerning the nature of the generalizable learning which was responsible for the improvement in distance estimation. Gibson and Bergman (1954) proposed that what was learned was ". . . a *conceptual scale* of yards in a psychophysical relationship with stimulation provided primarily by a receding stretch of ground" (p. 481). This scale, like a calibrated ruler, has boundaries or anchors at both ends, segregated units, and differentiated portions which are fractions or multiples of the unit. The improvement which was noted can be attributed to three achievements:

1
The development of closer psychophysical correspondence between the conceptual yard scale and the optic array provided by the ground
2
A stabilization of the scale's anchor points and its units
3
An increasing differentiation along the stimulus dimension

Gibson notes that while the conceptual scale is in correspondence with the optical gradients correlated with the ground surface, it is not tied to the particular ground surface used during the training trials.

In two subsequent experiments, Gibson, Bergman, and Purdy (1955) examined the role of the hypothesized conceptual scale by explicitly teaching each S a scale of distance. Experiment I examined the effect of the scale on judgments of absolute distance. Experiment II was concerned with the effect on judgments of relative distance. Two groups of Ss served in Exp. I. The Ss in both groups made a series of judgments of eighteen different distances. The outdoor setting and experimental procedure were the same as in the earlier study by Gibson and Bergman (1954). Group E received prior training on a different outdoor field. The training task required S to make ten *corrected* fractionation judgments of the bounded field. Near and far anchors were provided by S's station point and a large marker labeled "300 yards." The only raised object was a fire hydrant, 10 yards in front of S. The hydrant served to demarcate the unit of the scale. Group C received no prior training.

The results were unequivocal. Group C's error score was significantly greater than Group E's. The mean estimates of Group E were more accurate than those of Group C for fifteen of the eighteen target distances. In addition, the variability was lower for Group E. A comparison between Group E's distance judgments and the judgments of the experimental group in the earlier study (Gibson & Bergman, 1954) suggests that the two types of training had comparable effects. Scale training was almost as effective as the earlier training involving correction of distance judgments. Apparently the efficiency of the latter training procedure was not discernibly enhanced by having the training and test on the same ground.

In Exp. II, Gibson et al. (1955) tested the same two groups again. However, the test judgments differed from those in Exp. I. Using a combination of the method of limits and the method of constant stimuli, S was required to compare three standard distances with a variable distance target. The standard and variable could not be viewed simultaneously. The question of interest concerned the effect of scale training on differential sensitivity to distance. The main finding was that the difference limen was not significantly lowered by prior scale training. Despite this failure Gibson et al. are not ready to conclude that differentiation within the distance dimension cannot be improved by training. They suggest that a greater amount of training on a task more similar to the test of relative judgments might be necessary to produce a lowering of the difference limen for distance.

A more recent experiment by Wohlwill (1964) completes our review of the experimental literature. The conditions of Wohlwill's experiment differed considerably from those which prevailed in the experiments of Gibson et al. (1954, 1955). Wohlwill obtained bisection judgments of relatively short distances (45 and 90 centimeters) along the floor of a large viewing box. The floor of the box was either blank white or covered by a densely packed random distribution of star shapes on a white background. The experiment was a 2 × 3 factorial design. All Ss made a series of pretest and posttest bisection judgments and apparent-size judgments. Intervening between the two series of judgments were three different types of training. In the "control" training condition S made a series of eight bisections of a 90-centimeter distance. In the "high-low" training condition S made bisection judgments, four each from two observation points which were at different heights from the floor of the box. In the "scale" training condition S fractionated the largest standard distance into fifths. The fractionation series was repeated four times. Half the Ss assigned to each type of training received correction following each training trial; the remaining Ss received no correction.

In a previous study conducted under similar conditions but without the introduction of practice, Wohlwill (1963) had found a significant tendency for bisections to exhibit distance overestimation. The same tendency was observed in the pretest of the present experiment. The question then concerns the fate of this tendency as a function of practice. Difference scores derived from comparing the errors on the second half of the pretest with those on the first half of the posttest were analyzed. Only the correction variable proved to be a significant source of variance. Correction produced significant decrease in error; noncorrection did not. Difference between types of training did not affect the difference scores significantly. Generally, practice was ineffective in eliminating the overconstancy error.

The judgments of size did vary as a result of the practice variable. The mean constant error on the posttest was greater than on the pretest. The correlation between the size and distance judgment errors also changed from a significant positive correlation on the pretest to a nonsignificant correlation on the posttest. In other words, ". . . the effect of the distance training was to render the size judgments less directly dependent on perceived distance" (Wohlwill, 1964, pp. 409–410). This finding also reflects the limited effectiveness of the practice.

Gibson and Smith (1952) found comparable results in a study of the perception of size of pictured targets in photographs. An experimental group was given prior practice in estimating distances in photographs, and a control group made the size judgments without prior distance estimations. Although the corrected practice was found to improve the distance estimates of the experimental group, there was no evidence that judgments of size were significantly improved. Gibson and Smith attributed this lack of improvement to the highly specific nature of the learning produced by practice. They suggested that S merely learned "the association of a highly specific identifying clue" with a specific verbal distance estimate. "For training to have any generality, the continuity of the stimulus variables must be taken into account and *utilized in the training*. . . ." (Gibson and Smith, 1952, p. 17). If instead S responds to isolable clues, improvement will be confined to the training situation. While this interpretation is plausible for the situation of Gibson and Smith, it seems less appropriate for Wohlwill's (1964) experimental condition.

The experiments of Gibson and Wohlwill have demonstrated that training with correction can exert a limited facilitative effect on subsequent estimation of distance. One of the conditions which determine the magnitude of transfer has been indicated by Gibson. However, the conditions of transfer remain largely unexplored. Experimentation to explore these conditions might profitably begin with the similarity between the training and test situations. There are several similarities which could be examined in factorial combination: (1) similarity of operations for judging distance, (2) similarity of estimates which are required, e.g., bisection, trisection, and equidistance, (3) similarity of distance extents which are judged, and (4) similarity of background conditions. An experiment of this sort would help resolve the question of what is learned during training.

The effect of practice on
the perception of form

The effect of prior practice on the perception of form has rarely been investigated as an independent question. Instead, the investigations have been motivated by a desire to provide evidence relevant to more general theoretical orientations. The orientations which are related to the studies described in the first two sections are viewpoints associated with Gestalt psychology. The antiempiristic bias of Gestalt theory led to Gottschaldt's widely cited experiments (1926, 1929) on the influence of experience on the recognition of forms. The Gestalt emphasis on the organizational basis of form perception provided the rationale for Rubin's experiments (1921) on figural persistence and nonrecognition of reversed fields.

Figural persistence

In their analysis of form perception, the Gestalt psychologists, beginning with Rubin (1915), distinguished between figure and ground. This distinction referred to the general rule that in perceptual experience the visual world is articulated into segregated bounded shapes upon a more extensive phenomenally shapeless background. With the help of a variety of visual demonstrations the Gestalt psychologists hoped to isolate the factors that determine the figure-ground organization of meaningless, unfamiliar configurations. Koffka (1935) described six of these factors: orientation, relative size, enclosing and enclosed areas, internal articulation, Prägnanz, and Rubin's figural aftereffect. Rubin used the term "aftereffect" to refer to the tendency, observed in his experiments, for the current figure-ground organization to reproduce the immediately prior organization. Since the term "figural aftereffect" is currently used to designate a different phenomenon (Köhler & Wallach, 1944), the term "figural persistence" will be substituted for Rubin's term in the present discussion. Woodworth (1938, p. 631) has presented the following summary of Rubin's experiment:

■ Rubin prepared a large number of nonsense figures by cutting irregular portions out of cards and placing the cards before a lantern with green glass interposed so that on the screen there appeared an irregular green area surrounded by what was sensibly black. With a four-second exposure for each single figure, he presented a series of 9 figures, four times over, with instructions to see the enclosed green area as the figure, the black as ground. This was followed by a series of 9 similar figures with instructions to see the enclosing black area as the figure. The experimenter now shuffled these 18 figures with 9 new ones and presented them in mixed order, after an interval of 30–45 minutes, with instructions to remain passive as regards which part should be seen as figure, but to report in each case whether the figure was the enclosed or the enclosing portion and whether the field was recognized as one previously shown.

The results revealed a moderate tendency to see the same figure on the second exposure as in the original experience. As the subject had divided the field the first time into figure and ground, so he was likely to do the second time, even when remaining passive; 64 percent of the figures were seen in the same way as before, 33½ percent were seen with reversed figure and ground, and 2½ percent were seen in both ways. This carry-over of the same figure-ground organization of a given field from one exposure to another is called by Rubin the figural after-effect.

There has been relatively little direct experimental investigation of this phenomenon. There were two early studies (Dutton & Trail, 1933; Gottschaldt, 1926) which suggested certain restrictions on the generality of Rubin's results. Gottschaldt's findings led him to conclude that unless S expects a test and is set to look for familiar figures during the test, no persistence is observed. Dutton and Trail reported that the two modes of organization of Rubin's figures could not be achieved by all Ss. Only the most "obedient" Ss could see the enclosing portion as figure. This fact introduces an uncertainty regarding S's experience during the training. We cannot be certain that the Ss organized the training forms in a manner congruent with the instructions.

Rock and Kremen (1957) sought evidence of figural persistence in a modified version of Rubin's experiment. The chief modifications were these:

1
The training patterns were half-figures which ensured that the experience was with the intended unit.
2
The expectation of a forthcoming test which might lead S to look for familiar figures was eliminated.
3
The Ss were tested only once.
4
A control group was added which responded to the ambiguous figure-ground patterns without prior practice.

Figure 4 shows four of the test figures used by Rock and Kremen. The training figures were either the white or black halves of the test figures. These halves were exposed on a gray background identical to the background of the test figures. The training session consisted of eight 2-second exposures of each of eight training halves. There were two figures for each color-side (black, white—left, right) combination. The instructions led S to believe he was participating in an experiment on extrasensory perception. In the test, the eight ambiguous figures, which contained the trained halves, were presented along with ten new figures of the same type. Each figure was exposed for 1 second, and S reported the color and side of the portion which appeared as figure. Rock and Kremen (1957) found no evidence of figural persistence. The experimental and control Ss responded similarly to the ambiguous figure-ground patterns. Each of the two halves was perceived as figure by an approximately equal number of Ss.

Since Rock and Kremen (1957) modified Rubin's experiment in several ways, it is difficult to determine what is responsible for the discrepancy between the results of the two experiments. An experiment by Cornwell (1963) suggests an answer to this question. Cornwell attributed the failure of Rock and Kremen to reproduce Rubin's aftereffect to the absence from their training figures of the same black-white context that existed in their ambiguous test figures. Cornwell's (1963) experiment was a revised version of the Rock-Kremen study. The chief revision concerned the train-

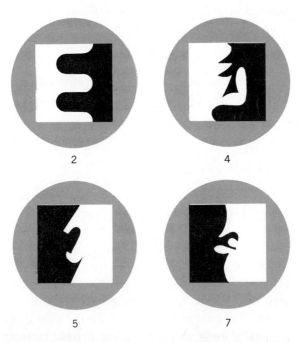

Figure 4. Samples of the ambiguous figure-ground test figures introduced by Rock and Kremen (1957) and used subsequently by Cornwell (1963).

ing figures. Rock and Kremen had used unambiguous black or white halves. Cornwell used the same black-white configurations in the training and test with one modification: in the training situations the contour between black and white was shifted laterally. This had the effect of eliminating the ambiguity; i.e., S tended to perceive one of the areas consistently as figure. In this way Cornwell was able to control S's organization of the training figures without affecting the "contextual relationship" between the training and test figures. The prediction was that ". . . if the same contour is later presented between black and white areas that are approximately balanced or equal, the S will tend to perceive the same area as figure that he perceived when the two areas were unequal" (Cornwell, 1963, p. 157). The results confirmed the prediction. It would appear that preservation of the stimulus context is essential for the effect.[9]

Although the reliability and validity of Rubin's observations continue to be questioned, there is sufficient additional evidence to support the hypothesis of figural persistence. Supporting evidence is available in a wide variety of experiments.

In a well-known study, Leeper (1935) showed that once S learned to organize or interpret a given visual configuration in a specific way, this operated immediately to render difficult the achievement of any other possible organization of the same configuration. One of the patterns was Boring's "my wife and my mother-in-law" figure. In the first phase of the experiment, half the Ss saw an unambiguous version of the "wife" and the other half saw an unambiguous version of the "mother-in-law." Leeper found that this prior experience controlled almost entirely the subsequent organization of the unambiguous composite.

Another effect of this general nature was reported by Epstein and Rock (1960). A series of experiments examined

---

[9] However, a subsequent study by the same author (Cornwell, 1964) failed to confirm the original findings (Cornwell, 1963). On the other hand, positive results have also been reported by Botha (1963) and Vetter (1965), using the original figures of Rock and Kremen. But the training procedures in the Botha and Vetter studies departed significantly from the pure exposure training intended by Rubin. Botha's Ss learned nonsense-syllable responses to the unambiguous halves. Vetter's Ss made esthetic judgments of each half during training. These procedures can be construed as forms of distinctiveness training and are somewhat inappropriate as a test of the figural-persistence phenomenon.

the relative influence of expectancy set and frequency and recency of prior exposure on S's figure-ground organization of Boring or Schafer-Murphy (1943) composites (see Figure 8) exposed tachistoscopically. The training consisted of a series of brief exposures of the unambiguous alternatives. By manipulating the composition of the preparatory series, expectancy, frequency, and recency were varied. The results showed an overwhelming tendency to organize the ambiguous composite so that the portion which appeared as figure corresponded to the most recently exposed unambiguous figure. The effect of recency was obtained even when expectancy set favored an alternative response. The occurrence of a recency effect under these conditions is presumptive evidence against a response-bias interpretation of the effect. The same selective figural persistence based on recency was observed in a later experiment by Epstein and DeShazo (1961).

An example of figural persistence somewhat similar to the recency effect is an interesting observation reported by Engel (1961, p. 303) in a study of stereoscopic perception. A pair of photographs of two different faces was presented in a stereoscope so as to stimulate corresponding retinal points. Ordinarily, if the two monocular fields do not differ greatly along some stimulus dimension, e.g., brightness, the two fields will appear to alternate. If the fields differ considerably, e.g., in degree of contrast, then one of the fields will predominate perceptually. Engel's experiment was in two stages, and each stage consisted of two phases.

In the first stage, Face A was first presented alone at maximum brightness, followed by the simultaneous presentation of Faces A and B. This sequence was continued with the brightness of Face B increasing from a very low level in the first cycle to a level equal to A on the last cycle. After each increase in illumination of B, S was asked to report what he saw. Engel found that B was never reported. Even when B and A had identical brightness, only A was perceived.

Then the second stage was initiated. This stage consisted of the reverse procedure: Face B was kept at the maximal brightness, while the intensity of A was reduced in successive decrements. On the last trial only B was illuminated. Despite the gradual physical disappearance of A and the sustained presence of B, S persistently reported Face A only, even on the last trial when only B was presented. These observations would seem to reflect the remarkable strength of the tendency for an originally perceived unambiguous figure to persist and determine the response elicited in an ambiguous stimulus situation.

The memory effect demonstrated by Wallach, O'Connell, and Neisser (1953) is another case of figural persistence. The experiment was in three stages:

1
A static shadow form was presented, and S reported its appearance. Most Ss reported seeing a two-dimensional random form in the plane of the translucent projection screen.
2
The actual form, which was a tridimensional wire form interposed between the back of the screen and a point source of light, was rotated. The rotation produced a continuous sequence of shadow transformations on the viewing screen. Once again S reported the appearance of the shadow forms. Instead of a sequence of deforming plane shadows, S perceived a single tridimensional rigid form turning in depth.
3
The original static shadow form was exposed again. The static form, which originally appeared flat, now appeared tridimensional. The tridimensional appearance produced by the turning exposure persisted and modified the appearance of the static form. This influence is highly specific, since the turning exposure did not affect the appearance of static forms which were not previously presented in rotation. The absence of generalization to nontrained forms reduces the likelihood that the memory effect was simply a carryover of a newly developed set or response bias for tridimensional reports.

Wallach et al. also observed that the static form, in its acquired tridimensional appearance, underwent spontaneous perspective alternations in depth. This observation is consistent with a perceptual interpretation of the memory effect (cf. Chapter 1).

Finally, a study involving the latency of figural articulation in inkblots may also provide relevant evidence. Atkinson and Ammons (1952) showed Ss four Rorschach inkblots (cards 1, 4, 5, 7), interspersed among fifty photographs. Each time an inkblot was presented, S was told ". . . what to 'see' in the inkblots" and to press a button when ". . . he clearly saw what he was supposed to in the inkblot" (p. 174). For example, S was instructed to see a "cat's face" in card 1 and a "man seated on a fire hydrant" in card 4. Response latency was the dependent variable. Of relevance to the hypothesis of figural persistence are the following two findings:

1
Mean latency of recognition decreased on successive exposures to each inkblot.
2
Once S had been trained to see a particular figure in a blot, an unusually long observation time was required for him to see a different figure in the same blot.

These two findings are consistent with the hypothesis of figural persistence. However, the experimental procedure leaves much to be desired, both in terms of stimulus specification as well as response definition.

The results of the experiments described above provide ample evidence that a previous mode of perceptual organization may persist beyond the initial occasion of stimulation and determine the current direction of organization. Still, relatively little is known about the conditions which determine the occurrence of figural persistence. A number of hypotheses are suggested by considering persistence to be a form of transfer. Thus, the transfer literature suggests that the time which elapses between training and test, and how this time is filled, will be an important consideration. Other variables are the amount of practice or training and the degree of similarity between the training and test figures. Although some information regarding the effects of these variables is available, further experimentation is required.

The explanations of figural persistence which have been advanced have been as varied as the diverse experimental contexts in which the phenomenon has been studied. One interpretation, which has been tested experimentally, was introduced by Epstein and DeShazo (1961) to account for the recency effect observed by Epstein and Rock (1960) with the Shafer-Murphy figures. Epstein and DeShazo interpreted the recency effect to be an influence of recent experience on the selection between equally available alternatives rather than an influence on the primary perceptual organization of the ambiguous figure-ground composite. The hypothesis was advanced that in the initial moments of exposure there occur rapid oscillations of figure and ground, and that the effect of the immediately preceding unambiguous exposure is to stabilize the oscillatory process in favor of the most recently perceived figure.

Evidence that a period of subliminal perceptual oscillation does occur was provided by the results of an experiment involving classical conditioning procedures. A discriminatory galvanic skin response (GSR) was conditioned to one of the unambiguous alternatives under circumstances that favored a recency effect of the other alternative. For example, profile A of the Schafer-Murphy composite (A/B) served as the conditioned stimulus (CS), while profile B was most recent, i.e., immediately preceded composite A/B. When A/B was presented, S should have seen B, but, at the same time, the GSR, which was conditioned to A only, should have been evoked. This follows from the assumption that prior to the exclusive appearance of B as figure, perceptual oscillation took place in which A was also represented. The results supported the hypothesis.

The hypothesis of perceptual oscillation is not intended to account for all instances of figural persistence. But it may successfully explain the cases where relatively simple, labile stimulus configurations are used. A case which satisfies this description is Adams's study (1954) of the perception of a reversible three-dimensional cube. S inspected a skeletal wire cube monocularly until a reversal occurred, i.e., an inversion of the perspective of the near and far faces. Both eyes were then covered for a 2-second period, after which S looked monocularly at the cube again. The influence of past experience is shown by the significant number of cases in which the reversed version of the cube was seen after training. The applicability of the oscillation hypothesis to this situation is fairly apparent. The hypothesis may also be applied to the memory effect of Wallach et al. (1953) and Engel's observation (1961) of monocular persistence.

Practice and the detection
of figures

The Gestalt psychologists did not absolutely deny that past experience affects perception. However, they did argue persuasively that experiential determinants are not as crucial as contemporary empiricism would suggest. These antiempiristic arguments were frequently buttressed by demonstrations and sometimes by experiments. One of these experiments, which became widely known and debated, was conducted by Gottschaldt (1926, 1929). The account which follows is based on Ellis's translation (1938) of Gottschaldt's work.

Gottschaldt's experiments were concerned with the effect of prior exposure to a form on subsequent detection of the form when it was embedded in a more complex form. "If 'experience' theories are correct, then the more *often* a certain figure . . . has been presented, the easier it should be to apprehend *this* figure when it appears in a larger one" (Gottschaldt, 1926, in Ellis, 1938, p. 263). Figure 5 shows a sample of the simple "*a* figures" and the complex "*b* figures." The *a* figure is embedded in the *b* figure. Five *a* figures were presented individually to two groups of subjects, under instruction to memorize the figures in preparation for a subsequent drawing task. Group I was shown each *a* figure three times; Group II received 520 presentations of each *a* figure. Following this practice, each of thirty-one *b* figures was presented once for 2 seconds. The Ss were asked ". . . to describe these *b* figures and were told that if their attention was attracted by anything in particular they should describe this in detail" (Gottschaldt, 1926, in Ellis, 1938, p. 268). The S's responses were classified in one of five categories ranging from the class in which ". . . the *a*-figure instantly stood out from *b* without any assistance" (p. 269) to the class in which ". . . no trace of *a* was perceived or suspected—the *b*-figure was described as *such* without

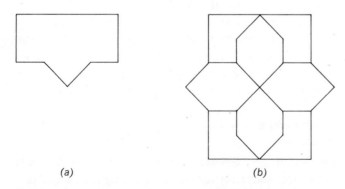

(a)   (b)

Figure 5. An *a* figure and a complex *b* figure in which the *a* figure is embedded.

reference to a" (p. 269). The results were unequivocal. In Group I, 91.3 percent of the responses were in the latter class; in Group II, this was true of 93.8 percent of the responses. In a subsequent experiment, Gottschaldt found that instructing S to assume an active search for a reduced the number of responses in the "no trace" class by 24 percent.

Gottschaldt concludes that prior experience or practice ". . . is practically without influence upon subsequent experience" (in Ellis, 1938, p. 277). The perception of forms is determined by internal principles of figural organization which have their basis in unlearned cortical field processes. These conclusions were vigorously endorsed by Koffka (1935) and Köhler (1947). More contemporary Gestalt-oriented writers have also attributed great significance to Gottschaldt's findings (Zuckerman & Rock, 1957).

Gottschaldt's findings regarding the ineffectualness of training have been challenged by Djang (1937). Djang used a series of twelve irregular figures composed of dotted lines. This was called the "simple series." Another series of twelve figures of a more complex nature was formed in such a way that each masked within it a figure of the simple series. The figures in the simple series were sorted into two halves of six each—forming the A series and the B series. The corresponding complex figures were sorted in the same way to form the A masked series and the B masked series. The A masked series then was used as the test series for the A series, and the B masked series was used as the control figures. Conversely, the B masked series was used as the test series for the B series and the A masked series used as control figures.

An observer learned either the A series figures or the B series figures by learning to draw them on repeated trials. Following this training he was shown figures from the two masked series to learn whether he saw any of the simple figures masked within them. The results of the experiment indicated that familiarity with the simple figures did significantly aid in seeing these figures when masked within more complex figures. Observers who first learned to draw the simple figures in the A series, for example, perceived more of these simple figures when concealed in the A masked series of complex figures than they saw of other unfamiliar simple figures concealed in the complex figures of the B masked series.

Further results of the same kind were reported by Hanawalt (1942). Prior to asking subjects to look for simple figures concealed in complex ones, Hanawalt gave them two kinds of experience. One was a kind of general practice in finding hidden figures in complex figures. In this procedure the simple figures used were different from the ones to be used in a criterial test. Another group of subjects was given specific practice in finding the same simple figures to be used in the criterial test. Performance of the subjects on the final criterial task of finding simple figures hidden in more complex ones indicated that general practice was inferior in its effects to specific practice but that performance on these test trials definitely was related to the amount of practice given the subjects. Some factors thought to be important in producing the improved performance attributable to practice included:

1
In practice the subject learned where to look for the simple figure.
2
Subjects learned to look for distinctive parts of the simple figures rather than for them as a whole.
3
Subjects learned to alter the figure-ground relations existing in the complex figures. Unessential parts tended to be perceived as ground against which the simple figures stood out.
4
With practice the amount of illusion seen in the complex figures decreased.
5
There apparently was a lowering of the threshold for discriminating the contour of the simple design from a number of closely repeated lines or units.

A more recent experiment by Francés (1963) also provided evidence that detection of the embedded figure is facilitated by previous exposure. Francés measured the time required by S to segregate the embedded figure with and without prior exposure to the simple figures. The results showed that prior exposure to the simple forms reduced the latency of segregation. The effect was limited to the group

which received exposure to the specific forms to be segregated. Other groups, which were preexposed to different,
similar, and dissimilar forms, did not show any reduction in
segregation time as compared with the control group which
received no prior exposure.

The investigations of Djang (1937) and Hanawalt (1942)
which *did* find significant effects of prior frequency on detection of embedded forms have been criticized on several
grounds. Zuckerman and Rock (1957) raised three objections:

1
Unlike the Ss in Gottschaldt's main experiments, the Ss in the
later studies by Djang and Hanawalt were instructed to search
for the *a* figure.
2
The complex *b* figures were inadequately constructed for the
purpose of concealment.
3
It is questionable that the Ss in the studies of Djang and
Hanawalt actually perceived the *a* figures.

These objections are not convincing. There is no reason to
look for the effects of prior practice exclusively under conditions in which no relevant motivation for the criterial task
exists. The fact that S is instructed to locate the *a* figure
does not disqualify the procedure as a test of the effects of
prior exposure. Most psychological variables are influenced
by performance set, and practice is no exception.

According to the second objection, Djang's experiment is
discredited because the complex *b* figures did not make
effective use of the principles of grouping to conceal the *a*
figures. We might note that this judgment is subjective. It is
not based on an empirical determination of the relative
frequency with which the portions of the *b* figure corresponding to the *a* figure are spontaneously isolated as figure prior
to any exposure to the *a* figure in isolation. The frequency
with which this occurs should be very much less for
Gottschaldt's *b* figures than for Djang's figures if the judgment of Zuckerman and Rock is correct. In fact, data of this
sort are essential if an experiment following Gottschaldt's
plan is to yield clear conclusions. Without knowledge of the
initial figural preferences we cannot assess the possibility

that another portion of the *b* figure, because of greater extra-experimental experience, has simply inhibited the appearance of the training figure. It should be noted that the *b* figure received only a single 2-second exposure. Under these conditions S would have no opportunity to respond to more than one portion of the *b* figure. However, even granting the argument that Djang's *b* figures are not as concealing as Gottschaldt's it is hard to see why this fact damages the validity of Djang's findings. A more reasonable conclusion is that the practice variable and the degree of concealment interact.

The third objection cannot be answered, but it can be applied with equal force to Gottschaldt's experiment. What basis is there for feeling confident that Gottschaldt's Ss, who failed to report the *a* figure, actually did not see the *a* figure? There is no firm basis for confidence on this point. As Postman (1963) has commented: "There are few cases in the history of perceptual experimentation in which the need for converging operations is as clearly illustrated as in the Gottschaldt experiments" (p. 68). Without these operations, there is no way to decide whether the Ss did not discriminate the *a* figure, discriminated the *a* figure perceptually but had no distinctive response with which to refer to it, or discriminated the *a* figure but simply preferred to report another figure. In fact, Schwartz (1961) has shown that practice effects are obtained with Gottschaldt's original figures if during the training the *a* figures are associated with distinctive familiar verbal responses (color names).

The foregoing critical analysis of the Gottschaldt experiment should not be construed as an attempt to establish the case for the critical role of prior exposure in form detection. The intention of the analysis is to suggest that this type of experiment is not very appropriate for examining the question. The Gottschaldt experiment obscures the chief objective. This is not the polemic objective of demonstrating the "victory" of past experience over grouping factors or vice versa. After all it is not untenable to grant that form perception is governed by innate organizational factors (see Fantz, 1961; Hershenson, 1964) but that practice can enhance discrimination of form. As an examination of the latter possibility the embedded-figures paradigm has nothing to recommend it.

The enrichment studies

This section will present a review of a series of animal experiments which have investigated the effects of preexposure to specific forms on subsequent visual form discrimination. The initial inspiration for these studies seems to have been Hebb's theory (1949) of form perception and more particularly an experiment reported informally by Hebb (1949, pp. 298–299). Two groups of rats were reared, one group in small cages in the laboratory and the other as pets in Hebb's home. The pet group exhibited superior performance on subsequent tests of problem solving. The superiority of the pet group suggested to Hebb that providing an early enriched environment could produce permanent facilitation of adult performance. The earliest enrichment studies (Forgays & Forgays, 1952; Hymovitch, 1952) were modeled after Hebb's study. These early studies did not focus on the effects of highly specific practice or experience, nor did they emphasize tests of perceptual discrimination. Instead they were investigations of the effects of prior experience in a diversified "rich" environment on performance in general tests of cognitive functioning. These early experiments have been excluded from consideration. This section will concentrate exclusively on the experiments which have specified the variations of prior stimulation more precisely and have as the criterion test a task involving visual discrimination.

An experiment by Gibson and Walk (1956) was among the first studies addressed specifically to the question of form discrimination. In this experiment and all those which follow, the experimental Ss were albino or hooded rats. The general plan of the Gibson-Walk study has served as a prototype for much of the subsequent work. Laboratory-born litters of rats were split into experimental and control groups. All rats were reared in identical cages with walls devoid of any pattern or textural variation. Only the cagemates, a water bottle, and food were visible. Four black metal forms were hung on the walls of the cages which housed the experimental animals, one on each wall. The forms were two *equilateral* triangles and two circles. The walls of the cages which housed the control animals were bare. The animals were reared in these cages until they were 90 days old. Then a discrimination task was introduced. Ten trials were given on each of 15 consecutive days in a V-shaped apparatus similar to that introduced by Grice (1948). The animals were required to learn to choose between a painted circle and a triangle in order to obtain food.

Figure 6 shows the percentage of correct responses on each day for the experimental and control groups. The superiority of the experimental group is obvious by inspection. Additional evidence of the superiority of the experimental group is provided by the fact that only one control animal attained the test criterion of eighteen out of twenty correct responses as compared with fifteen experimental animals. Gibson and Walk (1956) concluded that there is positive transfer from sheer prior exposure to stimuli, despite the lack of differential reinforcement.

In the Gibson-Walk experiment the training and test forms were identical. Does the facilitation which was observed depend on this relationship between the training and test forms? Gibson, Walk, Pick, and Tighe (1958) considered this question in the context of the broader question concerning

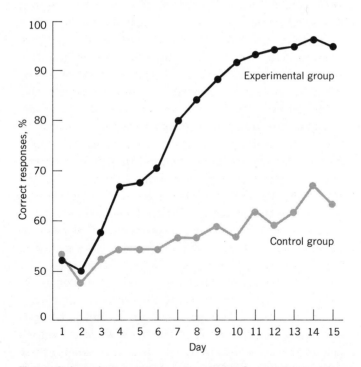

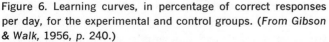

Figure 6. Learning curves, in percentage of correct responses per day, for the experimental and control groups. (*From Gibson & Walk*, 1956, p. 240.)

the generality or specificity of the transfer effect of prior exposure. "Is facilitation of discrimination by prolonged exposure a matter of identifying a *particular* pattern, or is some more general process responsible?" (Gibson et al., 1958, p. 584).

To examine this question four groups were tested. Group E_1 and Group C_1 were identical with the experimental and control groups of Gibson and Walk (1956). Group E_2 was reared like E_1, but the test required a discrimination between an *ellipse* and an *isosceles* triangle. Group C_2 was a control for Group E_2. The rats in Group C_2 learned the ellipse—isosceles triangle discrimination without prior exposure to any forms. As before, the animals were tested at the age of 90 days. The results were unequivocal. Both experimental groups were superior to their respective control groups. When the differences between E_1 and C_1 and between E_2 and C_2 were expressed as transfer scores, the average percent facilitation was found to be 14.5 for E_1 and 17.0 for E_2. Thus, the amount of facilitation produced by prior exposure seems to be independent of the relationship between the training and test stimuli.

Although the experimental results are clear, the generality of the conclusion may be questioned. Ellipses and isosceles triangles are, after all, only perspective transformations of the test stimuli. What is needed is a pair of training stimuli which have as little as possible in common with the test stimuli. In Exp. II Gibson et al. (1958) arranged such conditions. The plan of the experiment is shown in Table 13. Groups C_1 and E_1 are the standard conditions. Groups C_2 and E_2 were given the same training as C_1 and E_1, but they

Table 13
Summary of Exp. II of Gibson et al. (1958)

Groups	Training stimuli	Discrimination task	Mean no. of trials to reach criterion
C_1	None	T-C	162.5
C_2	None	H-V	137.2
E_1	T-C	T-C	133.8
E_2	T-C	H-V	130.0
CE_1	Rocks	T-C	138.9
CE_2	Rocks	H-V	138.5

NOTE: T, triangle; C, circle; H, horizontal stripes; V, vertical stripes.

were then required to discriminate between two patterns which differed greatly from the training forms—patterns of horizontal and vertical stripes. Groups CE_1 and CE_2 both were reared with irregularly formed "rocks" attached to the walls of their living cages. Group CE_1 was tested on the triangle-circle discrimination, CE_2 on the horizontal-vertical stripe discrimination. The last column of Table 13 shows the mean number of trials to reach criterion for the six groups. E_1 was superior to C_1, thus confirming the previous findings. However, the differences between E_2 and C_2 and between CE_1 and CE_2 were not significant. This would indicate that learning is highly specific. This evidence is weakened by the fact that the differences between E_1 and CE_1 and E_2 and CE_2 were not significant. We must conclude that the experiments of Gibson et al. (1958) have not clarified the question.

Forgus (1958a, 1958b) has reported two experiments which are relevant to an assessment of the question. Forgus hypothesized that transfer from early form exposure depended on the difference between the training and test pairs. More specifically, the hypothesis was advanced that the introduction of certain differences between the training and test pairs would produce more facilitation than exposure to the same pair during training and test. Four groups of rats learned a circle-triangle discrimination. Three experimental groups were tested after 52 days of exposure to forms painted on cardboard plaques, and one control group was tested after 52 days without exposure to forms. Experimental Group T had prior exposure to circle-triangle pairs. Experimental Group S received exposure to pairs composed of a circle and a triangular form whose angles (corners) had been deleted. Group A received exposure to pairs comprised of a circle and a triangular form with intact corners but with a segment deleted from each side. Group C was the control group.

Forgus (1958a) predicted that the positive transfer provided by preexposure would be greatest for Group S. Forgus reasoned that rats who are exposed to adjacent pairs of forms learn to respond to the pair as a unit. Therefore, their ability to respond discriminately to the pair in the test will be inhibited if the pair has been preexposed. (The contrary observations of Gibson et al. are not mentioned.) If a similar but different pair is preexposed, facilitation will be greater, since learning the test discrimination will not require that S disrupt a learned unit. Group S will exhibit most transfer (or least interference?), because the corners are the most salient aspects of triangular forms. The discrimination test was the same as that used by Gibson et al. The results showed that Group S was superior to the three remaining groups and that Groups T and A were superior to Group C. Forgus (1958b) confirmed this finding. He also found that discrimination between a circle and a noncontinuous angle was easier following preexposure to a continuous triangle as compared with preexposure to a noncontinuous triangle.

   Forgus's results show that transfer from prior exposure does depend on the similarity relationships between the exposure and test pairs. Forgus's interpretation of this effect is reasonable. A similar account can be formulated in terms of transfer theory. Since the two stimuli were exposed side by side in the rearing cage, S probably developed a common response to both. This would result in stimulus equivalence and inhibit performance on a test which required that S respond discriminately. This formulation suggests that the differences between the experimental groups reflect different amounts of negative transfer rather than differences in positive transfer. Still the experimental groups were superior to the control group. But the adequacy of the control group may be questioned. A better control condition would expose S to two adjacent visual patterns both of which differed greatly from the test pair. This would provide a basis for assessing the effects of learning to respond to a pair of shapes as a "unit" under conditions of very minimal specific transfer.

   In any event, it should be noted that Forgus's findings cannot decide the question raised by Gibson and Walk regarding the generality of the effects of prior exposure observed in their experiments. In the studies of Gibson et al. the forms were exposed separately, each on a different wall of the rearing cage, while Forgus preexposed the training forms in pairs. Therefore, the conditions of the Gibson studies may be more favorable for the development of distinctive responses to the two forms or for the development of a general ability to discriminate forms.

   The experiments considered thus far have all shown that discrimination is easier when it is preceded by prior exposure, as compared with a condition of no prior form exposure. In their experiment Gibson, Walk, and Tighe (1959) compared the ". . . greatest possible difference in visual stimulation." They compared a preexposure group with a group reared in total darkness. Presumably the difference between these groups on a form-discrimination task should be even greater than that observed when the preexposure group is compared with a standard control group. The results did not confirm this expectation. Furthermore, neither of the three groups (preexposure, dark-reared, standard-control) differed significantly on the discrimination test. Gibson et al. (1959) attribute the ineffectiveness of prior exposure to the fact that the forms presented during the preexposure period were painted forms instead of cutout metal forms (also see Gibson et al., 1958). When the forms are metal cutouts, transfer is observed; however, when they are painted on the walls of the cage, no facilitation is obtained. They suggest that the depth at the edges of the cutout forms makes them more "attention-getting" and more highly discriminable from the background than is the case for painted forms. Presumably painted forms are largely ignored by the animals [but see Forgus (1958a, 1958b) for evidence of positive transfer from prior exposure with painted forms].

In all the experiments considered thus far, the training has consisted of exposure to two different forms. The preference for this arrangement has the implication that the opportunity to "compare" different forms is an essential aspect of training. Gibson et al. (1958) examined this implication in an experiment which studied the effects of prior exposure to a *single* form. Half the experimental animals were reared with circle cutouts on the walls of the cage, and half with triangular cutouts. The control animals had no prior exposure. At 120 days of age, the rats performed a circle-triangle discrimination task. For half the Ss the preexposed form was the positive stimulus, and for the remaining Ss the novel form was positive. The main finding was that the experimental Ss were superior to the control Ss on the discrimination task. This was the case independently of which form was positive. The experimental Ss for whom the preexposed form was negative did exhibit a slight superiority, which probably can be attributed to novelty.

The results of this experiment show that prior exposure of a single form can facilitate discrimination between that form and another not previously seen. Unfortunately, the experiment did not include a condition in which both forms were preexposed. Thus, while we may conclude that the opportunity for comparison is not a necessary aspect of the training, we may not conclude that the exposure of single stimuli is as effective as exposure of a pair of different stimuli. It would be a simple matter to conduct an experiment to answer this question.

The procedure in the experiments which have been reviewed has been to commence preexposure from the onset of vision. (As a rule the eyes do not open until the rat is approximately 10 days old.) This practice is consistent with the emphasis in Hebb's theory on the special importance of early experience. However, there have been two experiments which have varied the age at which the preexposure has been given. The results are not in agreement. Forgus (1956) found that rats who had received preexposure during the first 41 days of life performed better on a form-discrimination task than rats who received later exposure. Gibson et al. (1959, Exp. II) did not corroborate this finding. They compared the effects of 40 days of exposure during the first 50 days of life with the effects of 40 days of exposure between 50 and 90 days of life. The two groups did not differ. However, it is difficult to assess this result. Age at exposure was confounded with the exposure-test interval. Since all Ss were tested at 90 days of age, the early-exposure group had a 40-day interval of no exposure between the termination of training and test, while the late-exposure group was tested immediately following termination of training. In addition, since Gibson et al. (1959) found that neither experimental group was superior to the control (no-exposure) group, it would appear that the conditions for testing the hypothesis were not created. In summary, the question of early versus late exposure remains undecided.

An investigation by Kerpelman (1965) concludes our examination of the evidence. Kerpelman noted that, as a rule, prior exposure has been accompanied by *nondifferential* reinforcement.

■ Spence (1936) postulated that nondifferential reinforcement of, for example, two stimuli raises the excitatory tendency of both. On introducing differential reinforcement (as in the discrimination task), enhancement of learning would be expected in Ss receiving prior nondifferential reinforcement (the preexposed Cornell experimental Ss) as compared to those receiving little or no prior reinforcement—differential or nondifferential —contiguous with the stimuli (the nonexposed Cornell control Ss). By this formulation the preexposed Ss in the Cornell experiments might be expected to learn the subsequent discrimination faster than the controls because, at the beginning of discrimination training, the stimuli for the former group were at a higher level of excitatory tendency than they were for the latter group (Kerpelman, 1965, pp. 257–258).

In brief, Kerpelman proposed that the superior performance of the preexposure group may be due to the nondifferential reinforcement, rather than to preexposure per se.

To investigate this possibility Kerpelman compared the performances of five groups of rats on a discrimination task following five conditions of pretraining: those in Group E_1 received 22 hours of daily exposure and were removed from the cages during the two 1-hour feeding periods. Those in E_2 received 22 hours of daily exposure and were fed in the cages for two 1-hour periods. Group E_1' was exposed to the forms for only 2 hours daily during nonfeeding periods. Group E_2' was exposed to the forms for two 1-hour periods during which they were fed. C was a control group, which was never preexposed to the forms. If Kerpelman's analysis is correct, only Groups E_2 and E_2' should be superior to Group C, since only these experimental groups received nondifferential reinforcement. Groups E_1 and E_1', which received no reinforcement in association with the forms, should not perform better than Group C.

The results are summarized in Table 14, which shows the results of a series of individual comparisons. The results for the 22-hour groups were compatible with the differentiation hypothesis. Thus the evidence is equivocal. In addition, there is the possibility that Kerpelman's procedure confounded the reinforcement conditions with conditions of attention. The animals in Groups E_2 and E_2' who received nondifferential reinforcement may also have been in a condition of heightened attention with regard to the forms. This possibility suggests itself because the forms were placed over the food tray and the food could not be carried from the tray. Therefore, the animals in Groups E_2 and E_2' spent 2 hours daily in close proximity to the stimulus forms. No such constraints were imposed on the animals in Groups E_1 and E_1'.

Despite several inconsistencies, the overall picture which

emerges from our review is compatible with the hypothesis that unreinforced exposure to visual forms facilitates discrimination between the forms. The degree of facilitation will depend on the extent to which S attends to the forms during the preexposure period. Furthermore, the degree of facilitation observed on a test of transfer may depend on the similarity relationships present between the preexposed and test forms. The nature of this dependence is unclear. Finally, the fact that positive transfer is observed when only single forms are preexposed suggests that learning how to compare is not the essential contribution of preexposure.

What accounts for the facilitation produced by prior exposure? Gibson et al. (1959) found that rats reared in total darkness were not deficient in performing a form-discrimination task. This finding shows that preexposure is not a necessary precondition for visual form discrimination. Apparently, rats can discriminate between forms without prior experience. It is questionable that preexposure would contribute significantly to this perceptual capacity. Therefore, it seems unlikely that the positive transfer which was observed in many of the experiments is due to a sharpening of S's capacity for perceptual discrimination.

A more plausible alternative is that the facilitation is due to the development, as a result of preexposure, of a disposition to base differential behavior on visual discrimina-

Table 14
Results of individual comparisons between groups*

	22-hour groups		2-hour groups	
	Differentia-tion prediction	Enrichment prediction	Differentia-tion prediction	Enrichment prediction
Measure	$E_2 = E_1 > C$	$E_2 > E_1 \geqq C$†	$E_2' = E_1' = C$	$E_2' > E_1' = C$
Trials to criterion	$E_2 > E_1 = C$		$E_2' = E_1' = C, E_2' > C$	
Initial errors	$E_2 > E_1 = C$		$E_2' = E_1' = C, E_2' > C$	
Repetitive errors	$E_2 = C = E_1, E_2 > E_1$‡		$E_2' = E_1' = C$	
Total errors	$E_2 = C = E_1, E_2 > E_1$		$E_2' = E_1' = C$	

* From Kerpelman, 1965, p. 261.
† Because of the possible operation of uncontrollable reinforcement contingencies in the presence of the stimuli in the absence of food, exact a priori predictions of the E_1-C difference could not be made within the enrichment framework.
‡ Sign > indicates significantly better performance. Sign = indicates performance levels did not differ significantly, although they may have differed nonsignificantly. For example, $E_2 = C = E_1$ means E_2 did not differ significantly from C, nor C from E_1, yet E_2 still may have differed significantly from E_1.

tions. The objection may be raised that the hypothesized disposition is not likely to develop, since reinforcement, i.e., reduction of hunger and thirst, was in no way contingent on the presence of specific forms. However, this arrangement does not preclude the possibility that the forms served as discriminative stimuli for other types of discriminatory behavior. This possibility existed for the animals that were preexposed to the test forms but did not exist for the control animals. If we may presume that the discrimination task involves two stages, learning that the criterial attribute is the difference between the forms and then learning E's arbitrary positive-negative distinction, then the control group is at a disadvantage. The control animals will need to use the early trials on the discrimination task in order to learn to use the perceived differences between the forms as a basis for responding, while the animals that received preexposure will use these trials to learn the discrimination. As a consequence, the experimental group will require fewer trials to master the discrimination task. Contributing to the plausibility of this account is the fact that rats, especially albinos, do not normally favor visual perception as a basis for behavior [see Barnett's (1963) handbook of the rat]. Prior to testing or elaborating this interpretation, or any other, it would be very valuable to obtain reliable records of the animal's behavior during the preexposure and nonexposure periods. None of the published reports contains any information about the rat's behavior during this criterial period. This is an unfortunate deficiency in a program of research devoted to studying the effects of prior experience on subsequent performance.[10]

---

[10] Another view that has been suggested about the effects of preexposure also merits consideration. It is generally conceded that in rats, stimulus changes (novelty, differential complexity, etc.) motivate approach behaviors (e.g., Berlyne, 1963). Animals preexposed to a given set of stimuli are more likely to respond on the basis of reward contingencies than animals either not preexposed or preexposed to only one of the stimuli. For these partially preexposed or nonpreexposed Ss, the stimuli are equally novel or one is more novel than the other, and such Ss may go through a long period of spontaneous alternation or response to differential complexity or exploratory behavior before "attending to the reward contingencies." That such phenomena can occur (exploration or complexity outweighing effects of reward) is seen in data by Sackett, Keith-Lee, and Treat (1963) for rats reared in isolation and tested as adults and by May, Beauchamp, and Pollack (1965) for normally reared rats. Thus, some possibly nonnegligible variance between preexposure and controls may be due to exploratory motives competing with both perceptual and reinforcement factors.

References

Adams, P. A. The effect of past experience on the perspective reversal of a tridimensional figure. *Amer. J. Psychol.*, 1954, **67**, 708–710.

Atkinson, R. C., & Ammons, R. B. Experiential factors in visual form perception. II. Latency as a function of repetition. *J. Exp. Psychol.*, 1952, **43**, 173–178.

Barnett, S. A. *The rat: a study in behavior.* Chicago: Aldine, 1963.

Berlyne, D. E. Motivational problems raised by exploratory and epistemic behavior. In S. Koch (Ed.), *Psychology: a study of a science.* Vol. 5. New York: McGraw-Hill, 1963.

Botha, E. Past experience and figure-ground perception. *Percept. Mot. Skills*, 1963, **16**, 283–288.

Cornwell, H. G. Prior experience as a determinant of figure-ground organization. *J. Exp. Psychol.*, 1963, **65**, 156–162.

Cornwell, H. G. Effect of training on figure-ground organization. *J. Exp. Psychol.*, 1964, **68**, 108–109.

Djang, S. The role of past experience in the visual apprehension of masked forms. *J. Exp. Psychol.*, 1937, **20**, 29–59.

Dutton, M. B., & Trail, P. M. A repetition of Rubin's figure-ground experiment. *Brit. J. Psychol.*, 1933, **23**, 289–400.

Ellis, W. D. *A source book of Gestalt psychology.* London: Routledge, 1938.

Engel, E. Binocular methods in psychological research. In F. P. Kilpatrick (Ed.), *Explorations in transactional psychology.* New York: New York Univer. Press, 1961.

Epstein, W., & DeShazo, D. Recency as a function of perceptual oscillation. *Amer. J. Psychol.*, 1961, **74**, 215–223.

Epstein, W., & Rock, I. Perceptual set as an artifact of recency. *Amer. J. Psychol.*, 1960, **73**, 214–228.

Fantz, R. L. The origin of form perception. *Scient. Amer.*, 1961, **204**, 66–72.

Forgays, D. G., & Forgays, J. W. The nature of the effect of free-environmental experience in the rat. *J. Comp. Physiol. Psychol.*, 1952, **45**, 322–328.

Forgus, R. H. Advantage of early over late perceptual experience in improving form discrimination. *Canad. J. Psychol.*, 1956, **10**, 147–155.

Forgus, R. H. The effect of different kinds of form preexposure on form discrimination learning. *J. Comp. Physiol. Psychol.*, 1958, **51**, 75–78. (a)

Forgus, R. H. The interaction between form preexposure and test requirements in determining form discrimination. *J. Comp. Physiol. Psychol.*, 1958, **51**, 588–591. (b)

Francés, R. *Le Développement perceptif.* Paris: Presses Univer. de France, 1962.

Francés, R. L'Apprentissage de la ségrégation perceptive. *Psychol. Française*, 1963, **8**, 16–27.

Gibson, E. J. Improvements in perceptual judgments as a function of controlled practice or training. *Psychol. Bull.*, 1953, **50**, 401–432.

Gibson, E. J., & Bergman, R. The effect of training on absolute estimation of distance over the ground. *J. Exp. Psychol.*, 1954, **48**, 473–482.

Gibson, E. J., Bergman, R., & Purdy, J. The effect of prior training with a scale of distance on absolute and relation judgments of distance over ground. *J. Exp. Psychol.*, 1955, **50**, 97–105.

Gibson, E. J., & Smith, JoAnn. The effect of training in distance estimation on the judgment of size-at-a-distance. *Human Resources Res. Center Res. Bull.*, Lackland Air Force Base, 1952, No. 52-39.

Gibson, E. J., & Walk, R. D. The effect of prolonged exposures to visually presented patterns on learning to discriminate them. *J. Comp. Physiol. Psychol.*, 1956, **49**, 239–242.

Gibson, E. J., Walk, R. D., Pick, H. L., & Tighe, T. J. The effect of prolonged exposure to visual patterns on learning to discriminate similar and different patterns. *J. Comp. Physiol. Psychol.*, 1958, **51**, 584–587.

Gibson, E. J., Walk, R. D., & Tighe, T. J. Enhancement and deprivation of visual stimulation during rearing as factors in visual discrimination learning. *J. Comp. Physiol. Psychol.*, 1959, **52**, 74–81.

Gottschaldt, K. Über den Einfluss der Erfahrung auf die Wahrnehmung von Figuren. I. *Psychol. Forsch.*, 1926, **8**, 261–317.

Gottschaldt, K. Über den Einfluss der Erfahrung auf die Wahrnehmung von Figuren. II. *Psychol. Forsch.*, 1929, **12**, 1–87.

Grice, G. R. The acquisition of a visual discrimination habit following response to a single stimulus. *J. Exp. Psychol.*, 1948, **38**, 633–642.

Hanawalt, N. G. The effect of practice upon the perception of simple designs masked by more complex figures. *J. Exp. Psychol.*, 1942, **31**, 134–148.

Hebb, D. O. *Organization of behavior: a neuropsychological theory.* New York: Wiley, 1949.

Hershenson, M. Visual discrimination in the human newborn. *J. Comp. Physiol. Psychol.*, 1964, **58**, 270–276.

Hymovitch, B. The effects of experimental variations on problem solving in the rat. *J. Comp. Physiol. Psychol.*, 1952, **45**, 313–321.

Kerpelman, L. C. Preexposure to visually presented forms and non-differential reinforcement in perceptual learning. *J. Exp. Psychol.*, 1965, **69**, 257–262.

Koffka, K. *Principles of Gestalt psychology.* New York: Harcourt, Brace & World, 1935.

Köhler, W. *Gestalt psychology.* New York: Liveright, 1947.

Köhler, W., & Wallach, H. Figural-aftereffects. *Proc. Amer. Phil. Soc.*, 1944, **88**, 269–357.

Leeper, R. A study of neglected portion of the field of learning;

the development of sensory organization. *J. Genet. Psychol.*, 1935, **46**, 41–75.

May, R. B., Beauchamp, K. L., & Pollock, S. Visual stimulus complexity and food vs. food alone as rewards for rats. *Psychonom. Sci.*, 1965, **3**, 403–404.

Postman, L. Perception and learning. In S. Koch (Ed.), *Psychology: a study of a science.* Vol. 5. New York: McGraw-Hill, 1963.

Rock, I., & Kremen, I. A re-examination of Rubin's figural aftereffect. *J. Exp. Psychol.*, 1957, **53**, 23–30.

Rubin, E. *Synoplevede Figurer.* Copenhagen: Gyldendalske, 1915.

Rubin, E. *Visuell wahrgenommene Figuren.* Copenhagen: Gyldendalske, 1921.

Sackett, G., Keith-Lee, P., & Treat, R. Food vs. perceptual complexity as rewards for rats previously subjected to sensory deprivation. *Science*, 1963, **141**, 518–520.

Schafer, R., & Murphy, G. The role of autism in a figure-ground relationship. *J. Exp. Psychol.*, 1943, **32**, 335–343.

Schwartz, C. B. Visual discrimination of camouflaged figures. Unpublished doctoral dissertation, Univer. of Calif. at Berkeley, 1961.

Spence, K. W. The nature of discrimination learning in animals. *Psychol. Rev.*, 1936, **43**, 427–449.

Vetter, R. J. Perception of ambiguous figure-ground patterns as a function of past experience. *Percept. Mot. Skills*, 1965, **20**, 183–188.

Wallach, H., O'Connell, D. N., & Neisser, U. The memory effect on visual perception of three dimensional form. *J. Exp. Psychol.*, 1953, **45**, 360–368.

Wohlwill, J. F. The development of "overconstancy" in space perception. In L. P. Lipsit & C. C. Spiker (Eds.), *Advances in child development and behavior.* New York: Academic, 1963.

Wohlwill, J. F. Changes in distance judgments as a function of corrected practice. *Percept. Mot. Skills*, 1964, **19**, 403–413.

Woodworth, R. S. *Experimental psychology.* New York: Holt, 1938.

Zuckerman, C. B., & Rock, I. A reappraisal of the roles of past experience and innate organizing processes in visual perception. *Psychol. Bull.*, 1957, **54**, 269–296.

Chapter six
Controlled practice or training:
II The acquired distinctiveness
of cues

In the chapter "Discrimination and Comparison," William James advanced the following hypothesis concerning the way in which experience improves discrimination: ". . . B and C, indistinguishable when compared together alone, may each contract adhesions with different associates, and the compounds thus formed may, as wholes, be judged very distinct. *The effect of practice in increasing discrimination must then, in part, be due to the reinforcing effect, upon an original slight difference between the terms, of additional differences between the diverse associates which they severally affect*" (James, 1890, pp. 510–511). The same hypothesis was reintroduced into contemporary psychology by Miller and Dollard (1941) in their discussion of the acquired distinctiveness of cues (ADC): ". . . learning to respond with highly distinctive names to similar stimulus situations should tend to lessen the generalization of other responses from one of these situations to another since the stimuli produced by responding with the distinctive name will tend to increase the difference in the stimulus pattern of the two situations" (p. 174).

The hypothesis of Miller and Dollard of the acquired distinctiveness of cues may be restated with the help of Figure 7. In Figure 7 the solid straight lines refer to associative linkages which actually may be observed by E. The wavy line and the broken line designate associative connections which are implied by the hypothesis. The existence of these associations is inferred. The inferential character of these intervening events is characteristic of mediational explanations (cf. Kendler, 1961). Two distinctive nonsense-syllable responses, *vax* and *neb*, are associated with two similar stimuli, nonsense forms F_1 and F_2. Each of the nonsense syllables produces an implicit distinctive cue S_{vax} and S_{neb}. The resulting stimulus compounds $S_{F_1} + S_{vax}$ and $S_{F_2} + S_{neb}$ may be presumed to be more dissimilar than the original stimulus pair. Therefore, stimulus generalization will be reduced, and discrimination will be enhanced. Also, on the basis of E. J. Gibson's (1940) analysis of the roles of generalization and differentiation in verbal learning, there should be more rapid acquisition of paired associates which have the predifferentiated forms as stimulus terms.

A similar model may be drawn to represent acquired equivalence. The essential difference between the procedures for producing distinctiveness and equivalence is that, in the latter case, the *same* response is attached to each form, thus enhancing their similarity. $S_{F_1} + S_{vax}$ and $S_{F_2} + S_{vax}$ are considered more similar than S_{F_1} and S_{F_2}. The model in Figure 7 can be expanded by increasing the number of stimulus-response components and by incorporating other likely variables. Goss (1955) has presented such expanded models. Among the variables considered by Goss are similarity relationships between the original stimuli and between the mediating responses, as well as the probabilities of the various associative contingencies in the model. We will treat these variables only when there is experimental evidence relevant to their evaluation.

In his review of the literature, Vanderplas (1963) has distinguished four different kinds of tasks which have been used as tests of the transfer effects of perceptual learning.

Discrimination   In the discrimination task, a pair of stimuli is presented, and S is required to state whether the members of the pair are the "same" or "different." Katz's

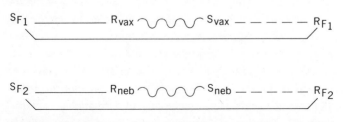

Figure 7. Mechanisms of acquired distinctiveness as postulated by Miller and Dollard. (*Adapted from Goss, 1955, p. 21.*)

study (1963) illustrates this procedure. Katz's Ss learned high associative-value nonsense syllables as labels for four randomly constructed geometric forms. Following this, the forms were exposed in pairs for brief durations, and S was required to report "same" or "different."

Recognition   In the recognition task, a set of stimuli is presented consisting of the stimuli presented during pre-training along with newly introduced stimuli, and S is required to state whether a stimulus is "old" or "new." In a study by Vanderplas and Garvin (1959) Ss learned nonsense labels for nonsense forms under conditions of paired-associates training. Following this training, they were required to select the nonsense forms from a set of forms which also contained similar new forms.

Identification   In the identification task, S is required to learn responses to the stimulus under the conditions of a paired-associates learning situation. Kurtz (1955) had Ss perform a preliminary discrimination task—they made same-different judgments of complex visual stimuli, e.g., simplified drawings of faces. Following this training task, Ss were required to learn a list of paired associates consisting of color names as responses and the faces as stimuli.

Motor   The motor task is essentially the same as the identification task, except that S is required to execute prescribed motor responses to each of the stimuli. For example, Gagne and Baker (1950) had Ss learn to associate a different letter with each of four different lights. In the transfer task, Ss were required to learn to manipulate a different switch in response to each of the lights.

The discussion in this chapter will be confined largely to studies which have used the discrimination and recognition tasks. Although all four tasks are appropriate for the examination of transfer of training as a *general* phenomenon, the discrimination and recognition tasks are especially suitable as tests of *perceptual* transfer. This is not to say that perceptual transfer is not involved in the identification and motor tasks. But as a measure of perceptual learning, these tasks, which involve both response learning and associative learning, are too complicated. The discrimination and recognition tasks do not involve response learning, nor do they involve the formation of specific associations. For this reason, these tasks are most suitable for the purpose of testing the discriminability of stimuli.

In addition to the above restrictions, one further restriction was imposed: among studies of discrimination and recognition, only those concerned with the discrimination or recognition of visual forms were considered. Several studies (e.g., Ellis, Bessemer, Devine, & Trafton, 1962; Ellis, Feuge, Long, & Pegram, 1964) which have been concerned with the effects of labeling on tactual discrimination of form will not be included. Discrimination of verbal stimuli will be excluded on the ground that discrimination of such stimuli is more likely to be based on nonvisual cues than on visual information. Also until recently, little attention has been given to specifying the properties of verbal items as perceptual stimuli.

Specifying the experimental operations required to test the hypothesis of acquired distinctiveness is not easy. Many of the methodological questions related to experiments on transfer of training, as well as studies of incidental learning, apply to the design of an experiment on ADC. These complexities were not obvious to the early investigators. However, subsequent analyses of Arnoult (1957), Wohlwill (1958), and Vanderplas (1958, 1963) have helped to clarify the methodological problems.

The availability of an alternative to the S-R interpretation of the effects of predifferentiation training also contributes to the importance of methodological considerations. (Actually, at least four different alternative explanations have been discussed in the literature, but the one to be described seems to be the chief contender.) The contending interpretation is derived from the differentiation theory of perceptual learning proposed by J. J. Gibson and E. J. Gibson (1955): ". . . we learn to perceive in this sense: that percepts change over time by progressive elaboration of qualities, feature, and dimensions of variation. . . . Perceptual learning, then, consists of responding to variables of physical stimulation not previously responded to" (p. 34).

Accordingly, the effect of labeling can be explained without reference to cue-producing responses. Labeling usually entails a procedure of training which forces S to attend to more aspects of the stimulus than he ordinarily would. This in turn leads to improved performance on a subsequent discrimination or recognition task. Thus, according to this view, labeling per se is incidental. Presumably, any procedure which would guarantee the same degree of selective attention during the pretraining would be equally effective. What is required to test this prediction is a comparison between a labeling condition and an "attention" condition without labeling. The latter condition is not easy to create, since it requires not only some guarantee that attention is equated but also assurance that S is not providing his own distinctive labels. This problem, as well as other methodological questions, will be considered as they arise in our review of the research on ADC.

Experimental investigations of the effect of the acquisition of distinctive responses on discrimination and recognition of visual forms

The earliest studies of this question were two experiments reported by Arnoult (1953). Three conditions of pretraining were used in Arnoult's experiments. Group C received ten learning trials in which different letters of the alphabet were paired with each of the five similar nonsense shapes later to be used in a discrimination test. The training of Group A was identical to Group C, except that the nonsense shapes were not those to be discriminated later. Group NP was not given any training preliminary to the discrimination task. The transfer task in Exp. I was a discrimination task. A novel "standard" shape was exposed together with a second shape. The latter shape was one of the shapes in the training sets for Groups C and A (D trials) or another copy of the "standard" (S trials). The Ss were instructed to report "same" or "different" as quickly as possible. The same discrimination task was used for all three groups. Arnoult's Exp. II differed from Exp. I only with regard to the transfer test. In Exp. II, the discrimination task of Exp. I was replaced by a recognition task. Each of the five nonsense shapes (learned by Group C) was exposed tachistoscopically alone, and S was required to identify the shape by selecting it from the set of five shapes. The accuracy and latency of the response were recorded.

Experiment I showed that the three groups did not differ significantly on either measure of performance. The results for Exp. II were comparable. In a supplementary analysis, the data were fractionated to determine whether interactions between training and rate of learning had masked the main effect. Experiment I provided no evidence of differences between poor and superior learners. However, in Exp. II, a significant difference was found between conditions C and A for the Ss who had performed best on the predifferentiation task. Arnoult concluded that the hypothesis of acquired distinctiveness was not supported. He suggested that a better test of the hypothesis might require more intensive pretraining.

Regardless of their outcomes, Arnoult's (1953) experiments could not have provided unequivocal support for the ADC hypothesis. An essential control condition was omitted, thus prohibiting any confident conclusions about the effect of labeling. This is a condition of attentive observation without labeling. As the experiments were designed, superior test performance under condition C could be due to labeling, but the same difference could also result from prior exposure to the forms later to be discriminated. Only condition C provided this preliminary exposure (familiarization).

Robinson (1955) examined the ADC hypothesis under conditions of more intensive preliminary training. The visual stimuli were ten fingerprints. The verbal labels were ten distinctive nicknames. Group D (distinctiveness training) learned to associate the names with the prints to a criterion of one errorless trial. Group E (equivalence training) learned to call five of the prints "cops" and the other five "robbers." Group S-D (differentiation training) was shown each of the ten prints serially and reported whether the currently presented print was the same as or different from the preceding print. Group NPT received no prior training. The transfer test was a discrimination task requiring ten same-different judgments. The mean errors and the mean latencies were compared. All the pretraining groups had significantly fewer errors and significantly lower latencies than Group NPT. However, the three pretraining groups did not differ on either measure. Thus, there was no evidence of acquired distinctiveness or equivalence as a result of labeling. On the basis of these findings and the retrospective reports of his Ss, Robinson concluded that pretraining is effective because it creates conditions for ". . . the finding of significant details enabling S to recognize a print and distinguish it from others" (Robinson, 1955, p. 114).

Robinson's experimental procedure introduces another methodological problem. As a consequence of differences in the difficulty of the training tasks, different amounts of practice will be required to achieve a common performance criterion for the tasks. Therefore, the number of exposures to the critical stimuli, e.g., the prints in Robinson's study, will be different for the three tasks. As a result, the training variable will be confounded with another variable, i.e., number of exposures. Robinson sought to resolve this difficulty by giving Groups E and S-D a number of postcriterial trials, to equate the number of exposures with the number received by Group D, whose task was most difficult. Underwood (1964), in another context, has questioned the adequacy of this resolution. In terms of Robinson's preferred hypothesis, a question may be raised concerning the validity of the assumption that the conditions of postcriterial practice encourage selective attention to the same degree as the conditions of precriterial practice.

Hake and Eriksen (1956) have called attention to an aspect of the paired-associates pretraining which may serve to limit its effectiveness. The letters of the alphabet, which were used by Arnoult (1953) and by Hake and Eriksen (1955) in a study of predifferentiation and identification, are not verbal responses which Ss are accustomed to using in labeling objects. The same may be said about the nicknames used as distinctive responses in Robinson's experiment (1955). Hake and Eriksen proposed that the ineffectiveness of labeling might be due to the fact that the learned labels ". . . have a minimum of relevance to the stimulus forms and . . . few private uncontrolled associations and significances for Ss prior to the experiment" (Hake & Eriksen, 1956, p. 235).

To overcome this limitation, Hake and Eriksen (1956) gave Ss practice in using letters of the alphabet as discriminatory responses prior to the paired-associates pretraining. Control Ss were not given this preliminary practice. The predifferentiation task consisted of 120 paired-associates learning trials with 12 metric nonsense forms as stimuli and either 2, 4, 6, or 12 letters as responses. The transfer test was a recognition task. The 12 predifferentiated forms were presented along with 12 new but similar forms, and S was required to indicate the 12 forms he had labeled on the preceding task.

Varying the number of distinctive labels associated with a constant number of stimuli has interesting implications. On the ADC hypothesis, the facilitating effect of prior labeling should be decreased by reducing the number of permissible responses. The same prediction is suggested by the proposal of Hake and Erikson (1955) that ". . . one advantage of learning verbal labels [in the paired associates-procedure] may be that it allows us to compare the distinctions which we make among the objects of the world with those made by others" (p. 161). When the number of labels is reduced, specificity of labeling is decreased and, therefore, ". . . the transfer effect should decrease also because the external criteria with which S can compare his own identifications of the stimuli during practice are more ambiguous" (Hake & Eriksen, 1955, p. 162). On the other hand, the differentiation hypothesis advanced by J. J. Gibson and E. J. Gibson (1955) would not necessarily predict variations of label specificity to affect transfer. This latter prediction is, in fact, supported by the results obtained by Robinson (1955) in the study described earlier and by Hake and Eriksen (1955) in a study which used an identification task as the transfer test.

The following were the main results of the experiment of Hake and Eriksen (1956). The experimental groups who received preliminary practice using letters as discriminatory responses were superior to the control groups on the paired-associates task. However, this superiority did not affect the performances of the experimental and control groups on the recognition task. Nor was there evidence of a significant main effect of the number of labels used in the paired-associates task on the number of forms correctly recognized on the transfer test. The only consistent effect on recognition which could be discovered emerged from an analysis of the within-subject correlation coefficients computed from the number of times each form was correctly labeled in the paired-associates predifferentiation task and correctly recognized on the recognition task. For the experimental Ss, those Ss who had received preliminary practice in labeling exhibited an increasing correlation with increasing number of labels. This was not the case for the control Ss.

None of the experiments, considered thus far, has produced unequivocal evidence in support of the ADC hypothesis. One concern in evaluating the adequacy of the experiments has been the question of amount of predifferentiation practice. In the experiments of Arnoult (1953) and Hake and Eriksen (1955, 1956) evidence was adduced to suggest the importance of amount of practice. Vanderplas and Garvin (1959b) studied this variable directly. They varied the amount of practice in a factorial design which combined four levels of practice with three levels of stimulus complexity and three levels of stimulus meaningfulness. Complexity was defined by the number of points (6, 12, or 24) at which the contour of the form changed direction. [For a justification of this definition, see Attneave (1957).] Meaningfulness was defined by the percentage of Ss who gave associative responses to each form (see Vanderplas & Garvin, 1959a).

In the training task, S was given 2, 4, 8, or 16 paced anticipation trials with a list of eight shape-trigram pairs. The trigrams had a Glaze associative value of 0 percent. On the test of recognition, S was shown a series of 16 cards each containing five shapes. On 8 of the cards, one of the shapes was a shape which had been labeled previously, and the other four were variations. On the remaining 8 cards all five shapes were variations. The S responded to each card either by selecting a shape if he thought that it was one of those seen previously in the paired-associates list or by saying "none" if he judged none of the shapes to be familiar.

Of main interest are the effects of variations of practice on performance of the recognition task. Vanderplas and Garvin (1959b) analyzed five types of responses: correct recognitions, selection of one of the five variations, incorrect "none" responses, selection of a variation when a correct shape was present, correct "none" responses. Levels of practice did not have a main effect on any of these dependent variables. We might note, however, that relatively little learning occurred during the paired-associates practice. The mean number of correct anticipations of the labels was

0.028, 0.72, 1.70, and 3.4 for 2, 4, 8, and 16 trials, respectively.

With regard to the remaining two factors, only complexity was significantly related to recognition. This relationship is not surprising or particularly instructive. There was also a significant complexity × practice interaction for the correct recognition responses, but this interaction is difficult to interpret because of the presence of a significant practice × complexity × meaningfulness interaction. The main effect of meaningfulness (associative value of the stimuli) was not significant. On a number of counts, one would expect stimulus meaningfulness to be a significant variable; therefore, the variable of meaningfulness should be reexamined. Two directions may be recommended for future experimentation. Greater differences in meaningfulness should be studied, e.g., low m nonsense syllables versus common nouns. In addition, properties other than Glaze's association value and Noble's associative frequency should be examined. Of special relevance is the extent to which the stimulus forms tend to evoke a consistent labeling response in a free labeling situation. Pfafflin (1960) found that differences in associative consistency influenced the amount and sign of the transfer from paired-associates labeling practice to a switch-pressing task. The transfer was positive for stimuli that were low in associative consistency and negative for stimuli that were high in associative consistency.

Experiments similar to the Vanderplas-Garvin study (1959b) have been reported by Ellis and Muller (1964) and by Vanderplas, Sanderson, and Vanderplas (1964). Ellis and Muller conducted a factorial experiment to examine the effects of shape complexity (6- or 24-point random shapes), three types of training (distinctiveness, equivalence, and "observation"), and four levels of practice (2, 4, 8, or 16 trials). Distinctiveness training involved practice in associating eight meaningful words to eight shapes. Equivalence training consisted of learning the label "wide" for four shapes and "narrow" for the remaining four shapes. The observation training consisted of exposures without labeling. The transfer test was a recognition task modeled after Vanderplas and Garvin (1959b).

Our concern is with the number of correct recognitions.

For this measure Ellis and Muller found a significant main effect of type of training and amount of practice. Complexity was not related significantly to correct recognitions. These latter two findings do not agree with the results of Vanderplas and Garvin (1959b). The interactions of practice with complexity, and training with complexity, were significant. The facilitating effect of increasing the amount of practice was greater for the more complex forms. The nature of the complexity × training interaction was such that "observation" training produced superior recognition for simple forms but labeling resulted in superior recognition for the more complex forms. Equivalence training consistently resulted in fewer correct recognitions than observation or distinctiveness training.

The results of the studies by Vanderplas and Garvin (1959b) and Ellis and Muller disagree with regard to the practice variable. The difference may be due entirely to the nature of the responses (labels) used in the two studies. Vanderplas and Garvin used trigrams with an associative value of 0 percent, while Ellis and Muller used meaningful words. It is a well-documented fact (e.g., Goss and Nodine, 1965; Underwood and Schultz, 1960) that variations of response meaningfulness will have pronounced effects on the acquisition and associative strength of paired associates. Therefore, we may assume that the difference in associative strength, produced by increasing the number of trials by a given amount, will be greater for the shape-word pairs than for the shape-syllable pairs. This assumption would account for the greater effectiveness of the practice variable in the Ellis-Muller experiment.

The results for the equivalence-distinctiveness comparison obtained by Ellis and Muller also appear to contradict the earlier findings of Robinson (1955) and Hake and Eriksen (1956). The findings of Ellis and Muller are confirmed in other experiments to be described shortly. For the moment, however, we might note that when the number of stimuli is held constant and the number of responses (labels) is varied, a correction must be made for the chance expectancies associated with the number of labels used. The scores on the paired-associates training task must be corrected, before the degree of learning on the training task can be ascertained for the different conditions, e.g., equivalence and distinctiveness training. [Procedures for making this correction are described by Hake and Eriksen (1956, p. 237) and Katz (1963, p. 426).] Without knowledge of the degree of prior learning, it is impossible to compare the transfer effects. Neither Robinson (1955) nor Ellis and Muller (1964) applied corrections; therefore, it is difficult to assess their findings.

Another experiment designed to compare the effects of distinctiveness and equivalence training was reported by Katz (1963). Katz had 7- to 9-year-old children perform a discrimination task, following one of three types of training: DL—four different high-association-value nonsense syllables were associated with four nonsense forms, which were described as "pictures of funny looking animals from Mars"; CL—two different syllables were associated with the forms; ML—no labels were associated with the forms, but S was instructed to count the forms as they appeared one at a time. The counting task was intended to minimize the possibility that S would introduce his own labels. This precaution was not observed in the other studies, which included an "observation" condition. The training consisted of a series of 150 trials. The transfer test was a series of twenty-eight tachistoscopic presentations of pairs of the training forms, and S made a judgment of same or different.

Analysis of the training data, after correction, showed no difference between conditions CL and DL. The important transfer measure is the number of "same" responses Ss made to the pairs composed of previously labeled, non-identical figures. Katz found that CL training resulted in significantly more "same" responses than DL and NL training. DL training resulted in significantly fewer "same" responses. Katz (1963) does not specify the level of complexity of the stimulus shapes. However, inspection of several figures, which are presented as illustrations, suggests that they are at the level of Ellis and Muller's high-complexity figures. Therefore, Katz's results can be regarded as confirming the results of Ellis and Muller.

Contradictory results have been reported by Vanderplas et al. (1964) in a more recent study. Vanderplas et al. examined the effects of shape complexity (6-point, 24-point) and associative value on discrimination and recognition tasks which followed 20 trials of practice. There were five conditions of practice: Group O simply observed. Group D was asked to observe the shapes as they appeared and note differences that might help them later. Group NS learned a different nonsense label for each of the six forms. Group W learned a different girls' name. Group C received no prior training. The results for the discrimination test were not significantly related to shape complexity, associative value, or type of training. There was a main effect of training and associative value on the recognition task, but no significant interactions. The results showed that Group D benefited most from training, while the least amount of transfer occurred for the NS group. This latter effect was independent of the level of form complexity.[11]

Summary of experimental findings regarding the influence of labeling

The experimental literature under review is replete with inconsistencies. Therefore, a set of summary statements will be useful.

Type of training   Labeling practice has been compared to a variety of conditions of observation without labeling. Robinson (1955) and Vanderplas et al. (1964), using a discrimination transfer test, found no difference between a labeling condition and a condition which required only discriminative observation (Robinson's Group S-D and Group D of Vanderplas et al.). The only positive results for a discrimination task were those reported by Katz (1963). When a recognition

---

[11] A novel approach to the question of the effects of labeling on form perception has been reported in a series of experiments by Donderi and Kane (1965). In one experiment, Ss learned two responses, "A" or "B," to three circles of different diameters. Two of the circles were associated with a common response, e.g., "A," and the remaining circle was associated with a unique response, e.g., "B." Then the circles were presented as luminous stimuli in a dark room, centered equiangularly around a fixation point. Under such conditions, luminous figures have been found to undergo a fading-disappearance-regeneration cycle much like that which is obtained with stabilized images (McKinney, 1963). Donderi and Kane report that when the responses to the circles are highly overlearned, there is a significant tendency for the common-response circles to disappear and regenerate together more frequently than any other pair.

transfer test was used, Ellis and Muller (1964) found that observation yielded greater transfer for simple forms but labeling yielded greater transfer for complex forms. On the other hand, Vanderplas et al. (1964), using the same forms, found superior recognition with their Group D for complex as well as simple forms.

Number of labels (specificity of responses)   Robinson (1955) and Hake and Eriksen (1956) varied the number of letters used to label a set of stimuli and found no significant effects. Robinson compared the effects of 10 and 2 labels for 10 prints. Hake and Eriksen compared 2, 4, 6, or 12 labels for 12 forms. Katz (1963) and Ellis and Muller (1964) did obtain significant differences related to differences in number of labels. Katz compared the effects of four and two 95 percent association-value syllables associated with four shapes and found more correct recognitions with the greater number of labels. Ellis and Muller compared the effects of eight and two meaningful words associated with shapes and confirmed Katz's finding.

Amount of practice   Contradictory results were obtained in two similar studies by Vanderplas and Garvin (1959b) and Ellis and Muller (1964). Vanderplas and Garvin did not obtain a significant effect, while Ellis and Muller found that increasing the number of paired-associates trials facilitated recognition.

Properties of the stimulus   Two stimulus properties, complexity and association value, have been studied with inconsistent results.

Concluding evaluation

The experimental data have provided only meager support for the hypothesis of acquired distinctiveness. Nor have the alternative hypotheses received significant support. None of the hypotheses are sufficient to predict the effect which a given experimental variation will have on discrimination or recognition. Under these conditions it might be justifiable to abandon all the proposed hypotheses. A more prudent response to this dilemma is to examine the possibility that the inconsistencies are due to imprecise specifications of the independent and dependent variables.

In the present connection, attention may be focused on the independent variable, and particularly on the labeling factor. There is reason to believe that specifications of the conditions of labeling, exclusively in terms of E's operations, are imprecise and misleading. This is so because such specification neglects the possibility that the S very frequently supplies his own distinctive responses. That Ss often engage in coding during paired-associates learning is recognized in the prevailing distinction between the functional and the nominal stimulus (Underwood, 1963). The nominal stimulus is the one presented by E. The functional stimulus is a transformed version of the nominal stimulus, which serves as the effective stimulus in the S-R connection. An analogous distinction may be made between the nominal and functional response. There is also justification for contending that self-generated labels will be more effective than labels introduced by E. "Ss who invent their own names or descriptive phrases for stimuli probably develop more relevant and useful mediators, for the words chosen are drawn from common language and are rich in associations and meanings and therefore assist transfer more than nonsense words of an unknown degree of distinctiveness" (Wright & Kagan, 1963, p. 71). In this connection, the criticisms of Hake and Eriksen (1956) should also be noted.

Rivera (1959) has proposed a similar distinction between the "overt responses" and the "perceptual responses." The overt responses are those ". . . which E requires S to give when different stimuli are presented," and the perceptual responses are ". . . those responses which constitute S's representation of the stimulus" (Rivera, 1959, p. 300). Rivera uses this distinction in a reexamination of the effects of varying the number of labels. Rivera proposes that the influence of this variable depends to a considerable degree on the concurrent covert introduction of perceptual responses.

Several observations, in an experiment reported by Rivera, lend support to this analysis. The Ss first learned ten or two letters to a set of ten fingerprints and then learned ten numbers to the same prints. In a postexperimental inquiry, the Ss who had learned two letters disclosed two distinguishable tendencies. There were those Ss who searched for a property common to the five prints associated with the same labels. However, most Ss proceeded differently. Most Ss singled out a distinctive property in each print and associated the label with that property. If it may be assumed that each distinctive property was implicitly assigned a distinctive label, i.e., a covert verbal description, then the intended difference between the experimental treatments will be vitiated. There will remain a difference between the number of *nominal* distinctive labels, but no difference between the number of *functional* distinctive labels. If this analysis is correct, then the results of the studies considered thus far do not necessarily invalidate the ADC and "attention to cues" hypotheses.

Rivera (1959) presents the findings of an experiment involving an identification transfer task to support his analysis. Group A learned to associate ten different letters to a set of ten fingerprints. Group C learned two letters, one for each arbitrarily determined subset of five prints. Group C was instructed not to look for common characteristics, and ". . . to memorize to each individual slide [print] its correct letter" (Rivera, 1959, p. 301). Group D also learned two letters, but under instructions which informed them that the prints had common properties and that ". . . the best way to do this [task] is to spot the common characteristics of the slides" (p. 301). The transfer task required S to learn the numbers 1 to 10 as responses for the prints. According to Rivera's analysis, Groups A and C should not differ; however, Group D should be inferior to Groups A and C on the transfer test. The results showed Groups A and C to be equivalent and C to be superior to D. However, the difference between A and D was not significant. There was, therefore, substantial if not conclusive confirmation of the expectations and support for the analysis which generated them.

The preceding analysis, upon elaboration, can be applied to account for the other experimental findings. For example, whether or not labeling, as compared with observation, affects subsequent discrimination or recognition may depend on the conditions of observation. Conditions which require S to make a judgment about the stimulus, e.g., Robinson's condition S-D (1955) and condition D of Vanderplas et al. (1964), are likely to encourage implicit labeling, largely eliminating any effective difference between this condition and the labeling condition. Other conditions of observation, which include a procedure for inhibiting implicit labeling, permit a true assessment of the effect of overt labeling.

The contention which is being advanced is that a decision concerning the validity of the several hypotheses must be deferred until greater control can be exercised over the response variable. Before this control can be achieved, the conditions which promote the introduction of implicit distinctive responses must be identified. Some of the variables which seem likely to be influential are the task instructions, complexity of the visual shapes which are presented during training, and the meaningfulness of the overt responses provided by *E*.

In addition to greater control of the occurrence of labeling, other aspects of the experimental conditions warrant closer scrutiny. In particular, we may note that paired-associates learning has been the exclusive procedure used to establish the distinctive or common responses. This preference is probably due to the prevailing inclination to view paired-associates learning as a form of conditioning. Since the Miller-Dollard hypothesis is part of a learning theory applied mainly to conditioning phenomena, paired-associates training has superficial appropriateness for testing the hypothesis.

Despite these considerations, there are at least two reasons for questioning the suitability of the procedure. First, the conditions of paired-associates training differ greatly from the conditions of the transfer tests of discrimination and recognition. Inasmuch as similarity of contexts is a variable which affects transfer (Deese, 1958, Ch. 9), it is legitimate to ask whether responses (labels) learned for shapes in a paired-associates context will indeed occur (transfer) explicitly or implicitly in a recognition or discrimination context. It is the implicit and essential premise of the experiments we have been considering that such transfer takes place. Obviously, if this premise is false, there would be no reason to expect an effect of prior labeling on discrimination or recognition. Parenthetically, this analysis also suggests an explanation for the fact that positive results are much more frequent for identification tasks as compared with the transfer tasks we have been considering. The identification transfer task and the paired-associates training task are highly similar to each other, thus optimizing the conditions for transfer.

The second reservation stems from a common, although not necessary, characteristic of paired-associates learning tasks which has been carried over into the training task of the ADC studies. The stimuli and responses are typically unrelated. In the present context, this characteristic has already been noted by Hake and Eriksen (1956). Letters, nonsense syllables, or randomly selected meaningful words have no structural or symbolic relationship to random shapes. The S may well learn the prescribed shape-label relationships, only to disregard these associations as arbitrary and, therefore, irrelevant for any subsequent task. It is doubtful that Hake and Eriksen (1956) have settled this question by their experiment. The main problem is to determine that the particular label is appropriate for the shape in question without using shapes which have a conventional, accepted label.

One procedure for accomplishing this objective is to have a S (S_1) supply his own labels and then rehearse them until he can apply them without error. For comparison purposes a second S (S_2) could be required to learn to associate the labels provided by S_1. If we may assume that the uncontrolled labeling of random shapes is largely idiosyncratic, then the labels will be less appropriate for S_2. A third S would receive only observation training. It is recognized that none of the hypotheses which have been considered, and certainly not the ADC hypothesis, explicitly requires that the labels have a special relationship to the stimuli. Still the discovery that this is a necessary condition could probably be accommodated by these hypotheses.

Our discussion has centered on the effectiveness of labeling. However, the experiments which have been reviewed have equally often exhibited an effect of observation. If our conjectures about uncontrolled implicit labeling are not accepted, how can the influence of observation training be explained? The problem is complicated by the fact that neither systematic reinforcement nor anticipation of a subsequent test seems to be a necessary condition for observation to have an effect. Two general hypotheses to account for this type of facilitation have been examined by Pick (1965):

1

Schema hypothesis. ". . . discrimination and identification involve matching sensory data or 'cues' about objects to prototypes or models of the objects which have been built up through repeated experience with the objects and 'stored' in memory. . . . Practice . . . would enable S to build up and refine the appropriate schemata" (pp. 331–332).

2

Distinctive-feature hypothesis. ". . . improvement of discrimination consists of learning the distinctive features of objects. . . . The function of practice . . . is to enable S to respond to an increasing number of stimulus variables and to discover which of these variables are 'critical' in the sense that they serve to distinguish between one object and another" (p. 332).

Pick's (1965) experiment was designed to examine these alternatives. The experiment consisted of a training stage followed by a transfer test. In the training stage, Ss were presented with a standard form, accompanied by three transformations of the standard and a second copy of the form. The task for S was to select the form which was the correct match. The Ss were kindergarten children. In the transfer test, Ss were assigned to one of three conditions. In the control condition, S was tested with three standards and three types of transformation, all of which were different from the ones used in training. In experimental condition I, Ss received the same standards, but these had to be distinguished from alternatives which represented new transformations of the standards. In experimental condition II new standards were used, but the alternatives were transformations of the type presented in training. The critical responses were the numbers of "confusion errors" on the transfer test. These errors were instances in which S selected a transformation instead of a true copy.

Confusion errors were most frequent for the control condition, least frequent for experimental condition II, and intermediate in frequency for experimental condition I. All the differences among the three conditions were significant. Thus there is evidence that both prototype and distinctive-feature learning occurs; however, the significant superiority of experimental condition I indicates that distinctive-feature learning is a more important source of positive transfer.

The distinctive-feature hypothesis has received support and can be plausibly used to account for several of the findings considered earlier. In particular the account seems suitable for the effects of observation training which has been given in the context of a discrimination task. The hypothesis is less acceptable as an account of the effects of sheer observation. In this latter case we need to be able to explain why the presumed abstraction of distinctive features occurs. In the case of observation in the context of a discrimination task, there are instructions which serve to induce a learning set which may encourage S to seek out distinctive features. However, in the case of sheer observation, the motivational determinants are not obvious. This same difficulty is present for the earlier version of this theory proposed by J. J. Gibson and E. J. Gibson (1955). Why does learning occur? This question remains unanswered in the exposition of the differentiation theory. An acceptable resolution of the question would enhance the value of the theory.

References

Arnoult, M. D. Transfer of pre-differentiation training in simple and multiple shape discrimination. *J. Exp. Psychol.*, 1953, **45**, 401–409.

Arnoult, M. D. Stimulus predifferentiation: some generalizations and hypotheses. *Psychol. Bull.*, 1957, **54**, 339–351.

Attneave, F. Physical determinants of the judged complexity of shapes. *J. Exp. Psychol.*, 1957, **53**, 221–227.

Deese, J. E. *Psychology of learning.* (2nd ed.) New York: McGraw-Hill, 1958.

Donderi, D. C., & Kane, E. Perceptual learning produced by common responses to different stimuli. *Canad. J. Psychol.*, 1965, **19**, 15–30.

Ellis, H. C., Bessemer, D. W., Devine, J. V., & Trafton, C. L. Recognition of random tactual shapes following predifferentiation training. *Perceptual Mot. Skills*, 1962, **10**, 99–102.

Ellis, H. C., Feuge, R. L., Long, K. K., & Pegram, V. G. Evidence for acquired equivalence of cues in a perceptual task. *Perc. Mot. Skills*, 1964, **19**, 159–162.

Ellis, H. C., & Muller, D. G. Transfer in perceptual learning following stimulus predifferentiation. *J. Exp. Psychol.*, 1964, **68**, 388–395.

Gagne, R. M., & Baker, Katherine E. Stimulus pre-differentiation as a factor in transfer of training. *J. Exp. Psychol.*, 1950, **40**, 439–451.

Gibson, E. J. A systematic application of the concepts of generalization and differentiation to verbal learning. *Psychol. Rev.*, 1940, **47**, 196–229.

Gibson, J. J., & Gibson, E. J. Perceptual learning: differentiation or enrichment? *Psychol. Rev.*, 1955, **62**, 33–40.

Goss, A. E. A stimulus-response analysis of the interaction of cue-producing and instrumental responses. *Psychol. Rev.*, 1955, **62**, 20–31.

Goss, A. E., & Nodine, C. F. *Paired-associates learning.* New York: Academic, 1965.

Hake, H. W., & Eriksen, C. W. Effect of number of permissible response categories on learning of a constant number of visual stimuli. *J. Exp. Psychol.*, 1955, **50**, 161–167.

Hake, H. W., & Eriksen, C. W. Role of response variables in recognition and identification of complex visual forms. *J. Exp. Psychol.*, 1956, **52**, 235–243.

James, W. *Principles of psychology.* New York: Holt, 1890.

Katz, P. A. Effects of labels on children's perception and discrimination learning. *J. Exp. Psychol.*, 1963, **66**, 423–428.

Kendler, H. H. Problems in problem solving research. In *Current trends in psychological theory: a bicentennial program.* Pittsburgh, Pa.: Univer. of Pittsburgh Press, 1961.

Kurtz, K. H. Discrimination of complex stimuli: the relationship of training and test stimuli in transfer or discrimination. *J. Exp. Psychol.*, 1955, **50**, 283–292.

McKinney, J. P. Disappearance of luminous designs. *Science*, 1963, **140**, 403–404.

Miller, N. E., & Dollard, J. *Social learning and imitation.* New Haven, Conn.: Yale Univer. Press, 1941.

Pfafflin, S. M. Stimulus meaning in stimulus predifferentiation. *J. Exp. Psychol.*, 1960, **59**, 269–274.

Pick, Anne D. Improvement of visual and tactual form discrimination. *J. Exp. Psychol.*, 1965, **69**, 331–339.

De Rivera, J. Some conditions governing the use of the cue-producing response as an explanatory device. *J. Exp. Psychol.*, 1959, **57**, 299–304.

Robinson, J. S. The effects of learning verbal labels for stimuli on their later discrimination. *J. Exp. Psychol.*, 1955, **49**, 112–114.

Underwood, B. J. Stimulus selection in verbal learning. In C. N. Cofer & Barbara S. Musgrave (Eds.), *Verbal behavior and learning.* New York: McGraw-Hill, 1963.

Underwood, B. J. Degree of learning and the measurement of forgetting. *J. Verb. Learn. Verb. Behav.*, 1964, 3, 112–129.

Underwood, B. J., & Schulz, R. W. *Meaningfulness and verbal learning.* Philadelphia: Lippincott, 1960.

Vanderplas, J. M. Transfer of training and its relation to perceptual learning and recognition. *Psychol. Rev.*, 1958, **65**, 375–385.

Vanderplas, J. M. Associative processes and task relations in perceptual learning. *Perc. Mot. Skills*, 1963, **16**, 501–509.

Vanderplas, J. M., & Garvin, E. A. The association value of random shapes. *J. Exp. Psychol.*, 1959, **57**, 147–154. (a)

Vanderplas, J. M., & Garvin, E. A. Complexity, association value, and practice as factors in shape recognition following paired-associates training. *J. Exp. Psychol.*, 1959, **57**, 155–163. (b)

Vanderplas, J. M., Sanderson, W. A., & Vanderplas, J. N. Some task-related determinants of transfer in perceptual learning. *Percept. Mot. Skills*, 1964, **18**, 71–80.

Wohlwill, J. F. The definition and analysis of perceptual learning. *Psychol. Rev.*, 1958, **65**, 283–295.

Wright, J. C., & Kagan, J. (Eds.) *Basic cognitive processes in children. Monogr. Soc. Res., Child Develm.*, 1963, **28**, No. 2.

Chapter seven
Controlled practice or training:
III The effect of reward
and punishment

In the decade following World War II, a new look became prominent in theoretical discussions of perception. This new look emphasized the role of motivational factors in perception. The argument was advanced that *exclusive* reliance on the "autochthonous" determinants, uncovered by the Gestalt psychologists and the psychophysical investigators, would never lead to a complete theory of perception. Additional determinants, rooted in the motivational system of the perceiver, needed to be taken into account. A vast program of experimentation was undertaken to demonstrate and elucidate the role of motivational factors in the determination of perception. Allport (1955, pp. 309–318) has listed six propositions for which support has been claimed:

■ 1
Bodily needs tend to determine what is perceived. . . .
2
Reward and punishment associated with the perceiving of objects tend to determine what is perceived. . . .
3
The values characteristic of the individual tend to determine the speed with which words related to those values are recognized. . . .
4
The values of objects tend to determine their perceived magnitudes. . . .
5
The personality characteristics of the individual predispose him to perceive things in a manner consistent with those characteristics.
6
Verbal stimuli that are emotionally disturbing or threatening

143

tend to require a longer recognition-time than neutral words, to be so misperceived as radically to alter their form or meaning, and to arouse their characteristic emotional reactions even before they are recognized.

The present discussion will deal with the second proposition exclusively. There has been ample coverage of the remaining questions in other sources (e.g., Allport, 1955; Brown, 1961; Dember, 1960; Jenkin, 1957). Furthermore the experiments conducted to study the second proposition have been more clearly designed as perceptual learning paradigms than the studies of the remaining propositions.

The earliest explicit formulation of the proposition appeared in a study by Proshansky and Murphy (1942). The purpose of this study was to demonstrate ". . . that perception develops positively in the direction of reward, tending away from the region of failure" (p. 296). This hypothesis was derived from the more general view that "perception . . . has other functions besides mediating correct reports. For one thing, it often fulfills a drive directly; one perceives as one wishes to perceive. One perceives in a way which has proved to be satisfying, or rewarding" (Proshansky & Murphy, 1942, p. 296). The term "autism," introduced by Bartlett (1932) in his classic study of remembering, was used to refer to this tendency for perception to be congruent with the perceiver's "wishes."

The influence of reinforcement
on figure-ground perception

An important early experiment was conducted by Schafer and Murphy (1943). In this experiment, monetary rewards and punishments were associated with two opposite complementary contour profiles. These are shown in Figure 8. The contours were made unambiguous by enclosing them in semicircles as shown in Figure 8. Following the period of reinforced exposures (and naming), the complementary profiles were combined to form an ambiguous composite. The hypothesis of autism suggested that the prior reinforcement history should selectively determine the response to the composite. The profile which was positively rewarded should be perceived as figure. The main finding was that fifty-four of the sixty-seven responses given to the first sixteen exposures of the composite specified the previously rewarded profile as figure.

A good deal of the experimental literature consists of responses to, and elaborations and criticisms of, this experiment. Rock and Fleck (1950) repeated the experiment of Schafer and Murphy with several minor modifications and failed to observe any significant effects of reinforcement on subsequent responses to the ambiguous composite. Several investigations have been reported which have tried to clarify the discrepancy between the findings of Schafer and Murphy and those of Rock and Fleck. Smith and Hochberg (1954) suggested that the specific monetary rewards (2 and 4 cents) used by Schafer and Murphy in 1943 may not have been effective when Rock and Fleck used them in 1950. In fact Rock and Fleck (1950) remarked that ". . . there is reason to doubt that the monetary reward and punishment succeeded in establishing the intended attitudes toward the different faces" (p. 774). This presumed limitation could be overcome by increasing the monetary amounts which served as reinforcements. However, Smith and Hochberg (1954) elected to eliminate the monetary reinforcements and to substitute electric shock. In the training series, one of the profiles was accompanied by electric shock, while the complementary profile was not shocked. Following fifteen exposures of each profile, there were thirty-two tachisto-scopic exposures of the composite, which were interspersed with thirty-one extraneous set-breaking figures. The results of this experiment were not impressive. The overall results showed a significant preference for the nonshocked profile. However, this effect is entirely the result of the performance of one of the two subgroups of Ss. The remaining subgroup

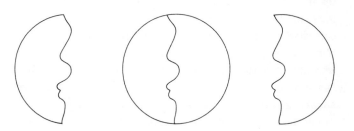

Figure 8. Contour profiles and ambiguous composite introduced by Schafer and Murphy (1943).

did not exhibit selective perception. These Ss reported the shocked and nonshocked alternatives with approximately equal frequency.

Smith and Hochberg (1954) also reported a second experiment which was like the study described above except that prior to the presentation of the composite, S was informed that two faces would appear in juxtaposition and that he should attempt to identify both. The results showed that 43 percent of the responses were correct identifications of *both* profiles. Of the remaining responses, 53 percent were nonshocked profiles, and 47 percent were shocked profiles. The difference between the shocked and nonshocked profiles was not significant. The finding that both profiles can be seen on a single exposure of the composite raises questions about the Schafer-Murphy effect. It is true that reports of both profiles did not occur frequently, except when Ss were instructed to expect this possibility. However, this may only mean that S will not give the "both" response unless he is assured that this response is acceptable to E. If S actually sees both alternatives but believes that a "both" response is prescribed, then he will probably give the response which has been associated with reward. These implications of Smith and Hochberg (1954) merit further examination.

Two experiments by Jackson (1954) were also directed at the discrepancy between the Schafer-Murphy study and the Rock-Fleck study. Jackson repeated the Schafer-Murphy study with only two essential changes: the amounts of the monetary rewards and punishments were increased, and S was paid for his participation. The results confirmed the Schafer-Murphy findings completely. A postexperimental interview was conducted to determine S's attitudes about the monetary rewards and punishments. On the basis of the interview two groups of Ss were distinguished. One group consisted of Ss who denied any concern with the monetary reinforcements, and the other group was comprised of Ss who admitted such concern. When the responses for these two groups were compared, the group expressing concern showed a significantly greater preference for the rewarded profile than the group which denied interest in the money. In fact, the latter group reported slightly more punished than reinforced profiles. The results of this comparison are compatible with the hypothesis of autism.

Unfortunately, the results of Exp. II reintroduced the original doubts. Experiment II was a replication of Exp. 1 which used a projector tachistoscope instead of the Dodge tachistoscope used by Rock and Fleck. With the projector tachistoscope the Schafer-Murphy results were not obtained. There are a variety of differences contingent on the type of tachistoscope which is used. For example, the image size was considerably greater for the projector tachistoscope than for the Dodge tachistoscope. Perhaps these differences are important. However, one must feel uneasy about an effect which is so highly specific.

Postman (1953) has objected to the usual interpretation of these studies. Postman raised the question ". . . whether rewards exercise their effects through need reduction or because they are emphasizers in Tolman's (1932) sense and provide the sensory effect of the stimulus with rich associative context" (Postman, 1953, p. 83). Ayllon and Sommer (1956) and Sommer (1957) have examined the emphasis hypothesis in a number of experiments. The earlier experiment involved two reinforcement conditions: reward versus neutral and punishment versus neutral. The emphasis hypothesis suggests that both the rewarded and the punished alternatives should be perceived more frequently than the neutral alternatives. There is even some suggestion in the literature (Tolman, Hall, & Bretnall, 1932) that punishment is a more effective emphasizer and, therefore, the punished alternative might be more frequently reported than the rewarded alternative. The autism hypothesis, on the other hand, requires that the rewarded alternative should be reported more frequently than the neutral one while the punished alternative should be reported less frequently than the neutral one. New training and test figures were employed, and presentation was in a Dodge tachistoscope. Monetary rewards (25 cents) and punishments were used. The results supported the autism hypothesis. The rewarded alternatives were reported more frequently than the neutral alternatives, while the punished alternatives were less frequently recognized (although this latter difference was not statistically significant).

Sommer (1957) examined this question again in a new experiment, which differed in two respects from the study described above: first, a reward-versus-punishment condition was added to the two previous conditions; second, the ambiguous test composites were presented as part of the series of exposures which included the unambiguous alternatives. Thus, S was tested during the course of the administration of reinforcement. In the previous experiments, the ambiguous test figures were presented in an unreinforced sequence following the termination of the reinforced unambiguous series.

The results which are summarized in Table 15 confirmed the findings of the earlier study. The rewarded alternatives were reported more frequently than punished or neutral alternatives. This supports the hypothesis of autism. However, contrary to the emphasis hypothesis, the punished alternative was not reported more frequently than the neutral alternative.

Another criticism of the Schafer-Murphy paradigm is implied by a number of observations reported by Rock and Fleck (1950). During the reinforced training the Ss were required to name the profile upon each exposure. Therefore, both seeing the profile and saying the name were reinforced. As a result, the probability of responding with the label of the reinforced profile is raised. The development of a response set could account for the preference for the reinforced profile without necessarily implicating perceptual selectivity. This possibility was examined in an experiment by Solley and Long (1958a). The stimuli were like those used by Schafer and Murphy. The chief innovation of the Solley-Long experiment was that S was asked to guess what was going to be exposed prior to each of the ten test presentations of the ambiguous composite. If the "response set" interpretation is correct, there ought to be a high positive correlation between S's guesses and the responses to the exposure of the test composite. Two experiments were conducted. Experiment I compared a (monetary) reward and

Table 15
Results of three reinforcement conditions

Condition	Perceived rewarded figure	Perceived neutral figure	Perceived punished figure	P
Reward vs. neutral	66	38		.01
Punishment vs. neutral		43	58	NS
Reward vs. punishment	31		16	.05

punishment condition. Experiment II compared a punishment and neutral (no reinforcement) condition.

The results are summarized in Table 16. The statistical analyses provided no evidence of a positive correlation between guessing and subsequent perceptual reports. Thus, there was no support for the response set interpretation of the "autism" effect. However, neither was there any evidence of autism in the perceptual reports of the Solley-Long Ss. In Exp. I, rewarded profiles were not reported more frequently than punished profiles. In Exp. II, the punished profiles were reported more frequently than neutral ones. This latter finding is more compatible with an emphasis hypothesis than a hypothesis of autism. As an explanation of the absence of an autism effect Santos and Murphy (1960) suggest that ". . . the guessing behavior which they required of the S might be regarded as an extinction phase which weakened the strength of 'expectancies' so that their influence was not adequately demonstrated" (p. 12). This explanation is not very convincing. It seems unlikely that a single unreinforced occurrence of a response (guess), in the absence of the stimulus, could result in extinction of the trained stimulus-response association.

Solley and Santos (1958) have reported an experiment which used verbal reinforcement in a study of the perception of the Necker cube. The stimuli which they used are illustrated in Figure 9. The test cube was a balanced cube whose appearance tends to fluctuate between two perspective alternatives. The cubes designated "left to right" and "right to left" are specially constructed to favor a single response. Solley and Santos were able to produce consistent, nonalternating responding to the balanced cube by giving verbal rewards in conjunction with presentation of the improved cubes. The experiment consisted of 101 exposures of the

Table 16
Contingency table of frequencies on trial 1

Guesses	Exp. I perceptual reports		Exp. II perceptual reports	
	Rewarded	Punished	Neutral	Punished
Rewarded	9	9	7	16
Punished	4	2	4	9
Total	13	11	11	25

left-to-right cube and 101 exposures of the right-to-left cube, along with 54 interspersed exposures of the balanced cube. One of the improved cubes was reinforced on approximately 70 percent of its exposures and the other on approximately 30 percent of its exposures. Each exposure lasted 2 seconds, and S identified the direction of each cube during the presentation. The reinforcements were approving remarks, e.g., "Uh-huh," "Good, you're doing fine." The reinforcements were given only if S identified the "improved" cube correctly.

The results showed that as the trials increased, there was an increasing tendency to report the rewarded perspective when the balance cube was presented. In the first block of nine interspersed balanced exposures, the responses were divided evenly between the two alternatives. In the last (sixth) block of balanced exposures, 8.5 of the 9 responses consisted of the rewarded alternative. Additional evidence of the effectiveness of reinforcement is provided by the results of a period of continuous exposure to the balanced cube. All six experimental Ss reported the rewarded alter-

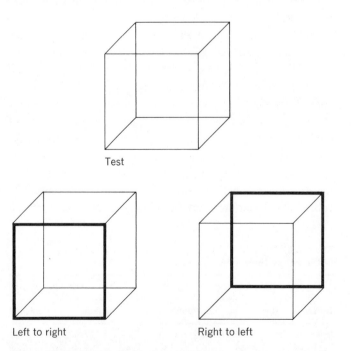

Test

Left to right   Right to left

Figure 9. Illustration of improved and test cubes as seen by the subject (face of cube is 2 by 2 inches).

native first and maintained this percept for a median time of 59 seconds before a perspective shift occurred. A control group who received no reinforcement distributed its initial responses between the alternatives and shifted after 5.17 seconds. The latter findings were confirmed in a separate experiment reported in the same paper. Solley and Santos (1958) conclude that ". . . there seems to be little doubt that verbal rewards can markedly restructure perception" (p. 192).

Although these results are clear, the generality of the conclusion has yet to be established. For example, Solley and Long (1958b) were less successful than Solley and Santos (1958) in demonstrating an effect of verbal reinforcement on the perception of the balanced cube. To reconcile this discrepancy, Solley and Santos suggest that ". . . rapport between E and S [is] a necessary condition for the effectiveness of the verbal reinforcement in this situation" (p. 199). This is a plausible suggestion. It seems likely that the value which S places on a verbal reinforcement will be partially dependent on how much he values the reinforcing agent. The literature on verbal conditioning supports this assertion.

The influence of reinforcement
on the perception of
spatial properties

The experiments which have been considered thus far have sought evidence of the effect of reinforcement in S's response to the presentation of ambiguous figure-ground or perspective patterns. These studies have been modeled after the early experiment by Schafer and Murphy (1943). Next we will consider the experiments which have sought to demonstrate the effects of reinforcement on the judgment of spatial properties, size, depth, and shape. These studies may be viewed as extensions of an early experiment by Proshansky and Murphy (1942). To demonstrate the influence of reinforcement on perception, Proshansky and Murphy conducted a three-stage experiment. In the pretraining stage, each experimental S gave estimates of the lengths of lines presented in darkness, estimates of the magnitude of a series of weights, and reports of the perceived direction of autokinetic movement. In the second stage (training), monetary rewards and punishments were introduced. For fourteen sessions, extending over seven weeks, Ss received reinforced exposures to the stimuli. Long lines, heavy weights, and movements of the stimulus light to the right were positively reinforced. Short lines, light weights, and movements to the left were negatively reinforced. The intermediate members of the series were sometimes reinforced positively, and sometimes negatively. In the final test stage, S again estimated the size and weight of the intermediate stimuli and the direction of autokinetic movement. A control group of three Ss followed the same procedure with the omission of the reinforcement during training.

Proshansky and Murphy found that estimates of the length and weight shifted significantly between the pretest and the posttest in the direction of the positively reinforced values. For example, the experimental Ss gave a mean estimate of 4.4 inches for the intermediate lines (3.5, 3.0, 2.5 inches) on the pretest and 5.5 inches on the posttest. For the intermediate weights (13, 12, 11 ounces), the pretraining estimate was 12.6 ounces, and the posttest estimate was 17.5 ounces. The results for the autokinetic effect were inconclusive. The estimates of the control Ss did not change between the pretest and posttest.

Two more recent investigations by McNamara (1959, 1960) will be considered next. McNamara's earlier study was concerned with the effects of reinforcement on the estimation of line length. The later study was concerned with the development of form constancy as a function of reward. McNamara's Exp. I (1959) was in three stages: In the *pretraining* stage Ss made five uncorrected judgments of subjective equality with the bisected-line illusion. The S adjusted the horizontal line to appear equal in length with the vertical line. In the second stage, the *training* stage, S made a series of sixty-six estimations of the separation between two parallel horizontal lines. During the first ten trials S's preference for overestimation or underestimation was determined. Reward, monetary or verbal, then was administered against S's preference and punishment in the direction of his preference. The *posttraining* stage was the same as the pretraining stage. The critical data were the difference scores obtained by comparing the pretraining and posttraining performances. The Ss who were reinforced for overestimating should change their performance on the post-training task to show greater overestimation and should have significantly larger posttest scores than Ss trained in under-estimation.

Figure 10 shows the performance changes over the sixty-six training trials in terms of the percent of overestimation per block of ten trials for four reinforcement conditions. Performance changes appear to be directly proportional to reward and inversely proportional to punishment. The rein-forcements were highly effective in establishing the desired error tendency. Table 17 shows the critical results. Inspection of the difference scores in Table 17 reveals a tendency for the Ss who were trained to overestimate to have larger posttest scores than Ss trained to underestimate.

In a corollary study, McNamara (1959, Exp. III) examined the possibility that the above results were due to the development of a response bias during training which generalized to the bisection task. Experiment III was like Experiment I with one essential difference involving the training stage: in Experiment I S made distance estimates of visually present stimuli; in Experiment III, S was asked to guess the separations of a series of concealed line pairs, basing their guesses on approximate estimates provided by E. If the results of Exp. I are due to response bias rather than perceptual modi-

Table 17
Changes in performance on bisection
illusion as a function of practice*

	Experiment I		Experiment III
S	Overestimation training	Underestimation training	Overestimation training
1	+25†	+ 4	2
2	+26	+ 2	11
3	+13	−19	0
4	+ 3	+ 6	15
5	+ 1	− 8	− 7
6	+ 6	+ 6	6
7	+14	+ 7	9
8	+13	+14	− 5
9	+17	− 5	13
10	+20	− 2	−12

* Adapted from McNamara, 1959, tables 1, 4.
† Scores are differences between pretraining and posttraining adjust-ments of horizontal line.

fication, then the training in Exp. III should have a similar effect. The results are shown in the last column of Table 17. Analysis of these data showed them to be significantly different (less overestimation) than the scores in the first column in Table 17 which were obtained in Exp. I. Furthermore, the scores in Exp. III did not differ from the scores of a control group which received no differential reinforcement during the training.

The results of McNamara's experiments supported the hypothesis regarding the influence of reward and punishment. We might note that the effect is restricted to overestimation. As Table 17 shows, the underestimation training did not succeed in inducing settings in which the adjustable bisecting line was shorter than the vertical.

McNamara (1960) has also reported two experiments dealing with the effects of reinforcement on the perception

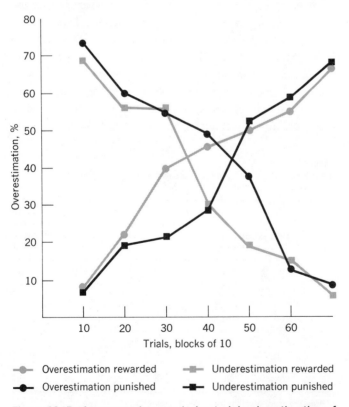

Figure 10. Performance changes during training in estimation of distance between parallel lines. (*From McNamara, 1959, p. 70.*)

of form. Experiment I was designed to show that rotation of a randomly contoured form in O's frontal plane would induce changes in the perception of that form. Experiment II proposed to show that the perceptual consequences of rotation would be lessened if rotation was preceded by a period of reinforcement with the figure.

In Exp. I forms *a* and *b* (see Figure 11) were presented in either 0°, 90°, 180°, or 270° rotation. (Figure 11 shows the forms in 0° rotation.) One group of eight Ss used a comparison device to match each of the angles in form *b* at each of the four rotation positions. A second group of ten Ss was shown form *a* four times in each of the four orientations and was asked to give the form a name. McNamara (1960) reasoned that ". . . if the perception of 'form' is variable due to rotation, it would be expected that Ss would give different names to the form as the form was rotated. However, if 'form' is invariant and basically *unlearned*, Ss would be expected to give a wide variety of responses *unrelated* to the position of the form in space" (p. 20). The

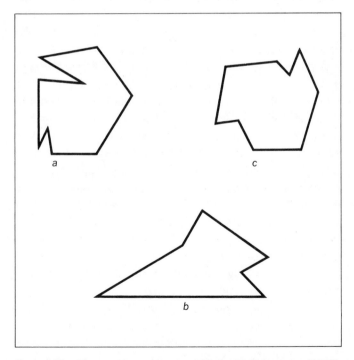

Figure 11. The random forms used in McNamara's (1960) experiments.

first prediction is straightforward; the second prediction, however, is unclear. One would be more inclined to predict that invariance of form perception would be accompanied by a reduction in the between-Ss naming variability.

The results for the angle-estimation task confirmed the expectation that the perception of angles would be a function of the rotation position. There was also a significant inter-action between the angle being judged and its rotation position. The results from the naming task were also clear. For each rotation position there was a clustering of responses around one or two names. For example, in the 0° position, nine of the ten Ss called figure *a* "face or head." Changes in the position of form *a* were accompanied by changes in naming. Thus, seven of the ten called form *a* "tent with flap" when it was in the 270° position. None of the Ss used this label for form *a* in the 0° position. The implication of the findings of Exp. I is that a form which undergoes rotation does not remain perceptually invariant.

McNamara's Exp. II (1960) was designed to test the proposition that prior association of reinforcement with the forms would make the perceptual judgments of the rotated forms more constant. There were two groups of Ss who received slightly different reinforcement treatments. Group 1 was given experience with the forms in a contrived weight-discrimination test in which the forms served as tokens worth 5 or 25 cents. The Ss were allowed to win the tokens and to take them to the Student Union, where they could be used as if they were money. Group 2 was given the same training except that the forms served as paper tokens which were presented in a booklet. The essential difference between the treatments was that Group 1 received a highly variable series of exposures to the forms. Since they were being handled *ad lib*, they were seen in a great variety of rotational posi-tions. Group 2 was exposed to fewer positions, since the booklet form of presentation tended to hold the viewing orientation relatively constant. In addition to these two groups there was a no-reward group.

The major prediction in Exp. II was that the Ss' responses would exhibit a decrease in within-variance as a function of rotation and an increase in between-subjects variance. Indi-vidual analysis of the three conditions did show evidence of a decrease in rotation effects. However, a comparison of the three groups did not specify any particular variable. The interaction of reward, angles, and rotation was highly significant. The implication is that any varied experience with forms, whether or not reinforced by *E*, will bring about a more constant percept.

The influence of reinforcement
on attention

This review of the experimental evidence will be concluded by considering two recent experiments on the perceptual consequences of conditioning attention. Prior to describing these studies the conceptualization of "attention" which underlies them must be discussed.

Historically, the word "attention" has frequently referred to a particular state of consciousness. This conceptualization is exemplified in Titchener's (1924) structural analysis. However, there has always been some recognition that attention involves behavior. Thus, in his description of attention, James (1890) remarked that ". . . *the accommodation or adjustment of the sensory organs*" (p. 434) is an essential aspect of attention. Contemporary writers (e.g., Berlyne, 1951; Berlyne, 1960; Guthrie & Edwards, 1950) have stressed the overt behavioral aspects to the exclusion of experiential properties.

One representative statement is provided by Solley and Murphy (1960): Attention is an act which precedes perception. Since it is an act with response-like properties, it is conditionable. "We believe that most acts of attending are conditioned along the lines of operant conditioning. That is, if an individual makes receptor adjustments, or some search behavior, and is immediately given a reinforcement stimulus, then the probability of his repeating that attentive response will increase" (Solley & Murphy, 1960, p. 188).

Fisch and McNamara (1963) have conducted a number of studies to examine this hypothesis. The general objective of these studies has been to show that perception can be influenced by prior training, which consists of reinforcing specific attentional responses. The particular perceptual effects which were sought were inferred from certain of Piaget's hypotheses (1950) concerning the relationship between attention and perception. Piaget proposed that a distortion factor exists in the perceptual system which tends to produce distortion of perception for any object in the center of the attentional field. For example, the "centration factor" will cause overestimation of the size of objects which are visually fixated. Piaget called this specific distortion the "error of the standard." Piaget also asserted that these distortions can be corrected by "decentralization or decentration," i.e., by a redirection of attention. These hypotheses of Piaget served as the basis for the predictions tested in the experiments of Fisch and McNamara (1963).

In one experiment, the hypothesis was tested that reinforcement for scanning the right or left areas of a Ganzfeld would affect the perceived magnitude of objects later presented in this portion of the field. "Specifically, verbal reinforcement for scanning in a right or left direction will produce a larger 'error of the standard' in a stimulus object which appears in the conditioned area of the field" (Fisch & McNamara, 1963, p. 893). In the first stage, the experimental S was asked to set a variable form to match the distance of a standard form. The left and right forms served alternately as standards. The depth judgments were made against the background of a gray Ganzfeld. Next, S performed 100 bisections of the Ganzfeld. S moved a vertical spindle laterally until the field was bisected. During these judgments positive and negative verbal reinforcements were administered with the purpose of training S to bisect the field in a manner opposite to his initial preference. For example, if S tended initially to bisect the field to the right of the true center, then he was induced by reinforcement to produce bisection judgments which were left of the true center. Finally, in the third stage, S repeated the original depth judgments. A control group of Ss were treated similarly except that their bisection training was not accompanied by reinforcement.

The main results concern the difference between the pretraining and posttraining depth judgments. If the bisection training has the effect of directing attending behavior toward the reinforced side, then a greater "error of the standard" should occur when the standard appears in the reinforced area. As a consequence of size overestimation of the standard, the comparison should be set nearer than the standard when the two appear equidistant. The results showed that thirteen of the fifteen experimental Ss behaved in agreement with the expectation that direction of training would result in greater error of the standard on the trained side. For example, if S had been trained to the left in the bisection task, then S would set the left form behind the right one on the posttest. The control Ss, who received bisection training without reinforcement, also gave posttest evidence of error of the standard but in the direction of their initial preference.

In a second experiment, Fisch and McNamara (1963) examined the effect of reinforced bisection training on direction of looking and consequent speed of object recognition. Following the bisection training Ss performed two recognition tests. In test 1 a number of slides each containing twenty small representational figures were exposed. Prior to each presentation S was asked to locate a specified figure by designating the quadrant in which it was contained. Each exposure lasted 5 seconds. Included in the series of twenty slides were four slides which did not actually contain an example of the required test figure. Test 2 was the same as test 1 and followed 1 week after test 1.

On the basis of the rationale presented earlier, Fisch and McNamara (1963) predicted that recognition would be superior for the figures presented on the trained side. For the slides which did not contain exemplars the expectation was that the Ss, who were forced to make location choices, would favor the locations which agreed with the direction of training.

In addition to the experimental group, a control group performed the two recognition tasks without prior bisection training. However, following the second test the control Ss performed the bisection test without reinforcement.

The results for the experimental group showed that nine of the thirteen Ss had shorter mean latencies for figures on the nonpreferred (trained) side than on the initially preferred side. The difference between the mean latencies for the two sides was significant. The control group showed significantly shorter latencies for the figures on the preferred side as determined by the posttest bisection task. However, the difference in favor of the preferred side for the control Ss was significantly smaller than the difference in favor of the nonpreferred side for the experimental Ss.

The results of test 2 showed that the experimental Ss had reverted to their original preference. The latencies were shorter on the initially preferred side than for figures on the trained side. It would appear that the effect of conditioning of attention was transient. The results for the control Ss on test 2 showed no significant difference between the figures on the two sides. This latter finding indicates the presence of a practice effect and makes uncertain any inferences based on the between-test differences for the experimental group.

An analysis of the results for the slides which did not contain exemplars did not show significant differences between the two sides for either the experimental or control group. There was evidence that the experimental Ss favored the nonpreferred side more than the control Ss.

Fisch and McNamara (1963) conclude that ". . . attention, conceptualized as an act, can be experimentally manipulated by means of a learning paradigm. Further, the method employed to influence attention, e.g., inducing general scanning behavior or a specific focusing of attention, has differential effects upon the subsequent perceptual organization of the field. . . . The predicted centration effect was observed" (pp. 906–907).

Conclusions and evaluations

The evidence concerning the role of reinforcement in determining perception has been reviewed under three headings: figure-ground perception, spatial properties, and attention. Although twenty-five years have elapsed since the first experiment by Proshansky and Murphy, the progress in this area has not been impressive. Nor is it likely that additional experiments of the same type will yield significant gains. With few exceptions the experiments have been inadequately designed. Neither the independent nor the dependent variables have been specified precisely. With regard to the independent variable three types of reinforcement have been used: monetary, electric shock, and verbal reinforcement. In each case questions may be raised about the efficacy of the reinforcing events. In the case of the monetary rewards and the verbal reinforcements there is reason to believe that S's interpretation of the experimental situation will determine the extent to which these monetary and verbal consequences will affect his behavior.

This is also true for the mild noxious shock used by Smith and Hochberg (1954). Perhaps this ambiguity could be handled by introducing special instructions or by using selected samples of Ss. For example, Ss who have a high need for approval (McClelland, 1958) could be used. Perhaps for these Ss certain verbal utterances may be confidently assumed to be positively or negatively reinforcing. However, even if this ambiguity is adequately resolved, cause for dissatisfaction would remain. The reinforcement procedures, although justified by precedent and analogy with conditioning procedures, are not very convincing. Even granting the contention that selective perception is learned as a result of differential reinforcement, it seems implausible that the reinforcements are of the sort used in the experiments. Compare the presentation of 4 cents with the profound consequences of the young child's learning to respond to the black marks on the printed page, instead of to the white interspaces. It also seems unlikely that adult Ss, with established perceptual functions and tendencies, will be affected very much by the introduction of small monetary sums or several approving "Uh-huhs." If any effect obtains, it is likely to be in the nature of response compliance rather than perceptual modification.

This argument leads to the second general weakness in the experiments which have been reviewed. With only few exceptions the experiments have not included procedures for determining whether the observed effects are to be properly assigned to the perceptual system. This deficiency is especially notable in the figure-ground studies. It is not possible to conclude, with any degree of confidence, whether Ss actually saw the reinforced portion of the composite as figure or only were encouraged to say it was figure. This question could be resolved by the introduction of converging operations or by the identification of secondary perceptual effects which are uniquely dependent on the perception of a specific portion as figure. (See Chapter 1 for a discussion of these procedures.)

As an example of the procedure of introducing converging operations, the *vexierversuch* (test trial), used so effectively by Goldiamond and Hawkins (1958), could be introduced.

This procedure calls for an additional test condition under which S is exposed to a blank tachistoscopic flash. In the case of the Schafer-Murphy figures, a tachistoscopic exposure of a blank circle would be more appropriate. The S's response to this test exposure, when it follows reinforcement training, will provide a basis for assessing the existence of a response bias.

The use of the second procedure requires the availability of a perceptual effect, not in any way involved in the training procedure, whose occurrence is dependent on figure-ground articulation. For example, Gelb and Granit (1923) reported that the portion of an ambiguous figure-ground pattern which was seen as figure was more resistant to the intrusion of another figure than was the portion seen as ground. Gelb and Granit found that the detection threshold for a colored spot of light was higher when the spot was projected onto the portion which appeared as figure. The spot had to be made more intense to be detected on the surface of the figure, as compared with the ground.

The findings of Gelb and Granit could be adapted to determine the nature of the effects produced by reinforcement. The procedure would be to project two light spots, one in each half of the composite, along with the exposure of the composite. The intensity level of the dots could be set at the detection threshold, as established by prior psychophysical investigation with a circle which was evenly divided by a straight vertical line. If the findings of Gelb and Granit can be accepted, then the following prediction can be made: On the premise that perceptual organization has been affected, the probability of detection will be lower for the spot which is projected on the portion reported as figure. On the other hand, if S's reports are due exclusively to a response bias, the two spots should be reported with equal frequency.

Another limitation of the experimental investigations is that the situations which have been investigated have been so special as to create serious doubts about the generality of the results. A series of experiments concerned with the determinants of the perception of the Schafer-Murphy composite hardly seems to be sufficient justification for the generalized proposition of autistic perception. The experiments which dealt with spatial properties and attention do provide some variety, but they are too few to alleviate the doubts. Until additional evidence is available, any conclusion about the proposition under consideration would be premature.

References

Allport, F. H. *Theories of perception and the concept of structure.* New York: Wiley, 1955.

Ayllon, T., & Sommer, R. Autism, emphasis, and figure-ground perception. *J. Psychol.,* 1956, **41,** 163–176.

Bartlett, F. C. *Remembering.* New York: Cambridge Univer. Press, 1932.

Berlyne, D. E. Attention, perception, and behavior theory. *Psychol. Rev.,* 1951, **58,** 137–146.

Berlyne, D. E. *Conflict, arousal, and curiosity.* New York: McGraw-Hill, 1960.

Brown, J. S. *The motivation of behavior.* New York: McGraw-Hill, 1961.

Dember, W. N. *The psychology of perception.* New York: Holt, 1960.

Fisch, R. I., & McNamara, H. J. Conditioning of attention as a factor in perceptual learning. *Percept. Mot. Skills,* 1963, **17,** 891–907.

Gelb, A., & Granit, R. Die Bedutung von "Figur" und "Grund" für die Farbenschwelle. *Z. Psychol.,* 1923, **93,** 83–118.

Goldiamond, I., & Hawkins, W. F. Vexierversuch: the log relationship between word-frequency and recognition obtained in the absence of stimulus words. *J. Exp. Psychol.,* 1958, **56,** 457–463.

Guthrie, E., & Edwards, A. L. *Psychology.* New York: Harper, 1950.

Jackson, D. N. A further examination of the role of autism in a visual figure-ground relationship. *J. Psychol.,* 1954, **38,** 339–357.

James, W. *Principles of psychology.* New York: Holt, 1890.

Jenkin, N. Affective processes in perception. *Psychol. Bull.,* 1957, **54,** 100–127.

McClelland, D. C. Risk taking in children with high and low need for achievement. In J. W. Atkinson (Ed.), *Motives in fantasy, action and society.* Princeton, N.J.: *Van Nostrand, 1958.*

McNamara, H. J. Nonveridical perception as a function of rewards and punishments. *Percept. Mot. Skills,* 1959, **9,** 67–80.

McNamara, H. J. The development of a form constancy as a function of reward. Unpublished doctoral dissertation, Univer. of Kansas, 1960.

Piaget, J. *The psychology of intelligence.* London: Kegan Paul, Trench, Trubner & Co., 1950.

Postman, L. The experimental analysis of motivational factors in perception. In J. S. Brown et al., *Current theory and research in motivation: a symposium.* Lincoln, Nebr.: Univer. of Nebraska Press, 1953, 58–108.

Proshansky, H., & Murphy, G. The effects of reward and punishment on perception. *J. Psychol.,* 1942, **13,** 295–305.

Rock, I., & Fleck, F. S. A re-examination of the effect of monetary reward and punishment in figure-ground perception. *J. Exp. Psychol.,* 1950, **40,** 766–776.

Santos, J. F., & Murphy, G. An Odyssey in perceptual learning. *Bull. Menninger Clin.,* 1960, **24,** 6–17.

Schafer, R., & Murphy, G. The role of autism in a figure-ground relationship. *J. Exp. Psychol.,* 1943, **32,** 335–343.

Smith, D. E., & Hochberg, J. E. The effect of "punishment" (electric shock) on figure-ground perception. *J. Psychol.,* 1954, **38,** 83–87.

Solley, C. M., & Long, J. Perceptual learning versus response set learning. *Percept. Mot. Skills.,* 1958, **8,** 235–240. (a)

Solley, C. M., & Long, J. When is "Un-Huh" reinforcing? *Percept. Mot. Skills,* 1958, **8,** 277. (b)

Solley, C. M., & Murphy, G. *Development of the perceptual world.* New York: Basic Books, 1960.

Solley, C. M., & Santos, J. Perceptual learning with partial verbal reinforcement. *Percept. Mot. Skills,* 1958, **8,** 183–193.

Sommer, R. The effects of rewards and punishments during perceptual organization. *J. Pers.,* 1957, **25,** 550–558.

Titchener, E. B. *The psychology of feeling and attention.* New York: Macmillan, 1924.

Tolman, E. C. *Purposive behavior in animals and men.* New York: Appleton-Century-Crofts, 1932.

Tolman, E. C., Hall, C. S., & Bretnall, E. P. A disproof of the law of effect and a substitution of the laws of emphasis, motivation and disruption. *J. Exp. Psychol.,* 1932, **15,** 601–614.

Chapter eight
Perceptual conflict

In this chapter a variety of perceptual conflicts will be considered. Three types of perceptual conflict may be usefully distinguished:

1
Conflicts involving independent, simultaneously present cues which have discrepant perceptual consequences
2
Conflicts involving the information provided by visual perception and the information provided by the consequences of purposeful action mediated by perception
3
Conflicts involving mutually exclusive contents which are simultaneously introduced into the perceptual system

Our chief concern will be with conflict resolution as an instance of perceptual learning.

Conflict between competing cues

There are many available cues for depth. In fact, except under conditions contrived in the laboratory, it is rare that circumstances arise in which only a single cue for depth is operative. Instead, it is typical of normal viewing that several means for determining spatial properties are simultaneously present. Furthermore, it is typical that these cues cooperate in determining perceived depth. For example, the gradients of optical texture and motion parallax indicate the same relative spatial ordering of objects in depth. However, suppose conditions are arranged for bringing two cues into conflict. What will be the perceptual consequences of such conflict?

The first investigator to arrange conditions of conflict was Wheatstone (1852). The arrangement required a pseudo-scope—a stereoscope which reverses each eye's view right or left.

■ Some very paradoxical results are obtained when objects in motion are viewed through the pseudoscope. When an object approaches, the magnitude of its picture on the retinae increases as in ordinary vision, but the inclination of the optic axes, instead of increasing, becomes less. . . . Now an enlargement of the picture on the retina invariably suggests approach, and a less convergence of the optic axis indicates that the object is at a greater distance; and we have thus two contradictory suggestions. . . . [The] continually enlarging picture on the retina makes it (the approaching object) appear to come toward the eyes, as it actually does, while at the same time it appears at every step at a greater distance beyond the fixed object (Wheatstone, 1852, pp. 15–16).

Over seventy years elapsed before the first systematic study of cue conflict was reported by Schriever (1925). Schriever's purpose was to determine the relative strengths of the various cues by pitting one against the other. For example, a solid of the shape shown in Figure 12 was photographed against a dark background and prepared as a pair of stereograms. When viewed in a stereoscope the concurrence of disparity, interposition, and light-shadow distribution produced a powerful depth effect. Now if the right and left stereograms are interchanged, the reversed disparity should, in the absence of other information, produce a pseudoscopic effect. However, Schriever found that the depth relief was not changed. Retinal disparity was ineffective. A combination of interposition and shading prevailed over disparity. In similar ways other cues were compared.

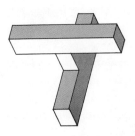

Figure 12. One of the solids used by Schriever (1925).

A number of striking demonstrations of cue conflict have been invented by Ames and the Transactionalist school (Kilpatrick, 1952, Ch. 2). Two of these are the balloon demonstration and the overlay demonstration. The balloon demonstration consists of two stationary balloons, side by side, whose size and brightness can be varied continuously and independently. If balloon A is made to increase continuously in size and diminish in brightness while balloon B decreases in size and increases in brightness, a cue conflict is produced. The size cue should produce a "looming" effect of A and a recession in depth of B. The brightness cue, on the other hand, favors apparent movement in the opposite direction.

Kilpatrick found that most observers reported movement in the direction favored by size change. The dominance of size change is explained by assuming that, as a result of past experience, the probability attached to the size-distance association is greater than the probability attached to the brightness-distance association. "Since in the past the prognostic reliability of size has been much greater than that of intensity of illumination, indications of size are given greater weight than are illumination indications in the extremely rapid, complex, evolving, and unconscious integration which is the perceptual process" (Kilpatrick, 1952, p. 8). This line of reasoning is like the hypotheses discussed in Ch. 2 of this book.

In the overlay demonstration, interposition is made to contradict the relative-size and known-size cues. The display is shown in Figure 13. The interposition cue determines the perceived relative positions of the surfaces despite the fact that this relative ordering is discrepant with the ordering favored by relative size and known size. Other investigations of perceptual conflict have been reported by Vernon (1937), Ittelson (1960, Ch. 9), and Wallach and Norris (1963).

The observations we have been considering reveal some of the ways in which cue conflict is resolved: oscillation between perceptual alternatives, dominance of one cue, and compromise in the form of a weaker effect than would be obtained by either cue alone. These observations have been used mainly to assess the relative strength of cues [e.g., Brunswik's (1956, pp. 50–52) use of Schriever's (1925) data]. The experiments and observations have only indirect

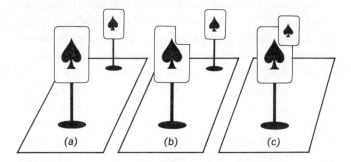

Figure 13. The overlay demonstration. In a dark room two play-ing cards are attached vertically to stands, one placed closer to the observer and the other more distant. Only the cards are visible, and the observer views them with one eye, thus being restricted to monocular depth cues. As illustrated in (a), the cue of relative size (and perhaps other monocular cues) clearly makes the distant card *look* more distant. Then a corner is clipped from the nearer card, as shown in (b), and the stand holding the farther card is moved to the left so that in the observer's retinal image its edges exactly fit the cutout edges of the nearer card. As shown in (c), the effect is clearly to make the more distant card now *appear to be in front of* the closer card. The cue of interposition contradicts and is sufficiently powerful to overcome the cue of relative size, thus resulting in a distorted perception of the two cards. (*From Krech & Crutch-field, 1958, p. 138.*)

relevance to the question of perceptual learning. However, two innovations, introduced by Wallach, change this situation significantly. The two innovations are (1) to expose S to the conflict situation continuously for a relatively extended ex-posure period and (2) to test the effectiveness of the cues individually before and after the exposure period. Suppose that dominant cue X and subordinate cue Y, pertaining to the same property, e.g., depth, are made to yield discrepant per-ceptual consequences. How will the normal relationship between Y and depth perception be affected by the intensive association of Y with the dominant but contradictory re-sponse favored by X? Will the normal relationship undergo modification as a result of the training? Wallach et al. have studied this question in a series of experiments on per-ceptual learning.

The cues which were involved in these studies (Wallach & Karsh, 1963a; Wallach & Karsh, 1963b; Wallach, Moore, &

Davidson, 1963) were the kinetic depth effect and retinal disparity. Both are depth cues, which usually cooperate in determining the perceived depth of small objects. Retinal disparity is a familiar cue, but the term "KDE," introduced by Wallach and O'Connell (1953), may require a brief explanation. The KDE is the perceived depth which results from the continuous changes of the retinal projection of the object due to rotation of the object or equivalent movement of the observer. Braunstein (1962) has reviewed the evidence related to the conditions for obtaining perceived depth as a result of motion. For the present it need only be noted that the KDE provides fairly accurate information concerning the shape and depth of the object (Epstein, 1965; Wallach & O'Connell, 1953).

Wallach, Moore, and Davidson (1963) produced the conflict by having S view turning wire forms through two specially devised mirror stereoscopes. These are sketched in Figure 14. The left-hand side of Figure 14 shows a *tele-stereoscopic* arrangement which has the effect of increasing the degree of binocular disparity and hence exaggerating the depth effect. The right-hand side shows an arrangement for reducing disparity. As Figure 14 shows, these changes in disparity are produced by varying the effective interocular distance. The telestereoscopic arrangement used by Wallach et al. increased the effective interocular distance by 7.6

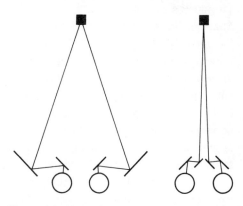

Figure 14. Arrangements in enhancing (left) and reducing (right) retinal disparity. The light paths from the target (square) to the eyes (circles) through the four mirrors of the telestereoscope are traced. (*From Wallach, Moore, & Davidson, 1963, p. 192.*)

centimeters. Since the normal interocular distance is 6.5 centimeters, the result is a doubling of normal disparity. Therefore, the depth of a tridimensional form, e.g., a wire cube, viewed through the telestereoscope appears greater than it is objectively.

In the first experiment, S began by judging the height and depth of a stationary wire cube (4.9-centimeter edge) which was viewed telestereoscopically. The mean height estimation was 5.71 centimeters, and the mean depth estimation was 9.96 centimeters. This latter estimate reflects the telestereoscopic exaggeration. Next, looking through the telestereoscope, S watched the cube rotating on a vertical axis which was continuous with one of its diagonals. Rotation continued for 10 minutes, at a speed of 12 rpm. The rotation and the concomitant projective transformations should provide a cue for the objective depth of the cube. Thus, the two cues gave conflicting indications of depth. After the 10-minute rotation period the S repeated the judgment of the depth of the stationary cube. A significant reduction of depth was observed. The postrotation depth estimate was 8.36, a reduction of 16 percent. Comparable results were found with several different wire forms, e.g., a slightly irregular pyramid.

In a corollary experiment, Wallach et al. (1963) found significant decreases in perceived depth for one form after 10 minutes of observing a second, different rotating form. Although the magnitude of the decrease was greatest when the rotating form and the test form were the same, there were significant decreases for all the training-test conditions formed by combinations of a diagonal cube, perpendicular cube, pyramid, elongated pyramid, and octahedron. This evidence of generalization suggests that the modification of perceived depth is not merely a carryover of information specific to the rotated training form. If this were the case no transfer to different forms would have been obtained.

In another corollary experiment Wallach et al. used the *iconoscopic* arrangement shown in the right half of Figure 14. This arrangement reduces the effective interocular distance and produces conditions which are the reverse of the main experiment. The prediction is that the postrotation estimate should significantly *exceed* the prerotation estimate. The results were consistent with this expectation.

Wallach et al. (1963) proposed that the changed depth estimate of the stationary figure, following rotation, represents a modification of the normal, preexperimental, correlation between disparity and perceived depth. This modification is considered to be an example of rapid perceptual learning. That the modification involves the disparity-depth relationship, and not the KDE-depth relationship, is made clear by the results of an experiment in which the posttest was a depth estimate of a monocularly viewed *rotating* form. There was no increase in estimated depth between the pretraining and the posttraining.

Does the learning which is observed in these experiments have characteristics in common with other types of learning? Figure 15 shows the training effects plotted against a logarithmic time scale. The curve is almost a straight line. As with other forms of learning the amount of perceptual modification (learning) is a function of practice, increasing with increasing exposure. Also, as is the case with other forms of learning, there is evidence that the modification can be

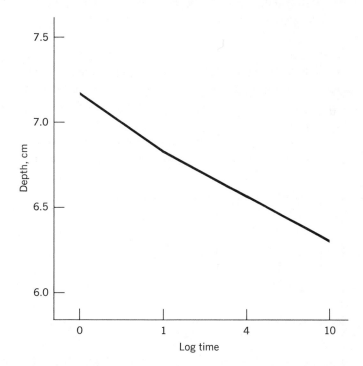

Figure 15. Changes in depth as a function of time. (*Adapted from Wallach, Moore, & Davidson, 1963, p. 200.*)

unlearned. If a rotating object is viewed by S without the stereoscope, this will partially cancel the depth decrease which results from the training, i.e., the stereoscopic observation of the rotating form.

Why does the learned modification of the disparity-depth relationship occur? The hypothesis favored by Wallach is that the modification is the result of a tendency to reduce perceptual discrepancy: ". . . when one set of cues is manipulated to cause the result of one perceptual process to differ from the other . . . a perceptual discrepancy comes into existence. A tendency to reduce this discrepancy through the modification of one of the two perceptual processes may be postulated as the cause of the training effect" (Wallach & Karsh, 1963a, p. 430).

Wallach and Karsh (1963a) obtained indirect support for their hypothesis in an experiment which examined the effect of training with two different forms. The forms are shown in Figure 16. The significant difference between the forms is that simultaneous transformations of length and orientation are produced when the form containing the diagonal lines is rotated. The left-hand form contains lines which are perpendicular to the axis of rotation, and, therefore, no changes in orientation accompany rotation. There is evidence (Wallach & O'Connell, 1953) that changes of *both* length and orientation are necessary for perceived depth to result from rotation. Therefore, only the "diagonal flag" will produce the KDE. Consequently, only telestereoscopic viewing of the diagonal flag will result in a "perceptual discrepancy." Rotation of the "vertical flag" will not lead to the KDE, and

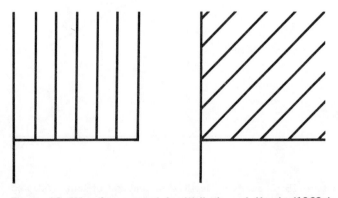

Figure 16. Wire forms used by Wallach and Karsh (1963a).

no perceptual discrepancy will be present. If the presence of a discrepancy is necessary, then the training effect should be restricted to the diagonal flag.

The main findings were that significant training effects were found for both forms but a significantly larger training effect was obtained for the diagonal flag. Wallach and Karsh (1963a) concluded that the presence of perceptual discrepancy is an important condition for the modification of disparity.

In the experiments considered thus far, evidence has been presented that a 10-minute training period can produce significant perceptual modification. In light of the long history of experience with the normal disparity-depth relation, how is it that modification occurs after only 10 minutes of training? Wallach and Karsh (1963b) offer two explanations:

1
The training period is a period of very concentrated learning, compared to extralaboratory experience.
2
Despite contrary impressions, stereoscopic depth perception is not highly durable and needs to be continually relearned.

Wallach and Karsh (1963b) reported two experiments to examine these explanations. In the first experiment, they demonstrated that if the telestereoscopic training is preceded by a short period of normal observation of the rotating form, then the effect of training is diminished. Wallach and Karsh suggest that this finding supports the first explanation, since it shows that concentrated training in support of the normal relation between disparity and depth can counteract the training effect. In the second experiment, Ss made binocular judgments of depth both before and after a 24-hour period of monocular disuse; i.e., one eye was covered for the full period. Wallach and Karsh found that there was a marked deterioration of stereoscopic depth perception after the 24-hour period. This finding is construed by Wallach and Karsh to mean that stereoscopic depth perception is highly modifiable and requires continuous practice and relearning.

Wallach's experiments are among the most interesting and instructive studies in the field of perceptual learning. And, as is frequently the case, they leave us with a set of questions for future investigation. Several of these will be discussed briefly.

1

Why is the training effect greater when the same form is used during training and test? Although Wallach et al. (1963) found that the training effect transferred to nontrained forms, the effect was greater for trained forms. This finding suggests that there are two components in the learning process. One is a general form of learning which consists of a modification of the generalized disparity-depth relationship. This modification accounts for the transfer to new forms. The second is learning specific to the form under observation. This information is useful only if the test form is the same one used in the training session. The addition of this specific component is responsible for the greater modification which is obtained when the forms in training and test are identical. It would be interesting to determine the learning curves for these two components separately. The curve shown in Figure 15 reflects the development of both components in combination. A procedure to separate these components would be to interrupt training after various durations of rotation and test with both the identical form and a different form. The curve for the latter condition should reflect only the general component; the curve for the identical form should reflect both components, and the difference between the curves can be construed as the development of the specific component.

2

What is the relationship between the training effect and the degree of preexperimental association between the cues? In the introductory remarks to this chapter, it was noted that it is typically the case that the depth cues are present in combination. Although empirical data are lacking, it is reasonable to conjecture that the frequency with which any set of two or more cues occurs in combination will vary. For example, binocular disparity and convergence will rarely be separated. On the other hand, relative size and relative brightness are certainly less frequently associated. And the KDE probably has a degree of association with disparity which is intermediate between the two aforementioned examples. The question under consideration is whether the effect of training will be the same for all three cases. The strength of the tendency toward resolution of the discrepancy between cues by modification of one cue may depend on the strength of the preexperimental cooperative association between the cues. In the case of a conflict situation involving cues that are only rarely associated, the conflict may be resolved by alternation rather than unilateral modification.

3

Will the degree of conflict affect the development and retention

of the acquired modification? To examine this question, procedures are required for defining the degree of conflict independently of the expected perceptual modification. A number of
procedures can be examined. The first is simply to vary the
discrepancy between the perceptual consequences of the opposing cues. For example, under condition 1 cue X leads to a
localization of the target at 1D, while cue Y leads to localization
at 2D. Under condition 2 cue X once more indicates 1D, but
cue Y has been manipulated to increase the apparent distance
of the target to 4D. The discrepancy has been trebled. A second
procedure is to increase the duration of time during which S is
exposed to the conflict. The assumption is that the intensity of
conflict increases as the exposure duration increases. A third
procedure is suggested by Schriever's work (1925). This procedure calls for an arrangement which combines *several* cues in
collaborative opposition to a single contradictory cue. Such an
arrangement might produce greater and more rapid modification
of the single cue than the one-versus-one conflict studied by
Wallach.

Conflict between
perception and action

This section will deal with cases in which the information
contained in the consequences of purposeful action conflict
with the information provided by visual perception. This type
of discrepancy will also be treated in Chapter 9, where the
literature on adaptation is discussed. The present discussion
will be restricted to two studies of perceptual learning in the
distorted room.

A variety of distorted rooms have been constructed [e.g.,
see Ittelson & Kilpatrick (1961)]. The experiments which
will be described in this section have used monocular rooms.
The desired appearance of these rooms is contingent on
monocular observation from a station point.

All monocular distorted rooms have two features in
common:

1
They are physical configurations which project to the eye at a
station point an optic array equivalent to the array which is
correlated with a normal rectangular room.
2
Despite the gross differences between the physical structures
of the variously constructed monocular rooms, they cannot be
distinguished by an observer whose eye is at the prescribed

station point. Neither can the distorted rooms be distinguished from a normal room. They all appear to be conventionally constructed rectangular rooms.

When objects are viewed in a distorted room, they assume anomalous appearances. For example, the sizes of objects are dramatically affected. There is an often-reprinted photograph of a mother and young child, standing in opposite far corners of a monocular room. An observer, viewing the contents of the room, reports a dwarflike adult woman and a giantlike little girl. Of course this report represents an exaggerated reversal of the actual relative sizes of the two people. Comparable anomalous size effects have also been demonstrated under more controlled conditions (Epstein, 1962). The anomalous perceptual appearances are not confined to apparent size. Effects on perceived shape and movement are also present.

The appearance of the distorted room is notably resistant to change. Several investigators have remarked that advance knowledge of the true construction of a distorted room rarely affects its appearance. "Even though S had just previously perceived the room as it objectively was with binocular vision, there was no complete carryover to monocular vision. This indicates that an intellectual awareness alone brought about by seeing the room in its objective shape . . . does not directly alter the mode of perception with monocular cues" (Weiner, 1956, p. 9).

Nor does it matter whether the knowledge is newly acquired or the product of repeated observations of the room. Perceptual modification will not occur merely as a consequence of a cognitive apprehension of the real nature of the room. However, there are other, less abstract, methods of learning about the room. Suppose two targets are marked at widely separated points on the back wall of a distorted room whose back wall is slanted in depth to the S's left. As a result of the slant-in-depth of the wall, the left-hand target will be physically more distant than the right-hand target. However, because the back wall appears to be frontoparallel, perpendicular to S's line of sight, the two target markers will appear to be equidistant. In the absence of contradictory information, the fact that perceived distance and physical distance are at variance does not constitute a condition of conflict. But if S is asked to perform a purpose-ful, self-correcting act related to the distance of the two targets, a condition of conflict will arise. A conflict will exist between the localizations provided by perception and the localizations indicated by the consequences of action. For example, if he attempts to throw a ball to the two markers in succession, he will discover that the two markers, which appear to be equidistant, nevertheless require throws which differ in force. The two experiments discussed in the follow-ing pages were concerned with determining whether the introduction of conflict leads to perceptual modification of the distorted room.

Kilpatrick's (1954) study was designed to answer three questions:

1
Would purposeful self-generated action in the distorted room result in a modification of the appearance of the room in the direction of veridicality?
2
Would the observation of equivalent actions executed by others result in comparable perceptual modification?
3
If modification occurs, what is its basis?

One alternative is that S engages in a "reweighting of visual cues" so that greater weight is assigned to specific "give-away" cues, e.g., defects in construction which betray the true shape of the room. A second alternative is that there is ". . . an actual learned alternation in the way in which a given stimulus pattern is perceived, a new perception which is not dependent on the utilization of give-away cues" (Kil-patrick, 1954, p. 363). Kilpatrick calls the first kind of learning "reorganizational" and the second type "formative."

Kilpatrick used three rooms: a normal 4- by 4-foot cubical room (room N) and two distorted rooms. Room L was larger on S's left than on his right. Room T was larger at the top than at the bottom. All three rooms were retinally equivalent. Preliminary tests showed that, with the head motionless and vision restricted to one eye, the three rooms were not dis-tinguishable. All three rooms were seen as normal. Following this preliminary test each S was given four training periods with room L. The Ss in Group A performed two tasks in each of the four periods. They attempted to throw a rubber ball to a number of targets on the real wall, and they traced the outline of the back wall with a long pole. Group NA merely viewed the interior of room L, while E performed the ball-throwing and wall-tracing tasks. Immediately after each training period S described the interior of one of the rooms. After each of the first two periods S described room L. After the third and fourth sessions descriptions of rooms N and T were obtained.

The following were the main results (also see Table 18):

1
The training produced a modification in the appearance of room L. Every S came to see room L more veridically.
2
When Ss were tested in rooms N and T, their descriptions differed from those which they provided in the pretest. Whereas rooms N and T appeared normal in the pretest, after the training with room L they appeared to have the shape of room L. The following are illustrative excerpts from one S's description of room N: The floor ". . . looks as if it slants down to the left . . . the left window of the center panel looks larger and like it is slanting down to the left on the bottom" (Kilpatrick, 1954, p. 367). Kilpatrick considers this transfer effect as evidence that the modification is a case of formative learning. Presumably, learning which was associated with specific give-away cues, present uniquely in room L, would not affect the appearance of different rooms.
3
Group NA showed the same evidence of learning as Group A.

Table 18
Reported changes in appearance of the three rooms after learning sessions for the action group (N = 6) and the no-action group (N = 6)*

	Reported room appearance			
	A group		NA group	
Condition of observation	No change	Changed in one or more aspects	No change	Changed in one or more aspects
L room:				
After 1st learning session	1	5	2	4
After 2nd learning session		6		6
Transfer:				
At the N room	1	5	2	4
At the T room		6	1	5

* From Kilpatrick, 1954, p. 367.

Apparently, self-generated activity is not essential. It is not at all clear why the information obtained by passive observation of the actions of others should be effective when other forms of advance information have no effect on the room's appearance (cf. page 176).

A similar study has been reported by Weiner (1956). There are several differences between Weiner's experiment and Kilpatrick's. In addition to the perception-action conflict, Weiner studied the effects of repeated exposure to conflicting perceptual information. This conflict was produced by introducing objects into the room. For example, a cigarette package was made to move across the room. As the package moved, it appeared to undergo continuous changes in size, while the room appeared normal and unchanging. The cigarette package's fluid appearance conflicted with S's established expectations regarding cigarette packages and may have provided information about the true shape of the room. In another "cue-demonstration," specially designed cards were introduced. The cards appeared initially to be distorted in shape and size; i.e., objectively they were rectangular with square designs, but they were perceived as trapezoidal with diamond designs. These are two examples of eleven perceptual demonstrations which were used. The distortions which were apparent in these demonstrations ". . . brought about conflict in S, i.e., a conflict between perceiving the distortion of the room and perceiving distortion of the objects" (Weiner, 1956, p. 30). In addition to these perceptual distortions, a stick-pointing task was used. The S was required to touch various points on the back wall with the end of a long pole.

Weiner found that the appearance of the room and its contents changed gradually. Initially, the room appeared to be normal, while its contents underwent distortion. But with continued exposure to the demonstrations and practice with the stick-pointing task, the perceptual distortions of the objects diminished and finally disappeared entirely. For example, the cigarette package appeared to be invariant in size and moving in depth. Accompanying the change in appearance of the objects was an alteration in the appearance of the room. The room was perceived veridically. These changes were not discrete modifications but progressed gradually over the course of the experiment. Weiner (1956) presents a detailed record of the verbal reports of one *S*, which illustrate this gradual development of learning.

Following this learning experience, *S* was exposed to a second room (B) which was objectively distorted but in a direction opposite to that of the first room (A). When the empty room B was viewed, *S* initially reported seeing a room like room A. This report is consistent with the results obtained by Kilpatrick (1954). However, Weiner carried the experiment one step further. He introduced the "perceptual demonstrations" into room B. Two striking observations were made. First, from the very outset the demonstrations presented in room B did *not* yield distortions. Thus, the moving cigarette package was perceived veridically, as was the case at the conclusion of the training in room A. Secondly, the appearance of room B altered with relative rapidity. Whereas one *S* required 20 hours of observation for the achievement of veridicality with room A, the same *S* required only 1 hour for this transformation to occur with room B.

■ It appears, therefore, that in addition to a perceptual stereotype *S* had developed *a generalized way of perceiving object-framework relationships,* so that objects could serve as invariant anchorings and could be perceived as invariant throughout transformation in the spatial context. . . . The newly-learned operation of organizing cues . . . was not restricted to functioning in a specific situation and was not tied to specific structural contents (Weiner, 1956, pp. 32–33).

What do the experiments of Kilpatrick and Weiner tell us about the perception-action conflict as a motive for perceptual learning? Action seems to have no special significance for perceptual learning. Action is important only as it introduces new cues that conflict with the cues available without active commerce with the environment. There was no evidence that conflicts arising from self-produced action led to accelerated or greater learning than cue conflicts arising from the observation of the actions of others or from discrepancies between two sources of perceptual information. These remarks are not intended as devaluation of the role of action in providing the conditions for perceptual learning. Outside the laboratory, self-generated action is probably the most effective, if not the exclusive, procedure for making contact with discrepant intramodal and intermodal information. In addition, any general conclusions about the role of action needs to take into account the adaptation literature which will be considered in Chapter 9.

Conflict between
competing contents

This section will consider briefly several investigations of conflict produced by the simultaneous introduction of competing contents. These experiments have not been designed explicitly for the study of perceptual learning. They have been concerned chiefly with the role of past experience in the resolution of perceptual conflict. However, the general procedure of these experiments may be adaptable for the study of perceptual learning.

A single procedure has dominated the investigations of this conflict. This procedure makes use of the fact that radically different stimuli, presented simultaneously to the two eyes, are not usually combined. Instead, the two stimuli are perceived alternately, with the rate of alternation increasing as exposure continues. This condition of presentation has been called "binocular rivalry." Woodworth (1938) and Vernon (1952) have reviewed the older studies of rivalry. Two general conclusions can be stated:

1
When parallel changes are made in both monocular fields, it is found that changes that normally favor efficient vision, e.g., increasing illumination and foveal projection, also favor rapid alternation.
2
When comparable changes are made in only one monocular field, then the dominance of that field is favored; i.e., S reports the contents of that field for a larger fraction of the total exposure time.

In the experiments reviewed by Woodworth and Vernon, the differences between the monocular fields were physical dimensions of stimulation. For example, a red square with ruled vertical lines was presented stereoscopically to one eye at the same time that the other eye was exposed to a green square with ruled horizontal lines. The major innovation of the experiments which will be discussed in this section is that the stimulus content has been meaningful and the difference between the rivalrous contents has had experiential significance.

The first experiment to examine stereoscopic perception under these conditions was reported by Engel (1956). Engel studied the responses to a condition of binocular rivalry in which the monocular presentations were different human male faces, one in an upright orientation, the other inverted. Engel reasoned that the long history of experience with normal upright faces would cause the upright face to be predominant in S's reports. The results agreed with Engel's prediction. Two forms of dominance of the upright face were observed. When the two faces were simultaneously perceived, the upright face had the appearance of a genuine figure whose integrity was being disturbed by another vaguely present face. When the two faces were perceived alternately, the upright face tended to remain longer in perception during the successive phases of alternation.

Comparable results were obtained in a similar experiment by Hastorf and Myro (1959). Hastorf and Myro contended that Engel's procedure may have introduced an ambiguity in S's task. Engel exposed the stereograms for 1 minute, following which a report was requested. During this minute a sequence of alternations occurred. In a sense, S was being asked to estimate the relative frequency or dominance of the two alternatives during the sequence. Hastorf and Myro (1959) suggested that a shorter exposure would guarantee ". . . that the relative predominance of right-side-up figures is not a function of mere estimation of the balance between two alternating stimuli" (p. 400). This was accomplished by limiting the exposure time to 0.1 or 0.2 second. The stimuli were pairs of stamps, containing pictures of heads in profile or photographs of men's faces. Hastorf and Myro found that upright faces were reported significantly more frequently than inverted faces.

Both experiments have presented evidence of monocular predominance based on a preference for upright orientations. This preference, insofar as it concerns structurally similar configurations such as human faces, is probably due to previous experience and learning. In subsequent experimentation, it would be well to take into account a possible confounding inherent in the use of human faces. An inverted face has a rather strange and unfamiliar appearance. Most importantly the inverted faces are not so readily described as upright faces. Therefore, there is the possibility that the greater frequency of reports of upright faces is simply a matter of the differences in the availability of descriptions of the faces in the two orientations.

Stimulated by Engel's study, two investigations have been conducted to study monocular predominance in binocular rivalry between contents which have differential cross-cultural significance. The general aim of these studies has been stated by Bagby (1957). They are ". . . concerned with discovering whether the cultural characteristics of conflicting visual presentations are differentially perceived by members of different societies. Presented with a situation of simul-taneous binocular rivalry, do subjects perceive more readily and consistently visual presentations of content drawn from their own culture than presentations of similar content from another society?" (p. 331).

Bagby's Ss (1957) were a group of twelve Mexicans and a group of twelve Eastern and Middle Western United States citizens. The two groups were matched for sex, age, educa-tion, occupation, and socioeconomic status. With only one exception, no S had traveled outside his country. The stimuli were ten pairs of stereograms. In each pair, one stereogram depicted a typical Mexican scene and the other a typical American scene. The following are two examples: (1) an American businessman and a Mexican peasant; (2) a base-ball scene and a bullfight scene. Each pair of stereograms was presented stereoscopically for a 1-minute viewing period, and S gave a running description of what he saw. The results based on the reports of the first 15 seconds of viewing are summarized in Table 19. The results clearly indicate that Ss reported scenes of their own culture as pre-

Table 19
Monocular predominance in the ten stereogram
pairs as a function of cultural differences*

Nationality and sex of subjects	N	No. where Mexicans dominate	No. where Americans dominate
Mexican:			
Males	6	44	16
Females	6	45	15
American:			
Males	6	7	53
Females	6	12	48

* Adapted from Bagby, 1957, p. 333.

dominant in binocular rivalry over scenes from another culture.

A study dealing with the effects of racial differences can be categorized with Bagby's experiment. Pettigrew, Allport, and Barnett (1958) used pairs of stereograms showing faces of white Europeans, full-blooded Bantus, "coloured," and Indians (Hindu or Moslem). A sequence of twenty pairs was exposed, each for 2 seconds, to Ss who were officially classified by the South African government as members of these four racial groups. The results did not reveal a significant tendency for monocular predominance which could be related to racial differences.

The general trend of the few experimental investigations indicates that perceptual conflicts, involving competing contents, are resolved by suppressing one of the alternatives in favor of the alternative which is congruent with past experience. However, the experiments do not provide any clues concerning the mechanisms that bring about the suppression of the incongruent alternative. Before hypotheses are devised to account for the selective suppression, further investigation is required to analyze the differences between contents. In each of the reported cases, the contents of the stereograms which were paired were not equally familiar. The frequency of exposure to inverted faces is much lower than the frequency of exposure to upright faces. Similarly, the scenes in Bagby's stereograms were not equally familiar to American and Mexican Ss. In each case, the monocular view that predominated was the view of the most frequently preexposed content. The question arises whether an explanation of the effects observed by Engel, by Hastorf and Myro, and by Bagby can be formulated entirely in terms of prior frequency, disregarding the factor of meaningfulness and other content dimensions.[12]

Concluding remarks

As the reader may have noted, there have been very few investigations of perceptual conflict. Yet it is justifiable to

[12] The controversial history of the perceptual-defense problem lends substance to this question [see Dember's review (1960)]. Although the status of perceptual defense is still undecided, it has become clear that many of the findings that were attributed to perceptual defense can be related more parsimoniously to differences in preexperimental familiarity and response availability.

conclude that the resolution of conflict can be an occasion for perceptual learning. Any more detailed conclusions must be deferred until more evidence is available. Of the three types of research described in this chapter, the investigations of Wallach et al. seem most promising. The independent and dependent variables can be precisely specified and controlled. There are many questions which remain to be answered. A number of these were considered in the earlier discussion of Wallach's experiments. Here one additional question will be mentioned. What determines the form of the resolution? Why does the resolution of the conflict between disparity and KDE take the form of a unilateral diminution of the efficacy of one of the cues? More generally, under what conditions will conflicts be resolved in a manner which leads to learning? Related to this question is the problem of identifying the factors which determine the direction of the change. For example, in the case of Wallach's experiments only the significance of binocular disparity is affected. The KDE remains unaltered by the conflict. The answer is not to be found in the "abnormality" of disparity, since this fact has no special significance in the perceptual system. The abnormality is defined entirely in terms of E's operations. A highly plausible explanation is that the stronger cue dominates. However, there is little evidence regarding the relative strength of cues independently of their relative effects in a conflict situation. A variety of procedures have been used to establish a ranking of cues (see Woodworth & Schlosberg, 1954, Ch. 16), but the question is not settled. Therefore, it is not possible to predict precisely what will be learned.

References

Bagby, J. W. A cross cultural study of perceptual predominance in binocular rivalry. *J. Abnorm. Soc. Psychol.,* 1957, **54,** 331–334.

Braunstein, M. L. The perception of depth through motion. *Psychol. Bull.,* 1962, **59,** 422–433.

Brunswik, E. *Perception and the representative design of psychological experiments.* Berkeley, Calif.: Univer. of California Press, 1956.

Dember, W. N. *Psychology of perception.* New York: Holt, 1960. Ch. 9.

Engel, E. The role of content in binocular resolution. *Amer. J. Psychol.,* 1956, **69,** 87–91.

Epstein, W. A test of two interpretations of the apparent size effects in a distorted room. *J. Exp. Psychol.*, 1962, **63**, 124–128.

Epstein, W. Perceptual invariance in the kinetic depth effect. *Amer. J. Psychol.*, 1965, **78**, 301–303.

Hastorf, A. H., & Myro, G. The effect of meaning on binocular rivalry. *Amer. J. Psychol.*, 1959, **72**, 393–400.

Ittelson, W. H. *Visual space perception.* New York: Springer, 1960.

Ittelson, W. H., & Kilpatrick, F. P. The monocular and binocular distorted rooms. In F. P. Kilpatrick (Ed.), *Explorations in Transactional psychology.* New York: New York Univer. Press, 1961.

Kilpatrick, F. P. (Ed.) *Human behavior from the transactional point of view.* Office of Naval Research, Contract Nonr-496(01). Hanover, N.H.: Institute for Associated Research, 1952.

Kilpatrick, F. P. Two processes in perceptual learning. *J. Exp. Psychol.*, 1954, **47**, 362–370.

Krech, D., & Crutchfield, R. S. *Elements of psychology.* New York: Knopf, 1958.

Pettigrew, T., Allport, G., & Barnett, E. Binocular resolution and perception of race in South Africa. *Brit. J. Psychol.*, 1958, **49**, 265–278.

Schriever, W. Experimentelle Studien uber das stereoskopische Sehen. *Z. Psychol.*, 1925, **96**, 113–170.

Vernon, M. D. The perception of distance. *Brit. J. Psychol.*, 1937, **28**, 1–149.

Vernon, M. D. *A further study of visual perception.* New York: Cambridge Univer. Press, 1952.

Wallach, H., & Karsh, Eileen B. The modification of stereoscopic depth-perception and the kinetic depth effect. *Amer. J. Psychol.*, 1963, **76**, 429–437. (a)

Wallach, H., & Karsh, Eileen B. Why the modification of stereoscopic depth perception is so rapid. *Amer. J. Psychol.*, 1963, **76**, 413–420. (b)

Wallach, H., Moore, M. E., & Davidson, L. Modification of stereoscopic depth-perception. *Amer. J. Psychol.*, 1963, **76**, 191–204.

Wallach, H., & Norris, C. M. Accommodation as a distance cue. *Amer. J. Psychol.*, 1963, **76**, 659–664.

Wallach, H., & O'Connell, D. N. The kinetic depth effect. *J. Exp. Psychol.*, 1953, **45**, 205–217.

Weiner, M. Perceptual development in a distorted room: a phenomenological study. *Psychol. Monogr.*, 1956, **70**, No. 16.

Wheatstone, C. On some remarkable, and hitherto unobserved phenomena of binocular vision. *Phil. Mag. Ser.*, 1852, **4** (3), Part II, 504–523.

Woodworth, R. S. *Experimental psychology.* New York: Holt, 1938.

Woodworth, R. S., & Schlosberg, H. *Experimental psychology.* New York: Holt, 1954.

Chapter nine
Adaptation to
transformed stimulation

Adaptation and aftereffect are not recent discoveries. It has long been known that continuous exposure to unchanging stimulation will lead to shifts in the observer's response. The shift will be toward the response associated with the neutral, normative, or zero value of the stimulus dimension. Following this adaptational shift, aftereffects are observed. The general nature of the aftereffect is that the response elicited by a given stimulus value presented in the post-adaptive period is displaced from the preadaptational response toward the opposite or complementary response.

The concept of adaptation was introduced originally to explain certain facts of color vision [see Boring's history (1942), esp. pp. 157–164]. However, since then, adaptation has been studied in a wide variety of contexts (Helson, 1964). The objectives of the investigations that are examined in this chapter have been different from those which have motivated the authors of the classic studies of adaptation, e.g., investigations of light adaptation. In the latter studies, the aims have been to establish psychophysical relationships and to derive or test physiological hypotheses about visual processes. The authors of the investigations that constitute the literature relevant to this chapter have been interested in adaptation chiefly for other reasons:

1
The results of the adaptation studies are felt to have implications for a consideration of the origins of perception, e.g., whether perception is nativistically or empiristically based.
2
The conditions of optical distortion provide an opportunity for exploring the role of learning in determining perception.

The experimental optical devices disrupt the established correlations between distal and retinal stimuli and between perception and behavior. Will the S learn to behave adaptively despite the disruptions? More importantly, will veridical perception eventually be regained, and what conditions are essential for this type of perceptual learning? These are some of the primary questions which will be discussed in this chapter.

This chapter will deal mainly with the more contemporary research on adaptation. The contemporary work reflects the revival of interest in this problem which was stimulated by the publication of the Innsbruck studies (Kohler, 1951). But, prior to considering the Innsbruck studies, it will be instructive to review a number of older investigations by Czermak-Helmholtz (1863–1866), Stratton (1896, 1897a, 1897b), and Gibson (Gibson, 1933; Gibson and Radner, 1937).

Czermak-Helmholtz   In Vol. III of Helmholtz's treatise *Physiological Optics*, he devotes a section to a discussion of the determinants of perceived direction. After evaluating several possibilities, Helmholtz concluded ". . . that our judgments as to the direction of the visual axis are simply the result of the effort of the will involved in trying to alter the adjustment of the eyes" (Helmholtz, 1866, transl., 1925, vol. III, p. 245). Essentially, it was Helmholtz's contention that perceived direction depends on a "judgment of the direction of the gaze" and that this judgment will depend on the "impulses of the will" which we know to be necessary in order to bring the eye into an intended position. Helmholtz also contended that the only effect of the impulse of the will that is manifested in the eye is the change of position of the image on the retina for the new position of the eye. These changes are used to regulate the relationship between the impulse of the will and its effect.

In support of this latter assertion, Helmholtz described an experiment which he attributes to Czermak (1863). Czermak's study may be the earliest experimental investigation of adaptation to prismatically induced displacement of visual direction.

■ Take two glass prisms with refracting angles of about 16° or 18°, and place them in a spectacle frame, with their edges both turned toward the left. As seen through these glasses, the objects in the field of view will all apparently be shifted to the left of their real positions. At first, without bringing the hand into the field, look closely at some definite object within reach; and then close the eyes, and try to touch the object with the forefinger. The usual result will be to miss it by thrusting the hand too far to the left. But after trying for some little while, or more quickly still, by inserting the hand in the field and under the guidance of the eye, touching the objects with it for an instant, then on trying the above experiment again, we shall discover that now we do not miss the objects, but feel for them correctly. It is the same way when new objects are substituted for those with which we have become familiar. Having learned how to do this, suppose now we take off the prisms and remove the hand from the field of view, and then, after gazing steadily at some object, close our eyes and try to take hold of it. We then find that the hand will miss the object by being thrust too far to the right; until after several failures, our judgment of the direction of the eyes is rectified again (Helmholtz, 1866, transl., 1925, p. 246).

Helmholtz attributed the adaptive shift and its aftereffects to changes in the felt position of the eye. Czermak's study is a clear precursor of the modern eye-hand coordination experiments that will be discussed later in this chapter.

Stratton   Since Kepler's theoretical analysis (1571–1630) of the formation of the retinal image, it has been accepted that the retinal image is inverted. Kepler was the first to show unequivocally that the rays of light radiating from each point in an object are collected by the cornea and crystalline lens and focused at a point on the retinal surface. The array of retinal points will constitute a diminished and inverted retinal image of the object. Subsequently, Kepler's analysis was corroborated empirically by Scheiner (1575–1650), who removed a portion of the opaque outer layers at the back of the eyeball, making the retinal image directly visible.

It may seem curious that recognition of retinal inversion was delayed until Kepler's time, especially since systematic studies of optics and ophthalmological investigations of the eye were being conducted for five centuries prior to Kepler [see Polyak's (1943) historical review]. Even Leonardo da Vinci (1452–1519), who was, in most matters, very little restrained by the conventional knowledge of his time, believed that the image was erect. There must have been powerful factors at work to bolster this incorrect notion. Among these factors was the opinion that the image had to be erect since otherwise the visual world would not be erect. This opinion was predicated on the assumption that perceptual properties and retinal properties need to be isomorphic. Nor did the wish to designate an isomorphic correlate of perceived uprightness disappear with the knowledge of the inverted image. For example, Descartes (1686), in a pictorial representation of the projection of the retinas upon the brain and pineal gland, showed the fibers running to the pineal gland as decussated, i.e., crossed as in an X, so that the final image, formed in the pineal body, was reerected.

The conclusive demonstration that the image is inverted forced students of vision to confront the problem they had hoped to avoid: ". . . there occurs one mighty difficulty. Objects are painted in an inverted order on the bottom of the eye: the upper part of any object being painted on the lower part of the eye, and the lower part of the object on the upper part of the eye: and so also as to right and left. Since therefore the pictures are thus inverted, it is demanded how it comes to pass that we see the objects erect and in their natural posture?" (Berkeley, 1709, in Luce & Jessop, 1948, sec. 88).

The attempts to resolve the question of upright vision with an inverted image took two alternative forms. One resolution involved reerecting the image at one stage of the visual process. Descartes' speculations, mentioned above, are of this nature. Another resolution of this type, based on the "law of projection" and the "law of direction," was advanced in the writings of Brewster (1831) and of LeConte (1895), who was a prominent nineteenth-century student of vision. The "law of projection" states that the mind receives impressions from the retina and projects them into space. The "law of direction" specifies the direction lines of the projection. The combined operation of these two laws has the effect of reerecting the percept. This argument is exemplified in the following excerpt from an article by LeConte.

■ Suppose I look at the horizon. A star . . . sends its ray into my eye . . . and it strikes a certain rod or cone on the lower half of the retinal concave. . . . The impression [is] referred back along the ray line to its proper place in space, and therefore, I see the star *above* the horizon. Now objects are made up entirely of such stars—i.e., radiant points—each sending its ray straight to the retinal concave, all crossing . . . making an inverted image. But each focal point of the image is referred back along its ray line to its own place; and thus the external image is reinverted in the act of external reference, and reconstructed in space in its true position as the sign and facsimile of the object that made it (LeConte, 1895, pp. 629–630).

Unfortunately for the advocates of this solution, the "law of projection" is fictitious, implying the existence of a homunculus which projects impressions or images. Furthermore, there is no awareness at any level of the directions of approach of light rays.

The advocates of the alternative resolution abandoned the requirement of isomorphism and the attempt to reerect the image. Instead, visually perceived uprightness was considered to be an acquired end product of the association of vision with touch or movements of the eye. This resolution is expressed in the following composite of the views of three of its advocates:

1
"That the visual sensations by themselves, without any previous experience, should evoke ideas as to a definite direction of the objects perceived, seems to me an absolutely unnecessary hypothesis" (Helmholtz, 1866, vol. III, pp. 251–252).
2
The orientation of the image on the retina is irrelevant. "Like every geometrical property of the image, so this one of its position, too, on passing into consciousness, is completely lost; and the position in which we see things is in no way prejudiced by the aforesaid position of the image on the retina" (Lotze, 1852, transl., 1886, p. 138; reprinted in Dember, 1964, pp. 131–142).
3
The sense of touch and the kinesthetic sensations provided by movements of the muscles give unequivocal information regarding localization. "It is certain that a man blind . . . from birth, would by the sense of feeling attain to have ideas of upper and lower. By the motion of his hand he might discern the situation [orientation] of any tangible object placed within his reach" (Berkeley, 1709, in Luce & Jessop, 1948, sec. 96).
4
Visual determination of orientation and localization is learned through association with touch and a variety of movements, particularly movements of the eye.

One of the implications of this empiristic theory is that, given an opportunity for visual-motor learning, the perceiver would eventually acquire adaptive perception and behavior, regardless of the orientation of the image on the retina. Even were the image to be experimentally reinverted so as to become "erect," the resulting disruption would only be temporary. Eventually, vision would be reeducated by touch, and the preexperimental perceptual world would be reinstated. Stratton was the first to test this implication experimentally.

Stratton's (1896, 1897a, 1897b) experiments are among the most widely cited experiments in the history of psychology. Despite the importance attributed to these experiments, there is still widespread disagreement about the observations which Stratton made. Forty years after the experiments were completed, Higginson (1937) documented the disagreement in detail and proposed to resolve the matter. But Higginson's optimism was not confirmed. A lack of consensus is still evident. Did Stratton actually learn to see the world in exactly the same way as he did before putting on the inverting lenses, or did he only learn to adjust his behavior to a world which looked upside down? Did a modification of visual localization occur during the adaptation period, or was the essential modification solely proprioceptive, involving changes in the felt position of the body? These questions continue to be debated (Harris, 1965; Taylor, 1962; Walls, 1951b).

His objectives (1896, 1897b, reprinted in Dennis, 1949, pp. 24–40) were to test the projection theory and Lotze's version of the eye-movement theory. Both these theories, and especially the projection theory, make the inversion of the retinal image an important condition of upright vision. To examine this assumption, Stratton decided to ". . . substitute an upright retinal image for the normal inverted one and watch the result" (Dennis, 1949, p. 25).

The experimental apparatus was a tube, containing a lens system, placed in front of the right eye at a distance which allowed a visual field of 45° width. The lens system consisted of two pairs of double convex lenses of equal refractive power, placed at a distance from each other equal to the sum of their focal distances. The resulting image on the retina, formed by the light passing through the lens system, was inverted and reversed, i.e., erect in relation to the external field, with right and left reversed. The left eye was covered by opaque black paper.

The main experiment lasted eight days and included a total of 87 hours of wearing the inverting lens system. During the experiment, at all times when the lenses were not worn, both eyes were blindfolded. The experimental procedure did not include controlled tests of perception or perceptual-motor coordination. Stratton simply went about his daily activities and recorded his experiences.

"*First day*. The entire scene appeared upside down. When I moved my head . . . the whole field of things swept and swung before my eyes. . . . Inappropriate movements were constantly made. . . . The movement was then checked, . . . and finally, by a series of approximations and corrections, brought to the chosen point. . . . Relief was sometimes sought by shutting out of consideration the actual visual data." As the day wore on the scene was ". . . accepted more as it was immediately presented." But there was always the awareness of another scene in which objects were oriented in the preexperimental position. ". . . in general all things not actually in view returned to their older arrangement and were represented [imagined], if at all, as in normal [preexperimental] sight." Parts of the body were also affected. For example, ". . . anticipation of contact from bodies seen to be approaching arose as if particular places and directions in the visual field had the same meaning as in normal experience. When one side of my body approached an object in view, the actual feeling of contact came from the side opposite to that from which I had expected it" (Dennis, 1949, pp. 27–30). These excerpts from Stratton's report of his experience during the first day of exposure show that optical inversion and left-right reversal produced significant modifications of perception and disruption of normal visual-motor coordination.

The critical question concerns the changes of perception and visually guided behavior during the extended period of exposure to the optical transformations. By the fourth day, Stratton reported a growing tendency to imagine the unseen parts of the scene as ". . . in harmonious spatial relation with the things I saw." In other words, the scene outside his field of vision was visualized as inverted.

In addition, Stratton found that new sensory-motor coordinations developed. For example, it became standard practice to start with the right hand, not the left, to grasp an object that was seen to the left although it lay objectively to the right. By the eighth day, everything appeared "harmonious" and normal. But this appearance of normalcy obtained *only* ". . . when the new localization of the body was vivid." The "new localization" of the body which Stratton mentions apparently refers to an inversion of the body image with respect to the real body. As long as this new localization was in force, the scene had a normal appearance, as it should since the felt localization of the body and the seen localization of the visual scene would be congruent. Apparently, Stratton learned to feel himself upside down, and also to feel normal in this state.

It is not clear from Stratton's report whether adaptation involved perceptual restructuring of the directions of space as well as learned motor adjustments and kinesthetic adaptation. The general impression that is communicated by Stratton in several places is that visually determined localization of up and down was not affected. This impression is supported indirectly by Stratton's description of his experience when the lenses were removed, at the end of the eighth day: "On opening my eyes, the scene had a strange familiarity. The visual arrangement was immediately recognized as the old one of preexperimental days; yet the reversal of everything from the order to which I had grown accustomed during the past week, gave the scene a surprising, bewildering air. . . . It was hardly the feeling, though, that things were upside down" (Dennis, 1949, p. 39).

The absence of an up-down aftereffect strongly suggests that no perceptual adaptation took place for inversion. At the same time the aftereffects seem to indicate some degree of perceptual adaptation to other aspects of the optical distortion. "When I turned my body or my head, objects seemed to sweep before me as if they themselves were in motion. The 'swinging of the scene, observed so continuously during the first days of the experiment, had thus returned with great vividness" (Dennis, 1949, p. 39). The presence of a motion aftereffect testifies to the perceptual nature of Stratton's adaptation to the optically induced motion.

Stratton concluded that the inverted position of the retinal image is not essential to upright vision. Stratton based this conclusion primarily on his demonstrated ability to learn to behave adaptively despite the optical reinversion. But this evidence of adaptive or correct performance does not necessarily entail the conclusion that the inversion of the image is irrelevant to visual localization of up and down. Behavioral adaptation could indeed result from a restoration of pre-experimental appearances. For example, upon initial exposure to the lens system, a man might appear to be oriented with his feet above his head, while at the end of the exposure period he might appear oriented with his head above his feet. If this were the case, then Stratton's conclusion would be supported. However, this is not the only basis for the recovery of adaptive behavior. Another basis would be the development of a rule of responding which reverses the usual correlations between visual localizations and motor responses, e.g., reaching down for a target which appears to be up. In other words, the restoration of adaptive behavior may mean only that the inhibitory effects of alterations in the relationship between seen and actual positions can be overcome when there is opportunity for the learning of new sensory-motor coordinations.

Stratton's work remains ambiguous, even if it is agreed that eventually the scene came to look normal and upright. The ambiguity stems from the fact that the appearance of normalcy could result from either a visual modification or a proprioceptive modification. According to the first alternative, at the outset of the exposure period, excitation of a point in the upper portion of the retina elicits the visual localization "down." After adaptation, excitation of the same retinal point elicits the visual localization "up." According to the second alternative, the underlying modification is proprioceptive and not visual. This interpretation is stressed in the summary of Stratton's work which was presented above. However, it should be recognized that it is purely speculative. Variants of this proprioceptive hypothesis can be found in Walls (1951b) and Harris (1965):

■ When Stratton first put on inverting lenses, he felt gravity pulling *away* from the seen location of the floor: "the general feeling was that the seen room was upside down; the body of the observer . . . was felt as the standard and as having an upright position (1897, p. 348)." But gradually Stratton began to feel that his feet, then his legs and arms, then most of his body, were all in "the place where the new visual perception reported them to be." The new proprioceptive localization was not stable—sometimes he even seemed to feel his limbs in both the normal and the new locations at once (1897, p. 465)—but when the legs and body were clearly felt to be in the new place, so, of necessity, were the gravitational pulls. Because the direction of the pull of gravity is, by definition, *down*, objects seen to lie in the same direction from the head as the legs were felt to be, were perceived as down. So the floor looked "down," making the room look "right side up" (Harris, 1965, pp. 429–430).

It is not possible to determine which of these alternatives interprets Stratton's work most correctly. Nor have the subsequent experiments on optical inversion settled the matter. Ewert (1930) set out to repeat Stratton's experiments. Some of the differences between Ewert's and Stratton's experiments were that (1) Ewert used a binocular optical system, (2) Ewert's exposure periods were longer, ranging from 175 to 195 hours, and (3) Ewert introduced a number of controlled tests. The primary question is whether the preexperimental visual world was eventually regained.

To determine this matter, Ewert devised two simple orientation "tests," which he administered on each of the 14 days of the experiment. In one test S looked down upon a series of seven different-colored blocks, placed on a table top, in a straight line extending from S's observation point. The S was asked to designate the nearest and farthest blocks by calling out their colors. The results were unequivocal: "The illusory disorientation effect which the lenses produced remained the same throughout the experiment. Down and up and right and left judgments were consistently exchanged. Responses were 100% consistent inversions" (Ewert, 1930, p. 345).

This result should be contrasted with the improvement which Ewert observed in a series of motor tasks, e.g., touch localization. Comparable results were reported by Peterson and Peterson (1938). No perceptual adaptation to the inversion of up and down was observed after 14 days of optical inversion.

Snyder and Pronko (1952) conducted a long-term investigation similar to Ewert's. However, because of their exclusive emphasis on motor adaptation, their work contributes only little to the specific question under examination. In agreement with the earlier studies they found that new visual-motor coordinations can be learned, so that performance is not permanently hindered by optical inversion. In a follow-up study, Snyder and Snyder (1957) also confirmed the finding of Peterson and Peterson (1938) that the learned visual-motor coordinations are very resistant to forgetting. Two years after the conclusion of the original experiment and without intervening practice under conditions of optical inversion, performance, upon resumption of optical inversion, was not significantly poorer than at the conclusion of the 30-day period 2 years earlier.

In concluding our discussion of vision with optical inversion, several studies summarized by Kohler (1951, transl., 1964) will be considered. These studies were conducted between 1947 and 1950 at the University of Innsbruck in Austria. Three experiments, lasting 6, 9, and 10 days, were conducted. The optical device was a mirror attached to the forehead, immediately above the eyes, like a cap visor. Unlike the optical systems used by the earlier investigators, the mirror system produced inversion of up and down, but not reversal of left and right.

In Exp. I, which lasted 6 days, there was marked improvement of motor performance, but the perceptual effects were inconsistent. The S's ". . . perceptions were only sporadically right side up." When the mirror was removed, ". . . the S occasionally saw upright objects as inverted, but only for the first few minutes" (Kohler, 1951, transl., 1964, p. 31).

In Exp. II, which lasted 9 days, the results were more conclusive. "Correct veridical perception was achieved. . . . After four or five days, however, vision underwent a remarkable change: it seemed as if the verticality dimension had 'gotten lost.' To illustrate: two adjacent heads, one upright, were *both* perceived as upright. Gradually, more and more objects appeared right side up. After the spectacles were removed, however, objects appeared to revert to their upside-down position. . . . For a few minutes people and furniture seemed suspended from the 'ceiling' head downward" (Kohler, 1951, transl., 1964, p. 32).

Experiment III, which lasted 10 days (123 hours), identified several of the conditions which favored the emergence of upright vision: (1) ". . . when the S was permitted to reach for and touch an object . . . the object, first seen as inverted, now suddenly appeared to be right side up." (2)

"When the S was presented with a weight attached to the end of a line, he correctly perceived the relative position of the weight (to the line) as soon as he took the end of the line in his hand; and once the pendulum was seen correctly, the perception of more distant objects also became veridical." (3) "Familiarity with objects proved to be a third determining factor involved in veridical vision. A candle, at first seen in an inverted position, wick downward, was seen right side up as soon as it was lit" (Kohler, 1951, transl., 1964, p. 33).

The empiristic theory of space perception insisted that the orientation of the image on the retina was a matter of indifference, insofar as upright vision is concerned. We should note that when Berkeley, in his *Commonplace Book* (Ed. Luce, 1944), raised the question of the effects of optical inversion, the S whom he contemplated was a newborn infant. Unlike the adult Ss who have been studied by Stratton and his successors, the hypothetical newborn S is not confronted by the necessity of unlearning previously established relationships, prior to achieving veridical perception with optical inversion. In this sense, the experiments have not been conducted under the most favorable conditions.

What have these experiments demonstrated about the adaptability of perception? Is the inverted image necessary for upright vision, or can we learn to see an upright world with an erect, optically inverted image? The answer will depend on which of the several experiments one emphasizes. Stratton reported partial perceptual reorientation after 87 hours, but there is uncertainty whether Stratton's adaptation actually entailed modification of visual perception (see Walls, 1951b). Ewert and Peterson and Peterson found no evidence of the development of perceptual uprightness after exposure periods of as much as 195 hours. On the other hand, Kohler's descriptions of the pictorial quality of S's visual world indicates complete perceptual adaptation after 123 hours of exposure distributed over 10 days. But it is not certain whether Kohler's reports implicate visual or proprioceptive modifications (Harris, 1965).

It is possible that the discrepancies between these experiments are partially due to differences in the "side effects" produced by the various optical devices. For example, the experiments which obtained total adaptation used an optical system which only inverted the field, without simultaneously reversing right and left. On the other hand, the experiments that obtained zero adaptation used devices that not only reversed right and left but also produced an additional inversion in depth. Another factor that may account for the discrepancies is the type of activity that was permitted during the experimental period. Thus, the experiments which secured no evidence of adaptation were also the experiments which placed most restrictions on S's freedom and variety of movement; e.g., Ewert's Ss spent most of their waking hours performing laboratory tasks.

Finally, we may note that very few Ss have been used, a grand total of nine Ss, all of whom were sophisticated observers. Therefore, it is unlikely that individual differences or attitudinal variations were effectively controlled. In fact, Stratton remarked that the appearance of the scene often seemed to depend on the "factor of volition" or the "force of will." A striking effect of attitude of observation was reported by Snyder and Pronko (1952). Toward the end of the experiment S was observing the scene from a tall building: "Suddenly someone asked: Well, how do things look to you? Are they upside-down? The S replied: I wish you hadn't asked me. Things were all right until you popped the question at me. Now, when I recall how they *did* look *before* I put on these lenses, I must answer that they do look upside-down *now*. But until the moment that you asked me, I was absolutely unaware of it" (p. 113).

This concludes our discussion of the question of upright vision with an inverted image.[13] The subsequent sections will contain only a few direct references to this work. However, the reader will recognize that many of the contemporary questions have precedents in the older discussions.

[13] Several early studies, notably those by Wooster and Brown, have not been included because of their exclusive emphasis on the acquisition of motor skills. A useful review of these experiments can be found in Smith and Smith, *Perception and Motion* (1962), along with a new work which introduces the use of television as an investigatory tool. However, a curious observation made by Russian ophthalmological surgeons may be noted briefly: "Patients suffering from cataracts regained their sight when their corneas were used as focusing screens for projecting real images. By the time these images reached the retina they were right side up. This, however, did not disturb the patients, who, so the author maintains, soon began to perceive objects as right side up. Apparently, inversion of the retinal image is not a necessary prerequisite for veridical perception" (Kohler, 1951, transl., 1964, p. 31).

It is chiefly for this reason that the earlier work continues to merit attention in contemporary treatments of adaptation and perceptual learning.

Gibson   J. J. Gibson's experiments (Gibson, 1933; Gibson & Radner, 1937) dealt with adaptation and aftereffect in the perception of curved and tilted lines. Figure 17 presents a pictorial summary of one of Gibson's experiments. The Ss wore prisms for 1 hour, during which they explored vertical lines and edges both visually and tactually. The differential deflections of the light which passed through the prisms produced curvature of straight vertical lines. Gibson's Ss reported decreases in the phenomenal (perceived) curvature of lines during the course of the 1-hour exposure period. When the prisms were removed, an aftereffect was reported. The aftereffect was an apparent curvature of straight lines in the direction opposite to the prism-produced curvature. Subsequently, Gibson and Radner (1937) found that prismatic distortion was not an essential condition. The same effects were obtained when curved or tilted lines were continuously inspected by the naked eye. Gibson concluded that the only necessary condition for obtaining aftereffects was a preliminary period of continuous exposure to stimuli which

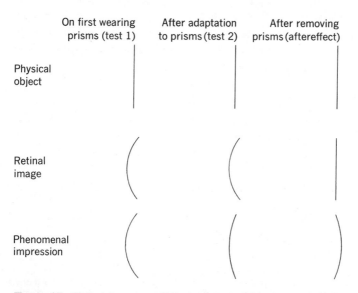

Figure 17. Pictorial representation of J. J. Gibson experiment on adaptation and aftereffect. (*From J. J. Gibson, 1933, p. 7.*)

deviated from the normative standard. Gibson's observations were largely neglected during the ensuing 20 years. However, interest in these phenomena has now been revived, and later we shall have occasion to consider them again.

The extended problem of adaptation to disarranged and rearranged optical stimulation

Most of the early work on the problem of adaptation to optically induced transformation was tied closely to the question of upright vision with inverted images. The question has been extended to include a great variety of optical distortions, and the theoretical significance of the findings has been interpreted more broadly.

Gibson (1964, pp. 7–8) has provided a useful listing of the optical transformations which have been studied. Most of these transformations will be described in greater detail in subsequent discussions.

1
Up-down reversal. This is a 180° inversion of the visual scene which has been accomplished by lens systems and by a mirror properly mounted on S's forehead.
2
Deflection with distortion. Wedge prisms worn before the eyes will produce deflections of the light rays, curvature of straight lines, and spectral dispersion in the form of visible chromatic fringes.
3
Shearing of the array on a midline. This has been achieved by using spectacles whose eyepieces are only half prismatic, the other half plain glass.
4
Bisecting the array with complementary colors. Each eyepiece is split into two halves. The color of one half is complementary to the color of the other half. Thus the light is subjected to a color transformation which depends on the direction of gaze.
5
Right-left reversal. This is accomplished with a totally reflecting prism which reverses right and left, without inverting up and down.

To these five transformations contained in Gibson's list, we may add the following three:

6

Tilting the visual field. Right-angled prisms have been used to rotate the field. The lateral displacements produced in this way are proportional to height in the field. The result is a visual field that is tilted from the vertical.

7

Continually varying distortions. For this purpose rotary prisms have been used. The rotary prisms, in front of each eye, are rotated at equal speeds, but in opposite directions around the line of sight. This produces a continually varying displacement of seen locations.

8

Minification. A convex mirror has been used to achieve minification, without affecting apparent distance.

The Innsbruck studies   The investigations conducted in the Innsbruck laboratories, and reported in Kohler's monograph (1951, transl., 1964), are probably most responsible for the renewal of interest in the study of adaptation. The Innsbruck studies are distinguished by their long duration, by the variety of transformations which were studied, and by their rich yield of provocative findings. The experiments may be conveniently divided into three main categories, based on the critical properties of the optical devices which were used: (1) studies which used inverting mirror devices, (2) studies which used distorting prisms, and (3) studies which used colored spectacles. The inversion experiments have been described in the preceding section. Of the remaining two types we will be concerned mainly with the experiments using wedge prisms, since adaptation to the transformations produced by such prisms has been the primary focus of the subsequent investigations.

Prior to examining the experimental work, a number of preliminary remarks about the optics of prisms may be helpful.[14] A prism is an optical substance bounded by surfaces that create a wedge. A pencil of light which passes through the prism is deviated from its original direction. An approximate rule for determining the prismatic deviation of a prism with a small apex angle is that the deviation will equal one-half the apex angle. Frequently, the measure of

[14] Ogle (1961, Ch. 4 ff.) presents an admirably concise and clear discussion of the optics of prisms in his introductory textbook on optics for ophthalmologists. The brief discussion offered here is based on Ogle's presentation.

prismatic deviation is expressed in prism diopters (pd). The diopter expresses the angular displacement of the image relative to the center of rotation of the eye behind the prism. For present purposes, all that is required is the fact that a prism diopter is equal to 0.57 arc degree. Therefore, the general rule for determining the prismatic deviation when the power of the prism is expressed in diopters is the same as the rule which holds for the specification in terms of apex angle. The deviation is about equal to one-half the prism diopters. For example, a 20-pd prism will produce an apparent deviation of 11° in the direction of the prism apex. This statement will be true only for incident rays which are perpendicular to the front face of the prism. Rays that enter at an oblique angle to the front face will be deviated to a greater degree. As a result, the retinal image of an object viewed through a prism will be distorted in several ways: the image will be laterally displaced, the edges of the object which are perpendicular to the apex-base meridian of the prism will be curved, and there will be a slanting of the image of all lines which are parallel to the apex-base meridian. These effects are illustrated in Figure 18.

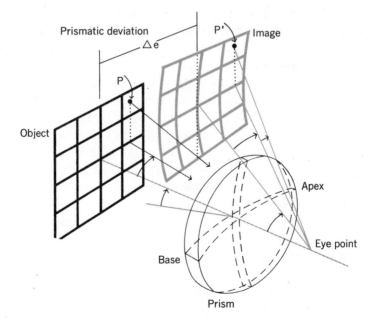

Figure 18. The distortion of the image of an extended object by a prism. (*From Ogle*, 1961, *p.* 75.)

There are other prismatic distortions, but only one other will be described. Boundaries between dark and light areas which are perpendicular to the base-apex meridian appear to have color fringes. This is due to the spectral dispersion produced by the differential deviation of short and long waves. Depending on the direction of light-dark change, the fringes will be yellowish-red or bluish-green.

If wedge prisms are inserted into goggles which are worn before the eyes, then the light entering the eye from reflecting surfaces, i.e., objects in the scene, will be transformed accordingly. The perceptual consequences will be apparent lateral displacement of objects, apparent curvature of straight lines, and color fringes. Although these distortions would be sufficiently disruptive, considered as static events, the disrupting effects of prismatic intervention are compounded when the wearer moves his head and his eyes behind the prisms. Accompanying these movements of the head and eye are continuous transformations of stimulation. Furthermore, because the eye is free to move behind the prism, the same retinal area on different occasions will be the locus of a virtually countless number of contrasting distortions. The result is that ". . . the same objects appear now enlarged, now reduced in size, and in the same retinal (foveal) area. One moment they slant to the left, the next they slant to the right. Right angles are transformed into acute angles one minute, while a minute later they are transformed into obtuse angles. Now something seems to move in one direction, now the same object moves in the opposite direction" (Kohler, 1951, transl., 1964, p. 61).

At the University of Innsbruck, a series of long-term studies, ranging in duration from 5 to 124 days, were undertaken to examine the effects of exposure to optical distortion. The Innsbruck studies were designed similarly to Stratton's studies. The Ss, usually members of the laboratory staff, wore experimental goggles and followed their normal daily routines. Heavy reliance was placed on S's introspective reports. Usually standardized objective laboratory tests of perception were not included.

The introspective reports were unequivocal. Upon initial exposure to the prismatic goggles, perception was a bewildering reflection of the continuous transformations produced by the prisms. However, eventually, veridical perception was largely restored and perceptual-motor coordination was re-gained. As a general rule, behavioral adaptation, represented by recovery of S's ability to perform motor acts correctly, was restored first. This is to say that S learned how to behave adaptively, e.g., reach for objects, before any signifi-cant degree of perceptual modification was observed. Per-ceptual adaptation required additional exposure. With regard to the perceptual adaptation which was eventually obtained, two general observations merit attention:

1
The rate of adaptation was not the same for the various dis-tortions introduced by the prism.
2
The degree of adaptation achieved in a specified exposure dura-tion was not the same for the various distortions.

For example, in an experiment lasting 23 days, Kohler (1951, transl., 1964) reported that ". . . apparent move-ments, distortions of angles, and disorientation disappeared almost completely; on the other hand, straight lines con-tinued to be seen as more or less curved" (p. 36).

When the prisms were removed, upon completion of the exposure duration, aftereffects were reported. Immediately upon removal of the spectacles perceptual distortions were once more observed. In some experiments the aftereffects were drastic. "What I experienced after I took off the spec-tacles was much worse than what I experienced when I first started wearing them. I felt as if I were drunk. Aftereffects continued for four days" (Kohler, 1951, transl., 1964, p. 34). These aftereffects were obtained following 10 days of continuous exposure to binocular spectacles containing 15-pd prisms. In other experiments, the aftereffects were less pronounced and less enduring. It is not clear, in the early experiments, how the differences in intensity and duration of the aftereffects should be explained. An obvious explanation is that the fate of the aftereffect is related to the rate and degree of adaptation. Indeed, the prevalent tendency to treat the aftereffect as a measure of adaptation presumes this relationship. Without questioning the general validity of this assumption, there are specific results of the Inns-bruck studies which are incompatible with this interpretation. For example, in one experiment, which lasted 9 days, ". . .

there was very little adaptation to curvature. . . . Nevertheless, there was a distinct bending aftereffect . . . [which]
lasted for only a few seconds, but reappeared with increased
intensity whenever she closed her eyes" (Kohler, 1951,
transl., 1964, p. 37).

Disregarding qualifying details for the moment, we may
conclude that perceptual learning occurred which had the
effect of shifting perception in the direction of veridicality,
despite the continuous presence of optical distortion. Perception changed while stimulation remained unchanged. In
addition, there was a transfer of learning which produced
aftereffects when uninterrupted stimulation was restored.

The experiments which will be described next differ from
those described previously. The essential difference involves
the nature of the optical medium which filled the eyepieces
of the experimental devices. In all the previous experiments
a single uniform optical medium was inserted in each eyepiece. Therefore, whatever the direction of gaze, the eye was
stimulated by light which was subjected to the same type
of transformation. In the experiments that concern us now,
each eyepiece in the spectacles was split into two halves,
each half with distinguishable effects on the light which
passed through it. Consequently, eye movements became
one of the codeterminants of the characteristics of the
retinal situation.

The "half-prism" experiments are so called because the
prisms inserted into each eyepiece of the experimental
goggles fitted only the upper or lower half of the frames.
In the particular experiment which will be discussed, 10-pd
spherically cut (convex-concave) prisms were inserted into
the upper halves of the eyepiece, and plain glass was
inserted into the lower halves.

Consider the fate of foveal optical stimulation in the
course of normal eye movements. When S turns his eye
upward, the fovea, as well as the rest of the retina, is
exposed to the full range of optical transformations. When
S turns his eye downward, the retina is exposed to normal,
undistorted stimulation. When he looks straight ahead, the
lower horizontal edge of the prism bisects his field, so that
half the retina is exposed to prismatic distortion while half
is exposed to normal stimulation. In addition, because of the
lateral displacement of the upper half of the field relative

to the lower half, a discontinuity is present between the upper and lower halves of the contours of objects.

The half-prism experiment lasted 50 days. Quantitative measures of adaptation and aftereffect were included, as well as the usual introspective analyses. The published introspective reports are quite detailed, but they will be summarized briefly. Four stages in the development of adaptation may be distinguished:

1

"Whenever I looked through the prism halves, the picture I saw was distorted; whenever I looked through the plain sections of the spectacles, the picture was undistorted" (Kohler, 1951, transl., 1964, p. 79).

2

In the second stage there was ". . . rapid progress of adaptation to the prismatic world [and] distinct aftereffects . . . in the unobstructed part of the visual field whenever the eyes move [downward]" (Kohler, 1951, transl., 1964, p. 82).

3

"As time goes on, I am becoming aware of the fact that my perceptual experiences are increasingly veridical. In other words, I no longer see marked distortions when I am looking through the prisms, and only weak aftereffects are present when I am looking through the lower section" (Kohler, 1951, transl., 1964, p. 82). But distortions appeared in both halves when, following prolonged viewing through one half, the eyes shifted to the other half.

4

In the final stage, adaptation was complete for the prismatic halves, and the aftereffects disappeared for the plain-glass viewing. Evidently, during this last stage, S's perceptions were the same whether they were based on optically transformed stimulation or optically undisturbed stimulation. The only exception to the rule of adaptation and veridicalization involved the lateral displacement and apparent discontinuity between the upper and lower halves of the visual scene. There was no adaptation to this anomaly, but S did learn to circumvent this distortion by avoiding the boundary between the prism and the plain glass, and by adjusting the direction of his scanning movements so as to minimize the discontinuity.

When the glasses were removed, the S experienced aftereffects, but these aftereffects were conditional on eye movement. Despite the fact that eye movements, in the absence of the experimental goggles, had no optical consequences, the perceptual consequences of eye movements were signficant. The aftereffects were noticeably greater when S turned his eyes upward, as contrasted with the effects observed when the eyes were turned downward. This difference was enhanced if S wore spectacles with eyepieces that were empty except for a thin wire which bisected each eyepiece at the original transition line between the prisms and the plain glass. "Always the aftereffects were stronger when seen through the upper half of the spectacles:——this even though the glass was missing from both eyepieces so that the *retinal images were the same in all cases*" (Kohler, 1951, transl., 1964, p. 85).

These aftereffects obviously depend on the total stimulus situation, rather than on retinal stimulation alone; they are conditional on eye movements. Therefore, Kohler labels them "situational," or "conditional," aftereffects. The after-effects were long-lasting; some appeared as late as 40 days after removal of the experimental spectacles. The various aftereffects diminished at different rates, but as a rule they disappeared earlier for downward looking than for upward looking.

The results of a number of objective tests corroborated the introspective reports. These were conducted daily for 90 days under four conditions: upward and downward vision, with and without the half-prism spectacles. The data curves, obtained with the spectacles, chart the course of adaptation over the 50-day exposure duration. The curves, without the spectacles, chart the development and dissipation of the aftereffects. The difference between the curves for upward and downward vision, without spectacles, defines the situational aftereffect.

Figure 19 shows three sets of curves, representing the results of three selected tests. In the curvature test, S was exposed to a series of luminous lines of varying degree of curvature, including a perfectly straight line. The S rated each of the individually presented lines as "markedly curved," "slightly curved," "very slightly curved," or "straight." The results are graphed in Figure 19a. The second test measured angular distortions by means of a frame with four movable sides which S adjusted to form a square. The results are graphed in Figure 19b (Kohler does not specify the character of the ordinate units). Lateral displacement was tested by a pointing task. The S turned a

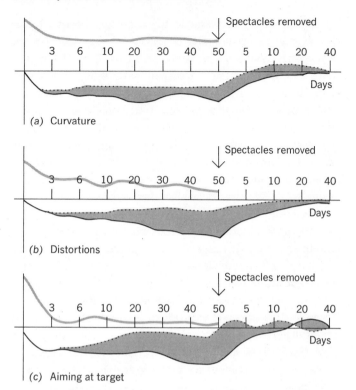

(a) Curvature

(b) Distortions

(c) Aiming at target

Figure 19. Results of objective tests in half-prism experiments. Magnitude of the effect (ordinate) is plotted against days of exposure. The heavy solid line graphs the results when S was looking up with the half-prisms in place. The thin solid line graphs the results when S looked up with the half-prisms removed. The dotted line shows the results when S looked down with the half-prisms removed. *(From Kohler, 1951, transl., 1964, p. 97.)*

pointer, which he could not see, so that it pointed directly at a dim electric bulb appearing in a dark room. The results are shown in Figure 19c.

Heavy solid lines show the results (deviations) when S was looking up with the half-prism spectacles in place. Therefore, these curves show the progress of adaptation over the 50 days of the experiment. Although there was adaptation in each case, the rate and amount of adaptation appear to be different for the three kinds of optical distortion. The thin solid lines show the results which were obtained when S looked up without the spectacles. These curves represent the magnitude and course of the aftereffects for upward vision. The aftereffect was a deviation in the opposite direction to the prism-produced errors. But obviously the magnitude of the aftereffect cannot be precisely predicted from the magnitude of the prism effect (level of adaptation). The dotted lines below the horizontal axes show the results when S looked down. These are the results for nonprismatic stimulation. The shaded areas call attention to the difference between S's settings, obtained without spectacles, for upward and downward vision. This is the difference in the aftereffect which was conditional on eye position. The effects were greater for upward than for downward vision.

Since the situational aftereffects are among the most striking findings of the Innsbruck studies, we will consider another example of this phenomenon. The example involves color perception and the effects of wearing two-toned spectacles. Each eyepiece contained a blue left half and a yellow right half. As the eyes turned left and right, the retinas were stimulated by blue and yellow light, respectively. In addition to introspective reports, the S was tested objectively each day. The S's task was to adjust a continuously variable color wheel, so that it appeared to be gray. These adjustments were made separately for eyes-left and eyes-right.

The rationale of the test is as follows: On the initial test, S's settings should be consistent with the law of complementaries. When looking left, through the blue half, S should require a yellow setting in order to perceive the wheel as gray; when looking right, through the yellow half, S should require a blue setting. If adaptation occurs in the course of extended exposure to the two-tone spectacles, then S should require progressively less saturated colors to compensate for the colors of the spectacles. In other words, the deviations of S's match from true gray should decrease. When the spectacles are removed, S's settings for subjective gray should reflect the previous adaptation in the form of predictable aftereffects. Evidence of situational aftereffects, dependent on eye position, would be obtained if S's setting for subjective gray were to vary according to the direction in which he is looking.

The results are illustrated in Figure 20. Figure 20a shows the color-wheel settings on the first day, for eyes left (2, 4) and eyes right (1, 3), with (1, 2) and without (3, 4) the spectacles. The results contained no surprises; they were

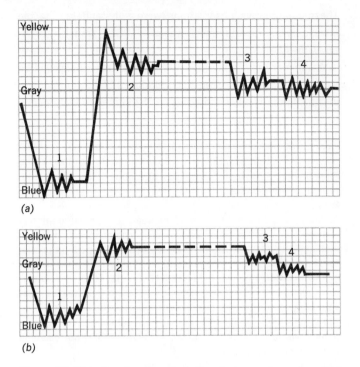

Figure 20. Results of color-adaptation test are shown by chart records made on the first day (a) and sixtieth day (b) of the experiment with blue-yellow goggles. On the first day the window of the test apparatus must be made strongly blue (1) to compensate for the yellow tint of the goggles and yellow (2) to compensate for the blue tint. When the goggles are removed after several hours, the aftereffects are negligible (3, 4). By the sixtieth day, however, the eye has adapted significantly to the color distortions produced by the goggles (b1, b2); when the goggles are removed, the complementary aftereffects are significant (b3, b 4). (From Kohler, 1962, p. 71.)

consistent with the principles of complementary colors. These settings, without spectacles, simply provide a base for determining the degree to which adaptation approached the preexperimental judgment. Figure 20b shows the settings obtained on the sixtieth day. Adaptation is evident in the desaturated colors selected by S (1 and 2). The situational aftereffects are evidenced in the differences, depending on eye position, which were present in S's settings *without* spectacles (3 and 4). In order to achieve a subjective gray, the color wheel had to be desaturated yellow when S was looking left and desaturated blue when S was looking right.

These quantitative observations were substantiated by the introspective reports (see Kohler, 1951, transl., 1964, pp. 108–115).

A summary of the findings of the Innsbruck studies will be useful. The results of two later studies will be interpolated in the summary, since they bear on the summary statements.

1

Wearers of wedge prisms learned to behave adaptively and displayed perceptual adaptation to the prism-produced distortions. This finding, first reported by Czermak, has been amply confirmed in later studies.

2

Adaptation occurred to differing degrees for the different distortions. This finding was confirmed in a later investigation by Pick and Hay (1964). The Ss of Pick and Hay wore 20-pd prisms for 3 or 42 days. The data presented in Table 20 are the results of the final tests on the 3-day and 42-day Ss, converted to percent adaptation for ease of comparison. Obviously there is great variability in the degree of compensation for the various distortions. It is not possible to compare the rank ordering of compensations in the Pick-Hay study, since Kohler did not examine this matter systematically.[15]

3

Upon removal of the prisms, aftereffects of varying intensity and duration were observed.

4

Wearers of half-prism spectacles also adapted, to the point that viewing the scene through the prism portion did not result in percepts which were different from those obtained through the plain portion. In both cases perception was veridical.

5

Upon removal of the half-prism spectacles, aftereffects were obtained, conditional on eye position. Kohler's experiments seem to have been the only studies of adaptation to half-prism spectacles. However, additional evidence of "gaze contingent" adaptations to prism-produced displacements has been reported by Pick and Hay (1966) and Hay and Pick (in press). These investigators did not use half-prisms. Instead, they examined the possibility that situational, gaze-contingent adaptations may

---

[15] Hajos and Ritter (1965) also have reported evidence that the course of adaptation differs for lateral displacement, curvature, and color fringes. However, the rank order of the magnitudes of the effects in the Hajos-Ritter study does not agree with the order obtained by Hay and Pick shown in Table 20. It is reasonable to expect that the relative rate of adaptation for the various distortions will not be the same under all conditions. The controlling variables have not been identified experimentally, but it is possible to derive some plausible guesses from the discussion in the remaining sections of this chapter.

Table 20
Percent adaptation of 3- and 42-day subjects
to various prismatic distortions*

| | % adaptation and 95% bounds | |
Distortion	3-day	42-day
1		
Overall horizontal image displacement		
a. Error in visually localizing an auditory target (visual-auditory)	44.6 ± 23.0	Not tested
b. Error in kinesthetilocalizing a visual target (visual-manual)	85.8 ± 26.1	90.1 ± 19.0
2		
Curvature of vertical straight lines	11.2 ± 2.4	30.0 ± 9.2
3		
Chromatic fringes at vertical contours	16.5 ± 5.6	33.9 ± 12.1
4		
Differential image displacement		
a. Tilting of horizontal lines with up-down head movement	8.4 ± 6.7	14.6 ± 6.8
b. Compression and expansion of fixated target with side-to-side head movement	0.8 ± 3.8	9.8 ± 7.2
c. Convergence of horizontal lines above and below eye level	Not tested	51.5 ± 30.8

* Adapted from Pick & Hay, 1964, p. 200.

result from the fact that prism spectacles distort the shape of the retinal image in a way that varies with the direction of gaze through the spectacles. In fact, precisely these gaze-contingent differences had led Kohler to conduct the half-prism experiments. In a number of well-designed studies Pick and Hay confirmed the existence of these situational aftereffects.
6
Results similar to the half-prism experiments were reported for the experiments with two-toned spectacles. Unfortunately, these results have not been corroborated in subsequent work (Harrington, 1965; McCullough, 1965). Harrington had Ss wear split-field glasses, consisting of a red (filter) left half and a green right half. The experiment was modeled after Kohler's two-tone study and lasted 146 days. The results were negative. No adaptation, in the form of decreasing saturation of matches, was observed. Nor was there any significant difference in the settings, made without spectacles, as a function of the direction of gaze. There is no obvious explanation of the discrepancy between Harrington's and Kohler's results. Nor does Harrington offer a resolution.

At this point, it may be appropriate to indicate an ambiguity in Kohler's specification of the conditions of the situational aftereffects. [Also see McCullough (1965) for a discussion of other difficulties.] Although there appears to be a contingent relationship between aftereffects and eye position, it is not possible to conclude that eye position per se is critical. Associated with pronounced shifts in eye position, e.g., right-left and up-down, are changes in phenomenal direction. Therefore, it is possible that the situational aftereffects are actually contingent upon egocentric localization rather than eye position. It should be noted, in this connection, that there is good reason for believing that a proprioceptive position sense is lacking for the eyes (Brindley & Merton, 1954).

There can be no question that the Innsbruck studies have contributed significantly to our awareness of the adaptability of the visual system. The observations reported in Kohler's monograph (1951, transl., 1964) were instrumental in arousing the current interest in the problem. However, the Innsbruck studies are disappointing in two respects:

1

Although the method of phenomenological introspection is admirably suited for discovering the general outlines of a problem, it is poorly suited for the purpose of discovering precise functional relationships. One searches in vain for data regarding the many obvious relationships which are suggested through analogy with other forms of learning. The following are a number of obvious examples. What is the rate of adaptation? How is the rate of dissipation of aftereffects related to the rate of adaptation? Will the degree of adaptation vary as a function of variations in amount of distortion and temporal distribution of exposure to distortion, e.g., massed versus spaced exposure? These questions, as well as many others, need to be answered, but for this purpose the phenomenological method must be abandoned, in favor of carefully controlled experiments.

2

A second reason for dissatisfaction is the absence of any clear and concerted effort to explain the occurrence of adaptation. There are hints to be found in various sources (Kohler, 1953; Kohler, 1962) and even an electrical model for the demonstration of the adaptation process (Kohler, 1956). But none of these more or less incidental hypotheses constitutes a coherent explanation. Perhaps the primary contribution of the Innsbruck studies to an explanation of adaptation is that they alert us to the possibility that movement, and feedback from movement, may play an imporant role. This suggestion regarding the role of movement has been independently developed and examined in an extensive series of studies by Held and his associates.

Early studies implicating movement

Three aspects of Held's experimental program may be distinguished:

1

The majority of Held's studies have been designed to demonstrate that adaptation to a variety of optically induced distortions depends on self-generated movement and the correlated "reafferent" visual stimulation.

2

Closely related are the studies whose main objective has been to partial out certain possible sources of confounding and thereby to eliminate alternatives to the reafference hypothesis.

3

In addition to these studies, there are a number of studies which have not involved optical distortion. Experiments have been conducted to show that self-produced movement is essential to the original development of perception.

Three early studies (Held & Gottlieb, 1958; Held & Hein, 1958; Held & Schlank, 1959) on "adaptation to disarranged eye-hand coordination" can serve to introduce Held's work. In these studies, conditions were arranged with the purpose of eliminating informational feedback to S regarding his performance on the criterial task. The technique originated by Held and Gottlieb, and revised by Held and Schlank (1959), is represented in Figure 21. The apparatus consisted of an upper and lower box separated by a half-silvered mirror (M_2). The target (T) was in the upper box, and S's hand was in the lower box. When only the upper box was illuminated, light from T passed through M_2 and was reflected from a fully reflecting first-surface mirror (M_1) to S's eyes, appearing as a virtual image at location T′ on the floor of the lower box. Under this condition, S's hand, although present in the lower box, was not visible. Therefore, his attempts to mark the location of the target were not guided by recognition of error. This condition is illustrated in Figure 21a. When only the lower box was illuminated, S could see his hand, but the target could not be seen. Since the hand is seen by successive reflection, through mirrors M_2 and M_1, it was seen at an increased optical distance. This condition is illustrated in Figure 21b. The chief difference between the arrangement shown in Figure 21 and the original arrangement introduced by Held and Gottlieb (1958) is that the latter used a 20-pd prism to produce lateral displacement, instead of a mirror system to produce increased optical distance.

The general plan of the Held-Hein (1958) and Held-Schlank (1959) experiments was as follows:

1
Preexposure test. With his hand unseen, S marked the apparent location of the target.
2
Exposure. S viewed the displaced image of his hand under one of three movement conditions: hand motionless, hand actively moved by S, hand passively moved by E.
3
Postexposure. S repeated the original localization task.

The exposure periods ranged from 3 to 6 minutes, and movements consisted of right-left arcs.

The results of the Held-Hein and Held-Schlank studies were unambiguous. The occurrence of adaptation was restricted to the condition of exposure which included active movement. For example, in the situation illustrated in Figure 21, six minutes of exposure to active movement of the hand resulted in a shift of 0.52 inch in the adaptive direction, but only a shift of 0.05 inch for the condition of passive movement. Since the views of the hand during the exposure period were the same for the active and passive condition of movement, the different degrees of adaptation cannot be attributed to purely optical factors. Held concluded that active movement is an essential condition of adaptation.

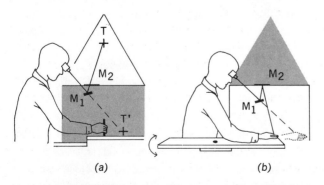

(a)   (b)

Figure 21. Schematic representation of S in the apparatus under two experimental conditions: (a), marking; (b), exposure. (*From Held & Schlank*, 1959, p. 604.)

The results obtained in the Held-Hein experiments and the Held-Schlank experiments have not been unequivocally corroborated. A study which did obtain confirmatory data was reported by Pick and Hay (1965). The experiment was designed to test the possibility that the finding by Held and Hein of greater adaptation for active exposure was due to the greater similarity between the exposure and test conditions for the active as contrasted with the passive exposure. This differential similarity stems from the fact that the test, for both exposure conditions, involved active movements of the hand. To explore the effects of similarity between exposure and test conditions, Pick and Hay conducted a 2 × 2 factorial experiment with two conditions of exposure, active and passive, and two conditions of testing, active and passive. During the condition of passive testing, S's hand was moved by E until S felt that his index finger was on target. During the exposure period, S viewed his moving hand for 5 minutes through a prism which produced a lateral displacement of 17°. The results showed a main effect of exposure conditions, in accordance with the finding of Held and Hein. But there were no significant effects associated with the testing conditions, or with the interaction between exposure and test conditions. Similar results have been reported by Singer and Day (1966). Thus, the account of the Held-Hein results, in terms of differential exposure-test similarity, was not supported.

An experiment that failed to obtain results consistent with the Held-Schlank study was reported by Weinstein, Sersen, and Weinstein (1964). Weinstein et al. used the Held-Schlank apparatus (see Figure 21) to test the effects of three types of exposure:

1
Self-produced movement of the optically displaced hand toward and away from the body
2
Same as condition 1, except that movement followed a left-right arc
3
Self-produced movement of the hand in a left-right arc, but without optical displacement

Different groups of Ss served under each exposure condition. All the groups exhibited *negative*, nonadaptive shifts. The means were $-2.10°$, $-3.21°$, and $-3.85°$ for conditions 1 through 3, respectively. Of the 15 Ss assigned to each exposure condition, only five Ss in condition 1, two in condition 2, and four in condition 3 exhibited positive adaptive shifts. Weinstein et al. concluded that they failed to replicate the results of Held and Schlank.

The results obtained by Weinstein et al. are clear-cut, but viewed in the context of their failure to obtain adaptation under any of their conditions it is questionable whether their findings have significance for an assessment of the role of self-produced movement. Obviously, if conditions are not suitable for demonstrating a particular phenomenon, it is not possible to examine the relationship between the phenomenon and some specific independent variable. However, apart from considerations of reafference, it is legitimate to seek an explanation of their failure to find adaptation. Although there is no immediately obvious explanation [however, see Held and Schlank (1964)], the fact that the greatest negative shift was obtained following condition 3 suggests the presence of uncontrolled determinants of localization, unrelated to optical displacement. This conjecture is also supported by the fact that the results did not merely show an absence of adaptation. A significant negative shift was obtained. Until these peculiarities are explained, the experiment by Weinstein et al. cannot figure prominently in an assessment of the reafference principle.

An experiment by Wallach, Kravitz, and Lindauer (1963) is also relevant to our assessment of the early studies by Held et al. The exposure conditions in the Wallach et al. study were designed to produce rapid adaptation to optically produced displacement. The procedure was based on the premise that perceptual learning is likely when two different conditions of stimulation which lead to discrepant perceptual consequences are simultaneously present (see Chapter 8).

To achieve this condition of conflict, Wallach et al. had S look at his legs during a 10-minute exposure to 20-pd prismatic displacement. S stood with his head bent forward looking down at the lower portion of his legs. During this period, S's head was maintained in a fixed, stationary position by a bite board. Thus, displaced vision was paired with another directional cue, the visual vertical. The legs paralleled a visual direction, and they also visually represented the vertical direction.

Two tests of adaptation were employed. The "pointing" test required S to point at a target without seeing his hand. The target was located 7° to the left of S. This test is comparable to the Held-Hein (1958) test. In the "forward direction" test, S had to judge when a target was straight ahead of him. This test is like the one employed by Held and Bossom (1961), to be described later.

The tests were made with the head stationary with and without prisms. Two experiments were performed, one under daylight conditions and one under dark-room conditions. Although there were differences between the results of the two experiments, only the results of the dark-room test will be reported. With the prisms on, the pointing test showed a significant shift of 4.15° away from the initial prismatically induced error of 11.52°. This represents an adaptive shift of 37.4 percent. With the prisms off, the pointing test showed a significant aftereffect of 3.76°. The results for the test of forward direction were comparable. There were significant adaptive shifts and significant, but smaller, aftereffects.

The experiments by Wallach et al. seem to provide examples of adaptation to displaced visual direction under conditions of passive exposure. Further evidence that active movements are unrelated to adaptation is provided by a subsidiary analysis reported by Wallach et al. In the dark-room experiment, Wallach et al. obtained records of the head movements which occurred despite the bite board. These records were obtained by means of a small mirror, attached to S's head which reflected a spot of light onto a scale attached to the wall. When S's head moved, the spot of light moved correlatively. Readings were taken at 30-second intervals. A rank-order correlation was computed to determine the association between the deviation of the head position and the magnitude of adaptation. The correlations for the two types of tests both approximated zero.

The reafference principle and the feedback model   Before describing additional evidence concerning the role of movement, let us consider the theoretical origin of the expectation that active movement is essential. The expectation has its origins in Von Holst's analysis (1954) of the special role of "reafferent" stimulation in determining perception. Several terms figure prominently in Von Holst's analysis. These terms are defined in the following excerpt from Von Holst's (1954) article:

■ The whole of the stimuli in whatever receptors I shall term *afference*, and in contradistinction to this I shall call the whole of the motor impulses *efference*. Efference can only be present when the ganglion cells are active; afference, on the contrary, can have two quite different sources: First, stimuli produced by muscular activity, which I shall call *reafference*; Second, stimuli produced by external factors, which I shall call *exafference*. Reafference is the necessary afferent reflexion caused by every motor impulse, exafference is independent of motor impulses (p. 89).

In Von Holst's terms, Held's findings show that reafferent visual stimulation, correlated with active hand movement, is a necessary condition for adaptation. Equivalent exafferent visual stimulation, correlated with passive hand movements, does not lead to shifts in eye-hand coordination.

In a number of elegant studies of the optomotor reflex in the fly *Eristalis*, Von Holst demonstrated that exafferent and reafferent visual stimulation have different consequences, even when they are optically equivalent. In fact, it may be stated as a general rule that reafference and exafference have different perceptual consequences. Exafference consisting of a symmetrically expanding image may yield the perception of continuously increasing size, with distance invariant. Reafference, which is optically identical, will usually lead to the perception of constant size and diminishing distance.

As another example, consider the optically equivalent movements of the image which may be produced by (1) moving the eye voluntarily and (2) having the eye moved mechanically, as can be accomplished by applying pressure to the eyeball with the finger. In the first case, the environment appears stationary; in the second case, the environment appears to move. Apparently, the two types of stimulation are distinguished on some basis. This capability is crucial. Without this ability, we might fail to distinguish a change of state from a change of position. Von Holst's chief

concern was to account for the organism's ability to distinguish exafference from reafference.

The explanation proposed by Von Holst required the
assumption that efferent impulses leave behind a centrally
stored image, or copy, of the efference. This image in the
central nervous system is called the "efference copy." Thus,
when the eye moves, an efference copy of the movement is
present ". . . to which the re-afference of this movement
compares as the negative of a photograph compares to its
print" (Von Holst, 1954, p. 91). Under normal conditions,
the reafference returns to the central nervous system and
nullifies the efference copy. As a result, the world does not
appear to move as the eyes move. The critical difference
between this situation involving reafference and the case of
exafference is that an efference copy is not available in the
latter case. The exafference is unmatched by an efference
copy, with the result that a perception of change arises.
The different effects of optically identical afferent and exafferent stimulation are due to the differential availability of
the efferent copy. In addition, the ability of the perceiver to
distinguish moving and resting objects when both produce
equivalent optical stimulation is based on this difference.

Held (1961) has expanded upon Von Holst's thinking, in
order to develop an account of the results of his adaptation
experiments. The model is illustrated in Figure 22. Held's
model shows a feedback cycle starting with an efferent signal

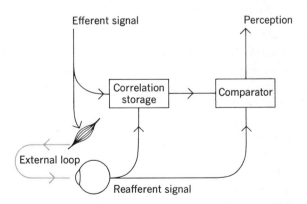

Figure 22. Schematized process assumed to underlie
the consequences of rearrangement, neonatal development, disarrangement, and deprivation. *(From Held,
1961, p. 30.)*

and culminating in the adjustive results of the reafferent signal. The following features distinguish Held's analysis from Von Holst's:

1

Von Holst's discussion emphasized eye movements, but Held's model is explicitly intended to deal with any motor system that can be the source of reafferent stimulation.

2

Since Von Holst was not concerned with changes over time, his model did not include explicit provisions for the storage of previously experienced efferent-afferent combinations. Held, on the other hand, is concerned with continuous phenomena. Therefore, Held introduced a memory component, the *correlation storage*, into the model.

3

Von Holst stressed the summative interactions between afferent stimulation and the efference signal (copy).

Instead of a summation, Held assumes that:

■ The reafferent signal is compared [in the comparator] with a signal selected from the Correlation Storage by the monitored efferent signal. The Correlation Storage acts as kind of a memory. . . . The currently monitored efferent signal is presumed to select the trace [of previous reafferent-efferent combinations] . . . containing the identical efferent part and to activate the reafferent trace combined with it. The resulting revived re-afferent signal is sent to the Comparator [see Figure 22] for comparison with the current re-afferent signal. The outcome of this comparison determines further performance (Held, 1961, p. 30).

Both Von Holst's and Held's models of sensory-motor interaction assign a special role to self-produced movement in maintaining a stable perceptual world and effective sensory-motor coordination. However, Held, who offers his model as the basis for an account of adaptation to optical distortion, does not supply a detailed illustration of its application to specific experimental situations. In fact, after an attempt to apply this account to the Held-Hein and Held-Schlank studies, we have concluded that the model is not an account of the process or mechanisms of adaptation. Rather it is an interpretation of the end product of adaptation. The model appears to be an elaborate answer to the question "What is modified when adaptation occurs?" rather than "How or why does the modification occur?"

The answer, which emerges from considerations of the model, is that adaptation consists neither of purely visual shifts, as Kohler suggested, or purely kinesthetic shifts, as Walls and Helmholtz maintained. But, instead, adaptation, according to this view, is a matter of establishing new reafferent-efferent associations. Since these new associations cannot be established, except as there are opportunities for the concurrence of efferent traces and reafference, active movement is necessary. But how or why these new associations are formed is not explained. The problem is all the more difficult, since in the Held-Hein and Held-Schlank studies the reafference-efference discrepancy has no functional consequences. Perhaps there is implied an intrinsic tendency in the central nervous system to minimize the discrepancy between reafference and efference. However, the Von Holst-Held model does not tell us how this comes about.

Further evidence regarding reafference and adaptation   In a series of experiments (Held, 1962; Held & Bossom, 1961; Held & Mikaelian, 1964; Mikaelian & Held, 1964), Held has tried to bolster his view regarding the critical role of reafference. The first experiment (Held & Bossom, 1961) to be considered dealt with adaptive shifts in egocentric localization, following self-generated and equivalent passive gross movements of the entire body. Egocentric localization was measured by having S orient himself so as to place a luminous target, in an otherwise dark room, straight ahead of him. The measures were obtained while S sat in the apparatus shown in Figure 23. S sat in a chair with his head held in a fixed position by a bite board. The upper part of his body was surrounded by a rotatable drum 5 feet in diameter. The target was located on the inside surface of the drum, at S's eye level. By exerting appropriate leg movements, S could rotate the chair around a vertical axis (b). An arrangement of arrow markers and protractors enabled E to determine the direction in which S faced, relative to the direction of the target.

Two experiments were conducted following the same general procedure:

1

Preexposure test of egocentric localization. The S made a series of judgments without prismatic intervention. S was instructed

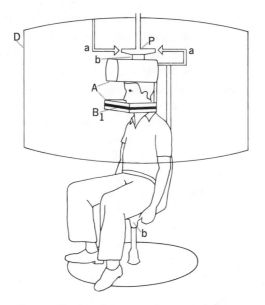

Figure 23. Apparatus used to measure egocentric localization: (A), shields forming aperture; (a), arrow indicators; (B), bite board;
(b), upper and lower bearings; (D), rotatable
drum; (P), protractor. (*From Held & Bossom,
1961, p. 34.*)

to rotate himself until the target appeared straight ahead of
him. The location of the target was varied from trial to trial by
rotating the drum.

2

Exposure. The Ss wore 20-pd trial-case prisms, fitted into
goggles. Two conditions of movement were studied. In one
condition, S walked freely along a typical outdoor campus path.
In the other condition, S sat in a wheel chair that was pushed
along the same path.

3

Postexposure test. The judgments of egocentric localization
obtained in the preexposure test were repeated without prismatic intervention.

Adaptation to prismatic distortion should be revealed as a
difference between the preexposure and postexposure localizations. The postexposure localizations should exhibit aftereffects (errors of localization) in the direction opposite to the
prism-induced errors.

In Exp. I the Ss were given four 1-hour exposures to
prismatic stimulation, two with base-right and two with

base-left prisms. Two 1-hour periods were spent in active movement, and two periods were spent in passive movement. Each S served under all four conditions, with a 24-hour interval between successive conditions. The mean shifts of localizations in degrees were 1.29 and −0.22 for the active and passive movement conditions, respectively. The shift for active movement was statistically significant and in the expected direction. This shift of 1.29° represented approximately 10 percent of full adaptation. The shift for passive movement was not significant.

Experiment II was similar to Exp. I, except that the exposure period was extended to 11 or 22 hours, spread over 2 or 4 days. The results of this extended experiment corroborated the findings of Exp. I. For example, subject B (Held & Bossom, 1961, p. 36, fig. 2) exhibited 100 percent adaptation after 22 hours of active exposure but 0 percent adaptation after passive exposure of the same duration. In other words, after 22 hours of active exposure S judged himself to be straight ahead of the target when he was actually 11° to the right. Following 22 hours of passive exposure, egocentric localization was perfectly accurate.

Although the results of the Held-Bossom experiment are straightforward, there are grounds for doubting whether they necessarily implicate the reafference principle. The doubt arises from considerations of other uncontrolled differences between the conditions of active and passive movement. In particular, there are likely to have been differences in the degree of attention and active visual sampling or exploration under the two conditions. When a S is passively conveyed, he is not as likely to engage in varied visual exploration, nor does he need to take the optical distortions into account in order to navigate the environment. On this basis alone, independently of reafference considerations, one might expect less adaptation for the passive Ss. To test this alternative interpretation, Held and Mikaelian (1964) conducted an experiment involving two conditions of movement, active walking and self-wheeling.

■ The interpretation implies that, if S had been required to propel himself by manipulating the wheels while seated in the chair, avoiding walls and other obstacles, he would then have compensated for the directional errors induced by the prism.

On the other hand, from our point of view the motor-sensory feedback generated by such movements of the arms should not have been appropriate for adapting egocentric localization as tested in the experiment (Held and Mikaelian, 1964, pp. 686–687).

The procedures and apparatus of this new experiment were like Exp. I of Held and Bossom (1961). The results showed an average shift of 4.1° in the expected direction after walking exposure and a nonsignificant shift of −0.40° following self-wheeling exposure. Held and Mikaelian conclude that a hypothesis of motivational or exploratory deficiency cannot account for the absence of adaptation under conditions of passive movement. Instead, the lack of compensation is due to the absence of reafference.

Another experiment designed to test the hypothesis of motivational or exploratory deficiency has been reported by Weinstein, Sersen, Fisher, and Weisinger (1964). Experiment I compared the shifts in egocentric localization which occurred following 1-hour prismatic exposure under four conditions: (1) a passive condition like that of Held and Bossom; (2) S moved both wheels nondifferentially while E steered the chair; (3) a blindfolded E pushed the chair in accordance with the steering direction provided by S; (4) S provided both locomotion and direction. Conditions 1 and 4 constituted a replication of the Held-Bossom experiment. Conditions 2 and 3 provided a test of the deficiency hypothesis. According to this hypothesis, reafference, contingent on self-produced movement, is not necessary. Adaptation will occur in the absence of reafference if the exafference is obtained under conditions which force S to attend to, and make decisions about, the environment. On this account, adaptation should occur during exposure under both conditions 3 and 4 but not under conditions 1 and 2.

The main finding was that all four exposure conditions led to small but significant adaptive shifts. The mean shifts, in the direction opposite the prism-induced displacement, were 1.09, 1.06, 0.77, and 0.72° for conditions 3, 4, 2, and 1, respectively. (Full compensation for prismatic deviation would lead to a shift 7° 25′.) The means for the four conditions did not differ significantly. These results are consistent with neither of the contesting hypotheses.

The experiments described thus far have examined the

role of reafference in criterial tests which involved eye-hand coordination and egocentric localization. In two additional experiments, the question has been examined for the case of adaptation to optically produced tilt. Since the Held (1962) and Mikaelian-Held (1964) studies are highly similar, only the latter study will be described. The general procedure and apparatus were like those of Held and Bossom, with the following differences:

1
An addition was made to the apparatus to permit E to deter-mine the apparent vertical by the method of adjustment.
2
During exposure, S wore right-angled prisms which rotated the visual field 20° counterclockwise, in addition to displacing the center of the field.

Ss began by making judgments of egocentric localization and the apparent vertical. Then S walked or was wheeled up and down a hallway. Finally, the original judgments were repeated.

The results for egocentric localization confirmed the earlier findings. There was a significant shift for the condition of active movement but no shift for the condition of passive movement. The tilt results, on the other hand, were somewhat ambiguous insofar as the reafference principle is concerned. The mean shift of tilt was 6.8° for active exposure and 1.9° for passive exposure. Although the shift for active exposure was significantly greater than for passive exposure, the latter shift differed significantly from zero. Adaptation to optically induced tilt was obtained in the absence of reafference.

Mikaelian and Held (1964) propose that the compensation for tilt observed with passive movement is due to the presence of the special conditions known to produce the Gibson type of aftereffect. The chief condition for generating this type of effect is a preliminary period of continuous exposure to lines which deviate from orientation norms. For example, Gibson and Radner (1937) found that following a continuous period of inspection of tilted lines, a vertical line appears tilted in the opposite direction. Since the hallway, which was viewed with the tilting prisms, was predominantly made up of lines in normative horizontal and vertical orientations, normalization occurred and an aftereffect was obtained even under the condition of passive movement.

In Exp. II Mikaelian and Held (1964) tested this interpretation by altering the exposure environment in a manner which eliminated the gridlike patterning which characterizes typical man-made environments. Exposure in such an environment should provide no opportunities for Gibson's normalization but should not affect the adaptation process, which is contingent upon reafference. Under these conditions no compensation for tilt should be obtained for the condition of passive exposure.

The exposure environment was a dark room on whose walls luminous spheres were hung at random. A S in the room could see only the luminous circles. A prismatic rotation of this visual field produced no significant change in the patterning. Nor did considerations arise concerning deviations from normalcy. Ss either walked back and forth in the room for 90 minutes or were transported over a similar path, standing on a dolly. The results were compatible with the interpretation of Held and Mikaelian. After active movements, there were significant shifts (aftereffects of adaptation) for both egocentric localization and apparent verticality. After passive movements, the mean shifts for both judgments were about zero.

Held and Mikaelian concluded that the adaptation during passive movement observed in Exp. I was of Gibson's type. Furthermore, the fact that adaptation occurred following active movement in the special environment of Exp. II showed that the tilt aftereffects were not simply instances of the Gibson aftereffect. The patterning of the environment in Exp. II was important only in ". . . serving as an agent in the production of reafferent stimulation contingent upon self-produced movement" (Mikaelian & Held, 1964, p. 262).

A comparison of the results of the two experiments of Mikaelian and Held yields an interesting observation. The magnitude of adaptation was lower in Exp. II than in Exp. I. It would appear that substituting the random aggregation of spheres for the normal indoor environments eliminated a factor that facilitates compensation for optical tilt. At least two alternative identifications of this factor can be considered:

1

Gibson-type normalization, which may act additively with the type of adaptation studied by Held, produces greater compensation when a normal environment is exposed.

2

The orientation histories of real objects in a conventional man-made environment impart to objects a preferred orientation that tends to impose itself on the atypical orientations which are optically induced.

An experiment by Morant and Beller (1965) lends plausibility to the second alternative. Morant and Beller have shown that the aftereffects of viewing an optically tilted field of vertical lines differ from the effects of viewing a field of objects optically tilted to the same degree. In general, the role which characteristics of the visual field may play in facilitating and inhibiting adaptation has not been explored.

An experiment by Held and Rekosh (1963) will conclude this review of the case for the role of reafference in adaptation. This experiment, which was concerned with curvature, was designed analogously to Exp. II of Mikaelian and Held. The intention was to examine the dependence of adaptation to prismatic curvature under conditions which did not confound the Gibson aftereffect with the hypothesized reafference-dependent aftereffect.

To accomplish this objective, an exposure environment was created such that when viewed prismatically the environment was not dominated by curvature to a degree different from that in the case for nonprismatic observation. For this purpose an exposure environment was used which consisted of a randomly distributed collection of irregular shapes. Held (1962) had earlier found that when viewed with a stationary head, this type of pattern did not yield a curvature aftereffect. Nor did nonprismatic exposure yield an aftereffect. In the present experiment, Held and Rekosh compared the aftereffects of exposure, obtained when S walked about with the effects obtained when he was wheeled around a similar path. When S, wearing prisms, moved or was moved through the environment, the relative retinal rates of displacements of the shapes were different from the rates correlated with the same movements in the absence of prisms. Compensation for this transformation should produce curvature aftereffects. According to the reafference hypothesis, the aftereffects should be present only for exposure which is accompanied by active movement. The results were consistent with this hypothesis.

The Mikaelian-Held and Held-Rekosh experiments are important in demonstrating movement-dependent adaptation free of confounding by the conditions for the Gibson-type aftereffect. This claim cannot be made for some of the earlier experiments, which provided exposures to natural and man-made environments. The Held-Rekosh experiment has additional significance. Hochberg (1963) has contended that Held's findings do not necessarily implicate modifications of visual space. Instead, Hochberg, commenting on the Mikaelian-Held experiment, argued that under the condition of active movement ". . . kinesthetic space will be rearranged toward fitting the visual framework, while passive observers, relieved of the necessity for acting in such a field, will retain their kinesthetic space relatively unaffected" (p. 544). Hochberg proposed that adaptation to curvature would not be subject to this reinterpretation, since curvature adaptation would implicate alterations in the geometrical relationship between points and lines within the visual field, instead of changes in the relation between the visual field and a nonvisual framework. The Held-Rekosh experiment satisfies this requirement. (Also see Held, 1963.)

Reafference and perceptual development   Both Kohler and Held have argued that the technique of optical distortion can serve as a tool for exploring the genesis of perception. The impression is given that the introduction of prismatic intervention reinstates the perceptual world as it existed originally, prior to perceptual development. Furthermore, it is contended that the process of adaptation and the process of development are analogous.

■ If development and compensation for rearrangement reflect the same process, then findings concerning the essential properties of movement—e.g., the need for self-produced movement . . . are equally applicable to development. We may then predict that the gross bodily movement required for visual-motor development must be self-produced movement. . . . [Reafference] is the source of ordered contact with the environment which is responsible for both the stability, under typical conditions, and the adaptability to certain atypical conditions (Held & Bossom, 1961, pp. 36–37).

The work of Riesen (Riesen, 1961; Riesen & Aarons, 1959) suggests that movement may be important in the development of perception. Riesen reported that kittens that were prevented from moving freely were deficient in visually guided behavior. However, in Riesen's studies there were significant differences between the variety and complexity of optical stimulation available to the restrained and unrestrained kittens. Therefore, it cannot be determined whether the deficiency observed by Riesen should be attributed to the lack of movement or to the lack of varied stimulation.

An experiment by Held and Hein (1963), which compared the performances of laboratory-reared kittens following active and passive movement, avoided this confounding. Pairs of kittens were reared in darkness until one kitten in each pair was able to move about in the experimental apparatus. Then each pair was exposed to the experimental environment for three hours daily. The apparatus and exposure environment are shown in Figure 24. The active animal (A) could move about the interior of a drum whose interior surface was covered with black and white stripes. The movements of kitten A were mechanically tranferred to kitten P. In this way kitten P was moved passively as a result of the active movements by kitten A. The rate and type of movement were

Figure 24. Apparatus for equating motion and consequent visual feedback for an actively moving S (A) and a passively moved S (P). (*From Held & Hein, 1963, p. 873.*)

the same for both kittens. In addition, they were both exposed to the same optical stimulation. The only difference
was that for kitten A the changes in stimulation were contingent on self-produced movement while for kitten P the
changes in stimulation were not dependent on active
movement.

The kittens were tested in three ways: visually guided
paw placement, avoidance of a visual cliff, blink to an
approaching object. The general question was whether the
kittens that moved actively would give evidence of superior
discriminatory capabilities. The results were unambiguous.
On the tests of visually guided paw placing and blinking, all
the active kittens exhibited the prescribed response, while
none of the passive kittens displayed the responses. On the
visual-cliff test, all the active kittens chose the "shallow"
side and avoided the "cliff" side (see Walk & Gibson, 1961,
for a description of this apparatus). This preference for the
shallow side was evident from the first day of testing. In
avoiding the cliff the active kittens exhibited a preference
also observed in normally reared kittens. The passive kittens,
on the other hand, distributed their descents about evenly
between the two sides. The absence of a significant preference for one side is usually taken as evidence of a lack of
the ability to discriminate depth (Epstein, 1964; Walk & Gibson, 1961). Held and Hein (1963) conclude that ". . . these
findings provide convincing evidence for a developmental
process, in at least one higher mammal, which requires
for its operation stimulus variation concurrent with and
systematically dependent upon self-produced movement"
(p. 876).

Hamilton and Bossom (1964) have tested the underlying
premise of the Held-Hein experiment in a different way. If
normal development and adaptation to optical distortion
depend on the same mechanisms, then we would expect that
the variables which regulate adaptation would also regulate
the dissipation of aftereffects. The aftereffects should diminish more rapidly after a postadaptational period filled by
active movement than after the same period without movement. To test this prediction Hamilton and Bossom used
the apparatus introduced by Held and Gottlieb (1958) in the
experiment on eye-hand coordination. During the exposure
to prismatic displacement, all Ss watched the self-movements
of their hand. Following the 15-minute exposure period, S

performed the initial adaptation test, which consisted of repeating the preexposure markings. Then a 15-minute dissipation period was initiated. There were two conditions of movement during this period: (1) a reafferent condition—S viewed the self-generated movements of his hand without prismatic displacement—and (2) a nonreafferent condition—S sat quietly in the dark.

The critical data are the decreases in the magnitude of the aftereffect with reafference (1) and without reafference (2). Hamilton and Bossom report their results in units of 0.1 with 1 inch equaling approximately a displacement of 3°. The average immediate aftereffect was 10.7. After 15 minutes the mean decrease in aftereffects was 8.6 and 5.4 for the reafferent and nonreafferent conditions, respectively. Both these decreases are significantly greater than zero, but they are *not* significantly different from each other. It would be useful to know how nearly these decreases approximated 100 percent dissipation. Unfortunately, Hamilton and Bossom do not provide separate data on the magnitude of the immediate aftereffect for the two groups. If, for any reason, the Ss who were assigned to the reafference condition had not adapted to as great a degree as the nonreafference Ss, the dissipation results would be biased in favor of the obtained outcome.

The fact that reafference does not appear necessary for the elimination of the aftereffects leads Hamilton and Bossom to question the general assumption that there are no differences between the processes underlying normal perceptual development and adaptation to prismatic distortion. Other evidence that reafference is not essential for the elimination of aftereffects is present in an experiment by Bossom and Hamilton (1963) with split-brain monkeys and in Hamilton's (1964) study of intermanual transfer. These findings challenge one of the chief assumptions of those who attribute great significance to the adaptation studies. However, we should note that the challenge is decisive only if we can accept the argument that all variables which are essential to the establishment of a state are also powerful determinants of its disruption. Putting the matter more specifically, we must assume that a factor X which governs acquisition also influences forgetting in the same way. There is no compelling a priori reason for this assumption. In fact, in some cases the experimental evidence strongly indicates that a given variable affects acquisition and forgetting in opposite directions. For example, distributed practice facilitates acquisition in classic and instrumental conditioning paradigms, but in general massed trials lead to faster extinction (Kimble, 1961, pp. 282–284).

Table 21 (p. 236) is a brief summary of the experiments which have investigated the influence of movement conditions on adaptation. The table shows that there is considerable evidence that self-produced movement facilitates adaptation to optical distortion. In several experiments, the most plausible interpretation of this finding is to emphasize the special contribution of reafferent visual stimulation. At the same time, there are several indications that movement-contingent stimulation is not always necessary. Adaptation has been reported under conditions of exafference and nonreafference. The evidence suggests that adaptation will occur in the absence of reafference (1) if S is forced to take the optical distortion into account in order to behave adaptively or (2) if S is confronted by a condition of perceptual conflict. In addition, there seems to be agreement that exposure to stimulus values which deviate from some normative state will lead to adaptation even for passive observation.[16]

It requires no more than a cursory knowledge of the history of controversy in experimental psychology to recognize the signs of a forthcoming protracted debate on the question "Is reafference necessary?" The probability is great that the final answer will not differ from the one implied in the previous paragraph. Reafference is one important determinant, but it is not essential for adaptation under all conditions. This conclusion would simply reaffirm the general observation that perceptual phenomena are multiply determined. Apart from requirements of an intact nervous system it would be difficult to specify absolutely necessary conditions for most perceptual phenomena.

What is learned?

The adaptation experiments show that the S who is exposed to optical distortion behaves differently at the end of the

---

[16] Also relevant to this conclusion are the findings of a number of studies that have not been reviewed in this chapter. See Howard, Craske, and Templeton (1965) and Singer and Day (1966).

exposure period, as compared with his behavior prior to, or at the initiation of, the exposure period. What underlying modification is responsible for the altered performance? What is learned or changed when a S adapts to optical distortion? This question has been raised earlier in the discussion of the inversion experiments. In that context, two different answers were considered. In a discussion of the studies of eye-hand coordination, Harris (1963a) has listed six alternatives:

1

"Conscious correction." When S first points at an object, viewed through a prism, he discovers that he has erred by pointing too far in the direction of the prism apex. Therefore, he *deliberately* corrects his performance by shifting away from the locus which seems visually correct. For example, if he finds that he has pointed too far to the left, he tries to aim farther right.

It is unlikely that this type of correction figures importantly in adaptation. The typical design of the adaptation experiment provides little opportunity or motivation for deliberate compensations for distortion. Also, if deliberate correction is the essential component of adaptation, aftereffects would not be expected. The S should give up the corrective actions when the prisms are removed, since corrections are obviously no longer appropriate. Pointing should be accurate.

2

"Visual change." The perceived location of objects may have changed. For example, prior to adaptation, a distal point correlated with central foveal stimulation will appear to be straight ahead. After adaptation, without altering eye, head, or body position, the distal point looks off to the side. Similarly, a target whose retinal image is off center may look straight ahead.

3

"Shift in perceptual axes." Adaptation may reflect a shift in the reference axes for all spatial perception. This interpretation is predicated on the assumption that perceptual space is unitary although it is the product of several modalities. Before adaptation, one axis of perceptual space is perpendicular to the frontal plane of the body, and this axis specifies the "straight ahead." After adaptation, the axis is rotated from its original position, and along with it all perceived directions are shifted.

4

"Visuo-motor recorrelation." Adaptation is neither a visual change nor an alteration of the motor response. Instead, it is a change in the correlation between visual imputs and motor responses. After adaptation, a given stimulus elicits a different response.

5

"Motor learning." Adaptation consists of learning new muscular responses to a particular perceived target location.

Table 21
Summary of studies of adaptation as a function of conditions of movement

Investigator	Optical distortion	Exposure Conditions	Test	Results
Held and Gottlieb (1958)	Lateral displacement	(1) Active hand movement; (2) passive hand movement	Target marking	Adaptation under condition 1 only.
Held and Schlank (1959)	Increased optical distance	Same as Held-Gottlieb	Same as Held-Gottlieb	Adaptation under condition 1 only.
Held and Bossom (1961)	Lateral displacement	(1) Walking outdoors; (2) passive wheel-chair conveyance	Egocentric localization	Adaptation under condition 1 only.
Held (1962)	Tilt	(1) Walk in hallway; (2) passive wheel-chair conveyance	Judgment of apparent vertical	Significant adaptation under both conditions but greater under condition 1.
Held and Hein (1963)	No distortion	(1) Self-produced movement inside a drum; (2) passive equivalent (kittens as Ss)	Paw placement, blink test, visual cliff	Only kitten reared under condition 1 responded normally.
Held and Rekosh (1963)	Curvature	(1) Walking in special environment; (2) dolly transport	Judgment of apparent straightness	Adaptation under condition 1 only.
Wallach, Kravitz, and Lindauer (1963)	Lateral displacement	Passive exposure under conditions of cue conflict	Pointing test and judgment of "straight ahead" with and without prisms	Adaptation exhibited in all testing conditions.
Weinstein, Sersen, and Weinstein (1964)	Increased optical distance	(1) Passive hand movement; (2) active hand movement; (3) active hand movement without prisms	Target marking	No positive adaptation under any conditions. All conditions yielded negative adaptation.

Author	Type of transformation	Conditions	Test	Results
Weinstein, Sersen, Fisher, and Weisinger (1964)	Lateral displacement	(1) Passive movement; (2) active nondirective movement; (3) direct only, passive movement; (4) active directive movement	Egocentric localization	Adaptation under all four conditions.
Held and Mikaelian (1964)	Lateral displacement	(1) Walking indoors; (2) self-propelled wheel-chair locomotion	Egocentric localization	Adaptation under condition 1 only.
Mikaelian and Held (1964)	Tilt	Exp. I: (1) walk in hallway, (2) passive wheel-chair conveyance; Exp. II: (1) walk in specially designed environment, (2) passive dolly conveyance	Egocentric localization and judgment of apparent vertical	Exp. I: egocentric localization showed adaptation only under condition 1, tilt adapted under both 1 and 2; Exp. II: adaptation only under condition 1.
Hamilton and Bossom (1964)	Increased optical distance	Active movement during adaptation period; either (1) active or (2) zero movement during dissipation period	Target marking	Adaptation and comparable amounts of dissipation of aftereffects under conditions 1 and 2.
Pick and Hay (1965)	Lateral displacement	(1) Active hand movements; (2) passive hand movement; passive and active test conditions	Target marking	Adaptation under condition 1 only. No difference between passive and active tests.

6

"Proprioceptive shift." In one form, this interpretation may be traced back to Helmholtz's analysis of Czermak's adaptation experiment (see page 189). Helmholtz contended that the underlying change was a modification of the judged, or felt, position of the eye. In Harrsi's discussion, the proprioceptive shift involves the hand. Prior to adaptation, the felt and actual positions of the hand correspond, but the hand visually appears to be elsewhere. One way in which this discrepancy can be resolved is for the hand to come to feel to be where it visually appears to be. According to the interpretation under consideration, adaptation consists of precisely such a proprioceptive shift. Thus, when the hand is pointing straight ahead, it is felt to be displaced to one side, in agreement with its visual location. When the hand is actually deviated from the straight ahead toward the prism base by an appropriate angle, it will look and feel to be straight ahead. Therefore, when the prisms are removed and S attempts to mark a target which appears straight ahead, he will move his (unseen) hand until it feels as if it is straight ahead of him. But, for the reasons just presented, this will leave his hand off to the side.

Although these six alternatives have been presented in the context of the eye-hand coordination experiments, they may be applied with varying degrees of credibility to the other adaptation experiments (Harris, 1963a; Harris, 1965). However, of more immediate interest are the experimental attempts to determine which of these interpretations is correct. Table 22 will help clarify the rationale of one type of experiment which has been designed for this purpose. The simplest description of Table 22 is that it shows the transfer predictions of the six interpretations when S is exposed to prismatic distortion and then is tested under the thirteen conditions listed in the left-hand column. Except for the test with normal vision, a plus (+) indicates that an adaptive shift is predicted which will be as large under the test condition as in pointing at a visual target.

Table 22 shows that several of the testing conditions are especially useful as a basis for deciding among the alternative interpretations. Helmholtz was the first investigator to propose this approach. In commenting on Czermak's study of displaced vision, Helmholtz contended that the underlying basis for the observed adaptation was a change in the judged position of the eye, and not a change in the felt position of the hand. Helmholtz suggested an experiment

Table 22
Test performance predicted by six interpretations of adaptation to displaced vision*

Test task	Proprioceptive change in the arm	Conscious correction	Visual perception	Frame of reference	Visuomotor recorrelation	Motor learning
Same as during adaptation†	+	+	+	+	+	+
Pointing at visual target without prisms	+		+	+	+	+
Pointing at visual target with unexposed hand		+	+	+		?
Verbal judgment of location of visual target		?	+	+		
Pointing at auditory target‡	+			+		+
Verbal judgment of location of auditory target‡				+		
Pointing straight ahead‡	+					+
Pointing at visual target with different arm movements	+	+	+	+	?	
Pointing at visual targets in different locations	?	+	+	+	?	
Judgment of distance between hands‡	+					
Judgment of location of passively moved adapted arm relative to visual target	+	+	+	+		
Pointing with adapted hand at unexposed hand‡	+					+
Pointing with unexposed hand at adapted hand‡	+					

* From Harris, 1965, p. 422.
† Except that (as with all the other tests) the subject cannot see his hand and receives no information about his accuracy.
‡ While blindfolded.
NOTE: The subject adapts by pointing with one arm, using a stereotyped arm movement, at a single target seen through prisms. A + indicates the prediction of an adaptive shift as large as that obtained with the task used during adaptation.

which he believed would substantiate this interpretation: ". . . if after having become used to looking through the prisms and finding the visible objects with the right hand, then we close our eyes and try to touch the same objects with the left hand, which has not been previously used, and which has not been in the field of view, we find that there will not be any difficulty about touching them with perfect certainty and precision" (Helmholtz, 1866, transl., 1925, vol. III, p. 247). Helmholtz reasoned that the occurrence of intermanual transfer necessarily implicates changes in components of the system that control reaching by either hand, such as "the judgment of the direction of the gaze." Lack of intermanual transfer would suggest that the underlying change affected only the exposed arm. It should be noted that Helmholtz never actually carried out his experimental proposal.[17]

Harris (1963a, 1963b) reported the first experiments designed to explore the basis of adaptation by means of a transfer experiment. Harris's experiments (1963a, 1963b) included six of the tests listed in Table 22. Experiment I involved the administration of four tests, both before and after a 3-minute period of wearing 20-pd prismatic spectacles. The following four tests were used:

1
With his unseen arm, extended under a table top, S pointed at one of five rods sticking up from the table top in a linear arrangement perpendicular to his line of sight.
2
With his eyes closed, S judged when a sound source, a clicker, was straight ahead.
3
With his eyes closed and the clicker behind one of the three central rods, S was instructed to point at the clicker.
4
With eyes closed, S pointed straight ahead.

During the 3-minute exposure period, S was able to see his hand, and he made ninety attempts to point at the central rod. In order to provide a basis for assessing intermanual

[17] An experiment by Kalil and Freedman (1966), which was published too late for detailed incorporation into this chapter, merits serious consideration in assessing Helmholtz's hypothesis. Kalil and Freedman secured photographic measurements of the eyes when S judged that he was looking straight ahead at a vertical rod. The measurements were obtained before and after exposure to the lateral displacement produced by 20-pd prisms. They found that the prisms produced lateral rotations of the eyes and that these persisted after the prisms were removed. S was not aware of these ocular rotations.

transfer, the tests before and after the exposure period were conducted with each hand separately.

Three aspects of the results will be reported, and their implications for the interpretations in Table 22 will be considered. There were two major findings: adaptation was exhibited to the same degree on all four tests, and adaptation was confined to the exposed hand. There was no intermanual transfer. A secondary finding was that the amount of adaptation was the same for all five target rods, even though only the central rod was used as a target in the exposure period.

Harris (1963a, 1963b) contends that only the hypothesis of proprioceptive shift is compatible with these findings. It will be helpful to review a number of the less obvious ways in which the findings contradict the various interpretations:

1
"Visual change." If, after adaptation, a target whose image is retinally centered looks off to the side, then S should point off to the side with the unexposed as well as the exposed hand. But there was no evidence of intermanual transfer. S pointed off to the side with the exposed hand but directly at the target with the unexposed hand.
2
"Visuo-motor recorrelation." This interpretation implies that adaptation will be confined to visual targets. However, Harris's experiment found adaptation for an auditory target localized with the eyes closed.
3
"Perceptual axes." This interpretation would predict intermanual transfer, but no evidence of intermanual transfer was obtained.
4
"Motor learning." The fact that the degree of adaptation was the same for the five rods seems to contradict this hypothesis. On this hypothesis, adaptation should be less for the peripheral rods, since the arm movements which are involved in pointing at these peripheral rods are different from those practiced in pointing at the central rod.

Harris concludes that the essential modification ". . . must involve a change in the felt position of the arm relative to the body. . . . The person comes to feel that his hand is where it looks as if it is" (Harris, 1963b, p. 813). Experiment II (Harris, 1963a) tested this interpretation more directly. Eight Ss made judgments of "interhand distance" both before and after a 3-minute exposure to prismatic displacement. If adaptation reflects a shift in the felt position of the exposed hand only, then judgments of interhand distance which follow adaptation should differ from those which precede adaptation. For example, a S who viewed his right hand through base-right prisms should come to feel his right hand to be to the left of its actual position. Therefore, he should feel his hands to be closer to each other than they are actually. Thus, if he is asked to judge a given interhand distance both before and after adaptation, the latter estimate should be smaller. In addition, if he is asked to produce a specified interhand distance, then following adaptation he should overestimate the distance. Eight other Ss made their first judgment of interhand distance after adaptation and their second judgment after a 3-minute period of nonprismatic exposure. Harris predicted that the two judgments would differ in the manner which can be deduced from the previous analysis.

During the exposure and dissipation periods, S performed the pointing task which was used in Exp. I. The method of magnitude production (Stevens, 1958) was used to obtain judgments of interhand distance. The S's hands were passively positioned, so that the adapted right hand was straight ahead and the left hand 7 inches to the left. This distance of 7 inches served as the standard and was assigned the number 10. The S's right hand was then moved to one of several new positions, separated by intervals of 1 inch, and S was instructed to move his left hand to produce distances of magnitudes 5, 7½, 10, 13, 20, 30, or 40.

Harris (1963a) presents a very detailed analysis of his findings. They may be summarized generally as follows: Following adaptation, the subjective interhand distances produced by Ss who wore base-left prisms were smaller than preceding adaptation; for base-right prisms interhand distance productions were greater following adaptation. The judgments following dissipation changed in the expected direction. Harris concluded that Exp. II provided direct evidence of a proprioceptive shift of the exposed hand during adaptation. Parenthetically, it may be noted that these findings are difficult to handle in terms of a motor-learning interpretation of adaptation. Since the adaptive shift is evident when S does not perform a motor response, i.e., when his hands are moved by E, the modification which underlies adaptation obviously cannot consist primarily of new motor learning. Additional direct evidence for the hypothesized change in felt position is obtained when S points with his unexposed arm at his stationary adapted arm. Efstathiou and Held (1964) have reported large significant shifts on this test. This shift occurred despite the fact that with his unexposed hand S can point correctly at other targets. Obviously, it is the felt position of the adapted hand which is responsible for the deviations from correct pointing.

Although Harris's results are unequivocal, there are certain differences between his procedures and the procedures of the investigators whose work was reviewed earlier, e.g., Held and Gottlieb (1958). Two differences that may be important are the following:

1
During the exposure period, Harris's Ss pointed at a target, while the Ss in the earlier studies merely moved their hands in a prescribed manner, without engaging in target practice.
2
Harris's exposure period was considerably briefer than the periods allowed by the previous investigators.

Subsequent experiments have shown that the first variation is not critical. However, the second variation may limit the generality of Harris's conclusions.

Hamilton (1964) has reported a study of intermanual transfer which used the apparatus and general procedures of the Held-Gottlieb (1958) study. Intermanual transfer was assessed by measuring aftereffects for the unexposed as well as the exposed hand. Under one condition, head movements were inhibited by placing S's head in a restraining device. Under a second condition, head movements were not restricted.

Hamilton (1964) found no evidence of intermanual transfer when movements of the head were restricted. There were significant aftereffects for the exposed hand but no significant aftereffects for the unexposed hand. This finding confirms Harris's finding under conditions entirely comparable to those which prevailed in the eye-hand coordination experiments which were reviewed earlier. The results obtained when head movement was not restricted did give evidence of intermanual transfer. There were significant aftereffects in the unexposed as well as the exposed hands, although the latter effects were significantly greater.

Hamilton suggests that under the conditions of free movement there are two changes which underlie adaptation: One change is a modification in the felt position of the hand. A second change involves "the sense of position of the neck-implication," i.e., the felt position of the neck and head. The latter change is the basis for the intermanual transfer to the unexposed hand. This interpretation would also explain why the aftereffects for the unexposed hand were smaller, since the unexposed hand would not be influenced by the changes in the felt position of the exposed hand. Hamilton's interpretation is obviously compatible with the hypothesis of proprioceptive shift favored by Harris.

A number of experiments by McLaughlin (McLaughlin & Bower, 1965a; McLaughlin & Bower, 1965b; McLaughlin & Rifkin, 1965) have also produced data which are consistent with Harris's hypothesis. McLaughin and Rifkin (1965) and McLaughlin and Bower (1965a) corroborated Harris's findings of changes in subjective straight ahead and auditory localization during adaptation to prismatic displacement of the hand. McLaughlin and Bower (1965b) have also reported a study of intermanual transfer. Each S received four series of tests in a single session. Each series consisted of the same nineteen judgments but in systematically varied order. The nineteen judgments were composed of four replications of a set of five judgments, with one judgment excluded. Each set consisted of the following five judgments: S set a vertical pointer at the subjective straight ahead, once with each hand; S set a pointer to coincide with a vertical line, once with each hand; and with full illumination and *only his right hand visible*, S repeated the "on line" judgment. The judgments were made while S looked through 20-pd prisms, with his head immobilized. This rather unusual procedure was designed to be used to examine intermanual transfer in tests of the subjective straight ahead and visual localization.

Figure 25 plots the means for each of the nineteen judgments. The course of adaptation can be traced by comparing successive instances of the same judgment. Intermanual transfer can be assessed by comparing the data points contributed by the right (exposed) and left hand for a given

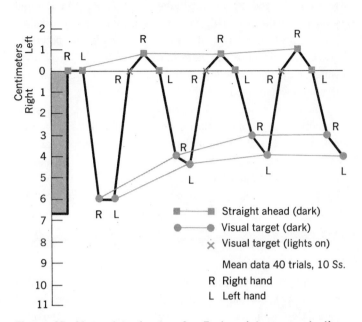

Figure 25. Mean data for ten Ss. Each point represents the mean of forty settings, four by each S. The zero point on the ordinate represents the veridical position of the visual target. Settings above zero represent settings to S's left; settings below zero represent settings to S's right. The thickened portion of the ordinate represents the direction and magnitude of the prism deviation. In half the trials the left-hand settings were made first, and in half the trials the prism deviation was to the left rather than to the right. The data have been transposed in order to make it possible to combine the results of all trials. (*From McLaughlin & Bower, 1965b, p. 69.*)

judgment. Figure 25 shows that the right hand provided evidence of adaptive shifts on both tests. Furthermore, there is no evidence of adaptive shift in straight ahead for the left (unexposed) hand. These findings confirm Harris's findings and support the proprioceptive hypothesis, but the results for the visual target marking do not agree with Harris's or Hamilton's observations. Figure 25 shows that intermanual transfer was almost complete for visual target marking.

McLaughlin and Bower (1965b) conclude that there are two components in adaptation to displacement: one is Harris's proprioceptive shift; the other component is ". . . a change in the apparent position of the visual target" which

McLaughlin and Bower attributed to a change in the felt position of the eye. This hypothesis is not very convincing, and before considering it seriously it would be better to search for uncontrolled determinants of visual localization which may have influenced S's response independently of the hand which was used.[18]

The experiments that have been reviewed tend, with some exception, to support Harris's hypothesis that a proprioceptive shift is the essential modification during adaptation to prismatic displacement of the hand. Other experimental evidence also seems most easily interpreted in terms of this hypothesis. For example, the evidence of interocular transfer of adaptation in split-brain monkeys (Bossom & Hamilton, 1963) and human Ss (Hajos & Ritter, 1965) is compatible with the hypothesis of proprioceptive shift. Wide acceptance of this hypothesis would represent a striking historical reversal. As was noted in the historical introduction to this chapter, the prevalent opinion among the philosophers of perception and many early psychologists, e.g., Berkeley (1709, in Luce & Jessop, 1948), Helmholtz (1866, transl., 1925), Dewey (1898), Carr (1925), was that vision is "educated" by touch. In the beginning, the only certain source of perceptual information is the tactual modality, and, through experience, vision comes to conform with touch. In the present context, this opinion would lead to the expectation that S will see his hand where he feels it to be. However, the evidence shows that the opposite is true. This evidence, together with other findings (e.g., Hay, Pick, & Ikeda, 1965; Neilsen, 1963; Rock & Victor, 1964) of visual dominance, seems to prepare the way for a diametrically opposed view of the dependency relationship between vision and touch.

A question of greater significance regarding the hypothesis of proprioceptive shift concerns its generality. Is the hypothesis plausible as an interpretation of the adaptation to other forms of distortion and other conditions of exposure? As yet (1965), there have been no published reports of experiments which have sought to assess the six alternative interpretations in a variety of adaptation situations other than the one discussed above. However, we did note the possibility of underlying proprioceptive shift in our discussion of Strat-

---

[18] However, see footnote 17 on p. 240 dealing with the findings reported by Kalil and Freedman (1966).

ton's inversion experiment. [Also see Walls (1951a, 1951b) on this point.] And Harris (1965) has made an extensive and persuasive argument that the generalized hypothesis of proprioceptive shift is an acceptable interpretation of the changes which underlie most adaptation to optical distortion. However, not all the cases yield to this interpretation with equal plausibility. For example, tilt adaptation and shifts in egocentric localization would seem to be readily interpreted as a change in the felt position of the head or body. On the other hand, an interpretation of curvature adaptation in terms of the proprioceptive hypothesis is not equally convincing; e.g., ". . . the S may feel that his eyes are moving in a straight line when they are actually tracing a curve" (Harris, 1965, p. 428).

Also remaining to be developed is an explicit hypothesis about the role of self-produced movement in affecting adaptation. If the hypothesis of proprioceptive shift is accepted, then it must also be concluded that self-produced movement is a precondition of this shift. Hamilton (1964) and Harris (1965) have suggested a number of possible ways to explain the importance of self-produced movement ". . . without postulating any motoric component in the end-product. For example, one might assume that the position sense during active movement differs from (and is more precise than) that during passive movement. Or motor changes may act as a catalyst that permits a joint's position sense to change" (Harris, 1965, p. 441). These aspects of the proprioceptive interpretation deserve further investigation.

Finally, one additional question needs to be considered: can conclusions regarding adaptation under conditions of long-term exposure be derived confidently from the studies of Harris, McLaughlin, and Hamilton, which involve very brief exposure durations? There is always the possibility that a number of different modifications occur but that the development of these changes requires different amounts of exposure to distortion. For example, a proprioceptive change may occur early during exposure, as Harris et al. found, to be followed or replaced later during the exposure period by a visual shift. In fact, this possibility is more than a conjecture. Hay and Pick (1966) have reported a series of three experiments on the effects of long-term exposure which lead them to conclude that the proprioceptive shift is only transient and is succeeded by a stable adaptation in the visual system. Their experiments follow the general outline suggested in Table 22, except that the tests were repeated at various times during the extended (40 days in Exp. I; 144 hours in Exp. II) exposure period. Six tests were used in Exp. II:

1
Eye-hand coordination. S marked a target, as in the Held-Gottlieb (1958) experiment.
2
Ear-hand coordination. S marked the location of a sound source while blindfolded.
3
Ear-eye coordination. S identified the visual direction of a sound source.
4
Eye-head coordination. S turned his head until he was directly facing a visible target. Shifts on this test implicate modified vision.
5
Ear-head coordination. S turned his head so that he was directly facing a sound source. Changes on this test would suggest modification of the auditory system.
6
Head-hand coordination. S pointed straight ahead of his nose, with his eyes shut. Shifts on this test identify changes in the felt position of the hand relative to the head.

During the exposure period, S wore 20-pd prismatic spectacles and walked about freely. The results are graphed in Figure 26. Early in the exposure period all the tests, with the exception of the ear-head tests, exhibited adaptive shifts. However, beginning with the 24-hour tests, those tests which implicated proprioceptive alterations displayed decreasing amounts of adaptive shift, while the tests which implicated visual modification displayed either increasing or sustained levels of adaptation. Hay and Pick (1966) conclude that ". . . the pattern of coordination changes shown in [Figure 26] is exactly that to be expected if a gradual adaptation in the visual system accompanies a rapid, largely transitory one in the proprioceptive system. The visual adaptation by itself accounts for the ear-eye and eye-head records; the transient proprioceptive adaptation by itself accounts for the ear-hand and head-hand records; and the two together account for the eye-hand record" (p. 155).

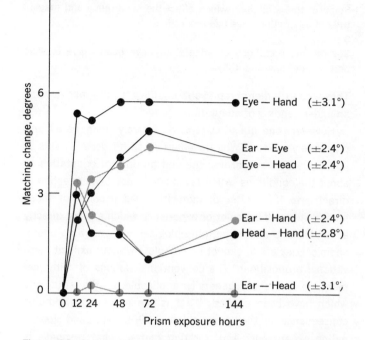

Figure 26. Changes in coordination on the six tests, using the preexposure measures as the base line. Positive changes are compensatory for the optical displacement or error producing for nonvisual tests in the direction opposite optical displacement. (*From Hay & Pick, 1966, p. 154.*)

The elaboration by Hay and Pick of Harris's approach has contributed importantly to a determination of the modifications which occur during exposure to optical distortion. There is good reason to believe that the finally accepted answer to the question "What is learned?" will incorporate two or three of the interpretations advanced by Harris, along with a specification of the conditions which favor the different types of modification.

Why does adaptation occur?

The studies which have been reviewed have made three important contributions:

1

They have provided controlled demonstrations of the organism's ability to adapt to a wide range of optical distortions.

2

Some of the conditions which affect the occurrence and magnitude of adaptation have been identified.

3

Several interpretations of adaptation have been made explicit and tested experimentally.

These contributions represent significant progress toward an understanding of adaptation.

However, one question remains entirely unanswered and only rarely asked: "Why do adaptive shifts occur?" This is not a question concerning the end product of adaptation or about the conditions which favor adaptation. The question is directed to the matter of motivation. An account of those modifications of behavior or experience which are not directly attributable to underlying physiological changes, e.g., photochemical depletion, cannot be complete without explicit motivational propositions. The conventional notions of reinforcement do not seem generally applicable to the situations which have been studied. What is the reinforcing stimulus consequence in the Held-Schlank (1959) eye-hand coordination experiment? And, for that matter, what response is being reinforced?

Except in the most cavalier application, it does not seem possible to offer a motivational account of adaptation in terms of conventional formulations of reinforcement, nor is a cognitive, information-processing interpretation (e.g., Weinstein, Sersen, Fisher, & Weisinger, 1964; Weinstein, Sersen, & Weinstein, 1964) able to explain why S's response is modified. The very fact that aftereffects occur makes a hypothesis of purposeful compensation implausible. Furthermore, in most experiments, it is difficult to determine what "decision-making processes" or cognitive deliberations S is supposed to be engaged in. Finally, in many of the situations S cannot possibly know whether his responses following adaptation are more appropriate or correct than preceding adaptation, since knowledge of results is not available to him.

The account which will be proposed seems to be implicit in many of the discussions of adaptation. The starting point is the observation that the conditions of the adaptation experiments are also conditions which create conflict. The conflict is in the form of a variety of discrepancies. These are chiefly of two general types, intersensory and intrasensory discrepancies. An example of the intersensory conflict is the discrepancy between visual and proprioceptive information, which has been described in detail in the previous section. An illustration of intrasensory conflict is provided by the experimental setting of Wallach, Kravitz, and Lindauer (1963).

A third source of conflict arises from a discrepancy between S's expectancies concerning the appearances of things and the way things actually appear when distorting devices intervene. This third type of discrepancy must be especially evident when S is permitted to move freely through a natural environment. One of or all these discrepancies are present in each of the adaptation situations. The presence of conflict or discrepancy may be a precondition for adaptation. Other evidence that conflict may be a favorable condition for perceptual learning was presented in Chapter 8.

It is obvious that the foregoing observations contribute to a motivational account of adaptation only if certain additional assumptions are made about the nature of conflict. The most general assumption is that discrepancies are disruptive and that there is a powerful tendency to eliminate discrepancies. Precedents for these assumptions may be found in more general discussions of conflict (e.g., Miller, in Koch, 1959; Festinger, 1957). Thus, the need to eliminate conflict is the motivational basis for the changes observed in adaptation experiments. While the foregoing analysis may be an acceptable account of the occurrence of change, the analysis does not specify the form which this change will take. Discrepancies may be nullified in a variety of ways, and an additional hypothesis is required to deal with the fact that certain forms of change seem to predominate. Here the reader may contribute his own speculation. These speculations will no doubt be very diverse. Two conjectures which seem implicit in the literature stress evolutionary selectivity and differential criterial validity. The investigations which would permit a decision between these and other alternatives have not been performed.[19]

---

[19] The reader who wishes to consider a different approach to the question of adaptation should see Taylor's book (1962). A simple summary statement of Taylor's admixture of mathematical set theory, cybernetic theory, and classic (circa 1943) Hullian S-R theory is impossible. The reader will have to make his own determination about the significance of Taylor's analysis for the questions of this chapter. Two excellent reviews are available to the reader who wishes guidelines to assist him, those of Hochberg (1965) and Pratt (1963).

References

Berkeley, G. An essay towards a new theory of vision. In A. A. Luce & T. E. Jessop (Eds.), *The works of George Berkeley Bishop of Cloyne.* New York: Nelson, 1948.

Boring, E. G. *Sensation and perception in the history of experimental psychology.* New York: Appleton-Century-Crofts, 1942.

Bossom, J., & Hamilton, C. R. Interocular transfer of prism-altered coordinations in split-brain monkeys. *J. Comp. Physiol. Psychol.,* 1963, **56,** 769–774.

Brewster, D. *Letters on natural magic, addressed to Sir Walter Scott.* London: J. Murray, 1831.

Brindley, G. S., & Merton, P. A. Absence of position sense in the eye. *J. Physiol.,* 1954, **153,** 127–130.

Dember, W. *Visual perception: the nineteenth century.* New York: Wiley, 1964.

Dennis, W. *Readings in general psychology.* Englewood Cliffs, N.J.: Prentice-Hall, 1949.

Descartes, R. *Tractatus de homine.* Amstelodami, 1686.

Efstathiou, Aglaia, & Held, R. Cross-modal transfer of adaptation to eye-hand rearrangement. Paper read at East. Psychol. Ass., Philadelphia, April, 1964.

Epstein, W. Experimental investigations of the genesis of visual space perception. *Psychol. Bull.,* 1964, **61,** 115–128.

Ewert, P. H. A study of the effect of inverted retinal stimulation upon spatially coordinated behavior. *Genet. Psychol. Monogr.,* 1930, **7,** 177–363.

Festinger, L. *A theory of cognitive dissonance.* New York: Harper & Row, 1957.

Gibson, J. J. Adaptation, aftereffect, and contrast in the perception of curved lines. *J. Exp. Psychol.,* 1933, **16,** 1–31.

Gibson, J. J. Introduction. In I. Kohler. The formation and transformation of the perceptual world. *Psychol. Issues,* 1964, **3,** No. 4.

Gibson, J. J., & Radner, Minnie. Adaptation, aftereffect, and contrast in the perception of tilted lines. I. Quantitative studies. *J. exp. Psychol.,* 1937, **20,** 453–467.

Hajos, A., & Ritter, M. Experiments to the problem of interocular transfer. *Acta Psychol.,* 1965, **24,** 81–90.

Hamilton, C. R. Intermanual transfer of adaptation to prisms. *Amer. J. Psychol.,* 1964, **77,** 457–462.

Hamilton, C. R., & Bossom, J. Decay of prism aftereffects. *J. Exp. Psychol.,* 1964, **67,** 148–150.

Harrington, T. L. Adaptation of humans to colored split-field glasses. *Psychonom. Sci.,* 1965, **3,** 71–72.

Harris, C. S. Adaptation to displaced vision: a proprioceptive change. (Doctoral dissertation, Harvard Univer.) Ann Arbor, Mich.: University Microfilms, 1963, No. 63–8162. (a)

Harris, C. S. Adaptation to displaced vision: visual, motor or proprioceptive change. *Science,* 1963, **140,** 812–813. (b)

Harris, C. S. Perceptual adaptation to inverted, reversed and displaced vision. *Psychol. Rev.*, 1965, **72**, 419–444.

Hay, J. C., & Pick, H. L., Jr. Visual and proprioceptive adaptation to optical displacement of the visual stimulus. *J. Exp. Psychol.*, 1966, **71**, 150–158.

Hay, J. C., & Pick, H. L., Jr. Gaze-contingent adaptation and prism orientation. *J. Exp. Psychol.*, in press.

Hay, J. C., Pick, H. L., Jr., & Ikeda, Karren. Visual capture produced by prism spectacles. *Psychonom. Sci.*, 1965, **2**, 215–216.

Held, R. Exposure-history as a factor in maintaining stability of perception and coordination. *J. Nerv. Ment. Dis.*, 1961, **32**, 26–32.

Held, R. Adaptation to rearrangement and visual-spatial after-effects. *Psychol. Beitrage*, 1962, **6**, 439–450.

Held, R. Movement-produced stimulation is important in prism-induced after-effects: a reply to Hochberg. *Percept. Mot. Skills*, 1963, **16**, 764.

Held, R., & Bossom, J. Neonatal deprivation and adult rearrangement: complementary techniques for analyzing plastic sensory-motor coordinations. *J. Comp. Physiol. Psychol.*, 1961, **54**, 33–37.

Held, R., & Gottlieb, N. Technique for studying adaptation to disarranged hand-eye coordination. *Percept. Mot. Skills*, 1958, **8**, 83–86.

Held, R., & Hein, A. Adaptation of disarranged hand-eye coordination contingent upon re-afferent stimulation. *Percept. Mot. Skills*, 1958, **8**, 87–90.

Held, R., & Hein, A. Movement-produced stimulation in the development of visually guided behavior. *J. Comp. Physiol. Psychol.*, 1963, **56**, 872–876.

Held, R., & Mikaelian, Harutune. Motor-sensory feedback versus need in adaptation to rearrangement. *Percept. Mot. Skills*, 1964, **18**, 685–688.

Held, R., & Rekosh, J. Motor sensory feedback and the geometry of visual space. *Science*, 1963, **141**, 722–723.

Held, R., & Schlank, M. Adaptation to disarranged eye-hand coordination in the distance dimension. *Amer. J. Psychol.*, 1959, **72**, 603–605.

Held, R. & Schlank, M. An attempt that failed to reproduce a study of disarranged eye-hand coordination. *Percept. Mot. Skills*, 1964, **19**, 301.

Helmholtz, H. von. *Physiological optics.* (Transl. by J. P. C. Southall.) Vol. III. Optical Society of America, 1925.

Helson, H. *Adaptation-level theory.* New York: Harper & Row, 1964.

Higginson, G. D. An examination of some phases of space perception. *Psychol. Rev.*, 1937, **44**, 77–96.

Hochberg, J. On the importance of movement-produced stimulation in prism-induced aftereffects. *Percept. Mot. Skills*, 1963, **16**, 544.

Hochberg, J. Review of J. G. Taylor, *The behavioral basis of perception. Amer. J. Psychol.*, 1965, **78**, 511–514.

Howard, I. P., Craske, B., & Templeton, W. B. Visuomotor adaptation to discordant exafferent stimulation. *J. Exp. Psychol.*, 1965, **70**, 189–191.

Kalil, R. E., & Freedman, S. J. Persistence of ocular rotation following compensation for displaced vision. *Percept. Mot. Skills*, 1966, **22**, 135–139.

Kimble, G. S. *Hilgard and Marquis' conditioning and learning.* New York: Appleton-Century-Crofts, 1961.

Kohler, I. Umgesunnung in Wahrehmungsbereich. *Pyramide*, 1953, **3**, 92–95, 109–113.

Kohler, I. Die Methode des Brillenversuchs in der Sahrnehmungspsychologie mit Bemerkungen zur Lehre von der Adaptation. (The use of distorting lenses as a method of studying the psychology of perception, with remarks on adaptation.) *Z. exp. angewand. Psychol.*, 1956, **3**, 381–417.

Kohler, I. Experiments with goggles. *Scient. Amer.*, 1962, **206**, 62–84.

Kohler, I. Über und Wandlungen der Wahrnehmungswelt. *SB Ost. Akad. Wiss.*, 1951, **227**, 1–118. (Transl. by H. Fiss, The formation and transformation of the perceptual world. *Phychol. Issues*, 1964, **3**, No. 4.)

LeConte, J. Erect vision and single vision. *Science*, 1895, **2**, 629–630.

Lotze, H. *Outlines of psychology.* (Transl. by G. T. Ladd.) Boston: Ginn, 1886.

Luce, A. A. (Ed.) Philosophical commentaries generally called the Commonplace Book: George Berkeley Bishop of Cloyne. London: Nelson, 1944.

McCullough, C. The conditioning of color perception. *Amer. J. Psychol.*, 1965, **78**, 362–378.

McLaughlin, S. C., & Bower, J. L. Auditory localization and judgments of straight ahead during adaptation to prism. *Psychonom. Sci.*, 1965, **2**, 283–284. (a)

McLaughlin, S. C., & Bower, J. L. Selective intermanual transfer of adaptive effects during adaptation to prism. *Psychonom. Sci.*, 1965, **3**, 69–70. (b)

McLaughlin, S. C., & Rifkin, K. I. Change in straight ahead during adaptation to prism. *Psychonom. Sci.*, 1965, **2**, 107–108.

Mikaelian, Harutune, & Held, R. Two types of adaptation to an optically-rotated visual field. *Amer. J. Psychol.*, 1964, **77**, 257–263.

Miller, N. E. Liberalization of basic S-R concepts: extension to conflict behavior, motivation and social learning. In S. Koch (Ed.), *Psychology: a study of a science.* Vol. 2. New York: McGraw-Hill, 1959.

Morant, R. B., & Beller, H. K. Adaptation to prismatically rotated visual fields. *Science*, 1965, **148**, 530–531.

255 Adaptation to transformed stimulation

Neilsen, T. L. Volition: a new experimental approach. *Scand. J. Psychol.*, 1963, **4**, 225–230.

Ogle, K. *Optics: an introduction for ophthalmologists.* New York: Saunders, 1961.

Peterson, J., & Peterson, J. K. Does practice with inverting lenses make vision normal? *Psychol. Monogr.*, 1938, **50**, 12–37.

Pick, H. L., Jr., & Hay, J. C. Adaptation to prismatic distortion. *Psychonom. Sci.*, 1964, **1**, 199–200.

Pick, H. L., Jr., & Hay, J. C. A passive test of the Held reaference hypothesis. *Percept. Mot. Skills*, 1965, **21**, 1070–1072.

Pick, H. L., Jr., & Hay, J. C. Gaze-contingent adaptation to prism spectacles. *Amer. J. Psychol.*, 1966, in press.

Polyak, S. The history of our knowledge of the structure and functioning of the eye. In P. Kornfeld (Ed.), *The human eye in anatomical transparencies.* Rochester, N.Y.: Bausch and Lomb, 1943.

Pratt, C. C. Review of J. G. Taylor, *The behavioral basis of perception. Contemp. Psychol.*, 1963, **8**, 257–258.

Riesen, A. H. Studying perceptual development using the technique of sensory deprivation. *J. Nerv. Ment. Dis.*, 1961, **132**, 21–25.

Riesen, A. H., & Aarons, L. Visual movement and intensity discrimination in cats after early deprivation of pattern vision. *J. Comp. Physiol. Psychol.*, 1959, **52**, 142–149.

Rock, I., & Victor, J. Vision and touch: an experimentally created conflict between the two senses. *Science*, 1964, **143** (3606), 594–596.

Singer, G., & Day, R. H. Spatial adaptation and aftereffect with optically transformed vision: effects of active and passive responding and the relationship between test and exposure responses. *J. Exp. Psychol.*, 1966, **71**, 725–731.

Smith, K. U., & Smith, W. M. *Perception and motion.* Philadelphia, Pa.: Saunders, 1962.

Snyder, F. W., & Pronko, N. H. *Vision with spatial inversion.* Wichita, Kans.: Univer. of Wichita Press, 1952.

Snyder, F. W., & Snyder, C. W. Vision with spatial inversion. A follow-up study. *Psychol. Rec.*, 1957, **7**, 20–31.

Stevens, S. S. Problems and methods of psychophysics. *Psychol. Bull.*, 1958, **54**, 177–196.

Stratton, G. M. Some preliminary experiments on vision without inversion of the retinal image. *Psychol. Rev.*, 1896, **3**, 611–617.

Stratton, G. M. Upright vision and the retinal image. *Psychol. Rev.*, 1897, **4**, 182–187. (a)

Stratton, G. M. Vision without inversion of the retinal image. *Psychol. Rev.*, 1897, **4**, 341–360; 463–481. (b)

Taylor, J. G. *The behavioral basis of perception.* New Haven, Conn.: Yale Univer. Press, 1962.

Von Holst, E. Relations between the central nervous system and the peripheral organs. *Brit. J. Anim. Behav.*, 1954, **2**, 89–94.

Walk, R. D., & Gibson, E. J. A comparative and analytic study of visual depth perception. *Psychol. Monogr.,* 1961, **75,** No. 15.

Wallach, H., Kravitz, J. H., & Lindauer, J. A passive condition for rapid adaption to displaced visual direction. *Amer. J. Psychol.,* 1963, **76,** 568–578.

Walls, G. L. The problem of visual direction. Part I. The history to 1900. *Amer. J. Optom., Arch. Amer. Acad. Optom.,* 1951, **28,** 55–83, (a)

Walls, G. L. The problem of visual direction. Part III. Experimental attacks and their results. *Amer. J. Optom., Arch. Amer. Acad. Optom.,* 1951, **28,** 173–212. (b)

Weinstein S., Sersen, E. A., Fisher, L., & Weisinger, M. Is reafference necessary for visual adaptation? *Percept. Mot. Skills,* 1964, **18,** 641–648.

Weinstein S., Sersen, E. A., & Weinstein, D. S. An attempt to replicate a study of disarranged eye-hand coordination. *Percept. Mot. Skills,* 1964, **18,** 629–632.

Chapter ten
Developmental studies of perception

The potential contribution of developmental studies has been aptly expressed by Hazlitt: "Nothing gives a better insight into the working of the mind than the study of the development of behavior . . . the man who has heard the beginning of a story is ipso facto a more reliable judge of the credibility of the ending than the man who has come in at the middle" (quoted in Munn, 1955, p. VI). In the context of this book, the emphasis will be on perceptual development. More specifically, the question of perceptual development will be explored to determine how this field of investigation can contribute to our knowledge of perceptual learning.

General observations

The ontogenetic development of perception has been a matter of long-standing interest among European psychologists. The emergence of Gestalt psychology, with its emphasis on innate organizational factors, stimulated efforts to determine whether perception followed a developmental course. Piaget's theoretical writings served as another very important stimulus for investigation. Piaget and his associates have contributed and continue to contribute extensively to the experimental literature. In contrast to the active interest among European psychologists, American psychologists during the first half of this century devoted little attention to the question of the development of perception. However, the post-World War II period has been marked by a notable intensification of interest in the psychology of perception, and with it a new interest in the developmental question. As a result, there exists at present a fairly extensive body of research literature. Summaries of this literature have been presented by Baldwin (1955, Ch. 3), Munn (1955, Ch. 8), E. J. Gibson and Olum (1960), Wohlwill (1960), and E. J. Gibson (1963).

In this chapter, no effort will be made to duplicate the coverage of Baldwin, Munn, E. J. Gibson, and Wohlwill. There is little to be gained by exhibiting, once again, the general state of disarray in the field. In addition, a good deal of research, summarized by the above reviewers, is characterized by inadequate experimental design and data analysis. As Wohlwill (1960) has observed, the studies place a ". . . heavy strain . . . on the reader's willingness to assume an attitude towards the mere possible" (p. 251). For these reasons, an extensive review of the literature will be eschewed in favor of a more detailed consideration of a number of illustrative studies.

The studies which have been selected are exceptions (certainly not the *only* ones) to Wohlwill's unfavorable characterization. They were selected in accordance with two minimal requirements:

1
Age was one of the independent variables, and an adequate number of values of the age variable were sampled. This can be accomplished either by a cross-sectional technique or a longitudinal technique. The selected studies have employed the former technique, which involves the use of independent age groups.
2
The experimental procedures and especially the constant factors, e.g., instructions, and dependent measures were carefully controlled.

Finally, experiments were favored which articulated or attempted to test an explicit hypothesis about the mechanisms or processes underlying the expected developmental change.

Additional comment is in order regarding two kinds of studies which were excluded for reasons other than those given previously. Investigations of sensory processes, which are considered to be related directly to specifiable properties of isolable receptor mechanisms, were excluded. The selections have been restricted to investigations of the perceptual phenomena which have been emphasized in the earlier chapters.

The second omission requires more extended explanation. Omitted are the growing number of investigations of the perceptual functioning of "naïve" organisms. The organisms in question are either deprived of visual stimulation from birth until the time of testing or are tested at the first practical moment following birth. The best representatives of this approach are the experiments of Walk and Gibson (1961), Fantz (1961), and Hershenson (1964).

These studies have used the stimulus-preference method, apparently originated by Staples (1932). The S is exposed to a number of discriminable (by an adult S) stimuli, and E observes whether S exhibits a preference for one of the stimuli. The preferential response is one already available in S's repertory, prior to the test. Two responses which have been used are fixation of a target and locomotion. If S exhibits a preference, then it is concluded that he has the capacity to discriminate between the stimuli. By suitable variations of the stimuli, it is possible to determine the specific property which is the discriminative cue. Failure to make a preferential response is often taken as evidence that S is unable to discriminate. If a significant preferential response is made by naïve Ss, then it is concluded that learning or previous exposure is not necessary for the perceptual function in question. The absence of a preferential response is taken to imply that learning is necessary for the emergence of the discriminative capacity.

Parenthetically, we may note that this rationale makes a positive conclusion about learning, contingent on demonstration of the null hypothesis. This is never a desirable requirement for support of a thesis. In this case, it is especially prejudicial, because the "nativistic" hypothesis does not make a one-directional prediction. Only significant preference is required, not preference for a given stimulus, designated in advance.

These investigations seem better suited for the exploration of the nativism-empiricism issue than for an examination of the developmental question [see Epstein (1964) for a discussion of the nativism-empiricism question and a summary of the experimental literature]. The finding that prior exposure or learning is not necessary for the original occurrence of discrimination in no way precludes the possibility of developmental changes as the organism ages. These changes may take the form of a capability for increasingly finer discriminations. It is noteworthy that the discrimination of gross differences has been required in most studies of naïve organisms. Perceptual development could consist of increasing differentiation, starting from an innate minimum discriminative capacity. It is also possible that increasng age may be accompanied by the development of error. Thus, the infant might exhibit perfect constancy, but overconstancy may develop as he grows older.

In summary, the findings of significant preference in naïve Ss is compatible with subsequent developmental change. The principal contribution of the naïve organism study, insofar as the developmental question is concerned, is that it allows E to extend the range of values of the age variable. But this contribution is not easily realized, since the tasks set for the infants are too easy for older Ss and those suitable for older Ss are too difficult for infants. Thus, there may be no single set of test conditions which can be used over the entire age range.

Nor are the results of a study of naïve organisms more useful in the case of the failure to observe a preferential response. Strictly speaking, under these circumstances, nothing can be concluded about perceptual learning. However, even if the conclusion is accepted that learning is necessary, nothing is known about the course of learning and its underlying mechanisms.

The investigations of naïve organisms are more informative when their procedures are expanded to include systematic variations of the relevant properties of visual stimulation. An example of this type of study is Hess's investigation (1950) of the development of the chick's responses to light-and-shade cues of depth. Chicks were reared under two different conditions of illumination. The control chicks were reared in cages illuminated from above. The experimental chicks were reared in cages that were illuminated from below. Thus, the two groups experienced different distributions of light and shade. A test was designed to explore the chicks' utilization of light-shade distribution as a cue for depth. The test was administered at 1-week intervals, beginning at 1 week following hatching and continuing to 7 weeks of age.

This type of study has several objectives:

1
Determination of the original status of a response
2
Determination of developmental changes in the response
3
An evaluation of the conditions that are responsible for the character of the observations made in exploring the first two questions

Unfortunately, studies of the type performed by Hess are still rare [see Walk & Gibson (1961), Epstein (1964), and Fantz (1965) for reviews of the studies of naïve organisms].

Methodological considerations

All methodological considerations which apply to the design and interpretation of experimental studies apply to the developmental studies. However, two specific requirements deserve to be reemphasized here. Excellent discussions of these requirements have been provided by E. J. Gibson and Olum (1960) and Kessen (1960).

Control of the independent variable   Two preliminary decisions are required of the investigator who wishes to make cross-sectional comparisons among different age groups. First, he must decide how much variation he can tolerate on dimensions other than age. This is almost a meaningless question unless the investigator has some clues concerning the identity of the age-correlated variations which are potentially confounding. He must be able to identify the variables which may be safely disregarded in the selection of Ss as well as the variables which must be taken into account. With this knowledge, he may select his samples at the various age levels so that the values of the relevant variables are randomly distributed within each sample. But this sampling procedure may not always be feasible and sometimes may be virtually impossible. Often E must use the restricted number of children who are readily available, regardless of considerations of their representativeness in relation to a larger population. In other cases, the ideal of random distribution is difficult to achieve because the variable in question is tied too closely to age differences. As an example, in a cross-sectional study of distance perception using groups ranging from 6 to 16 years it seems most unlikely that the range of heights could be distributed randomly among the age groups. There is reason to suspect that the angle of observation, which will vary as a function of height, may affect distance judgments. Therefore, it is incumbent upon the investigator who wishes to make statements of the form R = f(Age) to control the variations in height. Harway's experiment (1963), which will be described later, will illustrate how this control can be achieved.

A second decision regarding the age variable concerns the choice of the particular age groups to be included in the study. It is risky to draw conclusions about the course of development from data drawn from very few age groups. The risk is compounded when these few groups are either bunched together on the low end of the age scale or very widely separated. In both cases, the experiment will not be sensitive to the distinctive features which may characterize a developmental trend, e.g., nonlinear characteristics. The cross-sectional study should include a sufficient number of age groups, and the ages that are selected should tap the developmental period at successive stages throughout the full course of development.

Comparability of conditions   Investigators who have used the cross-sectional approach have frequently introduced variations in the procedures for the different groups. For example, a standard psychophysical method will be used for the older Ss, but a modified version will be used for the young children. Usually, the modification is justified on the ground that the children cannot understand or perform the required operations. Needless to say, modifications, whatever their exigency, can create problems in determining the comparability of the experimental conditions for the different groups. Therefore, two general rules have been proposed by methodologists [e.g., E. J. Gibson & Olum (1960); Wohlwill (1960)] in this field:

1
Differences between the procedures, applied to the various age groups, should be kept to the minimum necessary for the experimental purposes.

2
The modifications should not violate the methodological requirements of acceptable response measurement.

On the other side of the question, the E who uses identical
procedures for all age groups should ascertain that the
instructions and operations are interpreted similarly by all
Ss.

Illustrative investigations of the development of perception

This section will be devoted chiefly to a discussion of a few
selected investigations of the development of perception.
These studies have been concerned with the perceptual
phenomena which were treated in the previous chapters:
form perception, size-distance perception, and motion perception. All veteran experimenters have ruefully learned that
no single experiment can successfully settle a question to
everyone's satisfaction. The experiments which will be discussed are no exception to this discouraging rule. Therefore,
these studies are not being presented in the fond belief that
they offer final, definitive resolutions of their respective
problems. The main objective of this presentation is to
assess the potential of developmental studies whose primary
claim for our attention is not simply a welcoming attitude
toward the "mere possible." Consideration of these studies
may provide the reader with guidelines for a more systematic
developmental study of perception.

Perception of distance   A thorough review of the developmental studies of the perception of size and distance has
been presented by Wohlwill (1963). Our discussion will
begin with the investigations of distance perception reported
by Harway (1963) and Wohlwill (1963, 1965). Harway's
study is especially interesting because, unlike many of the
previous investigators, Harway attempted to assess the importance of two rationally selected age-correlated variables.
The two variables are height and interocular distance. Both
these factors vary systematically with age, and both may
affect distance perception. Increasing height may affect apparent distance by decreasing the differences subtended by a

specific horizontal stretch at different distances from S. Increases in interocular distance may enhance the effectiveness of binocular depth cues.

There were sixty Ss, grouped at five age levels, with median ages of 5 years 6 months, 7 years 2 months, 9 years 11 months, 11 years 9 months, and 23 years. The judgments followed a procedure introduced by Gilinsky (1951, 1960). The Ss stood at the end of a grass field and directed E to mark off successive 1-foot intervals. A 1-foot ruler, placed on the ground at S's feet, served as a standard. S was instructed to tell E when a marker in the field had been moved ". . . as far . . . as the ruler is long." The nearest 1-foot stretch began 1 foot from S, and nineteen successive 1-foot estimates were obtained for most Ss. (Some Ss provided such gross overestimates that the entire field was traversed before nineteen units were judged.) Each S provided judgments under two conditions: one at normal height, the other at an adjusted height. For the latter condition, the children stood on an adjustable platform, so that the total height was 5 feet 6½ inches for the children in all four groups. The adults' adjusted height was accomplished by requiring them to kneel.

Harway's task is analogous to that posed in a size-constancy experiment. The principal difference is that a horizontal extent is judged at varying distances, rather than a frontoparallel extent. In Harway's experiment, perfect distance constancy would be evidenced by invariantly accurate estimates of the successive 1-foot extents. Progressive underestimation of successive 1-foot extents is equivalent to progressive underconstancy. Figure 27 shows the average constant error for successive distance judgments obtained under the condition of normal height. The curves on the left of the graph represent the visual-angle functions for a 1-foot ruler at S's feet and nodal points at four representative heights.

Figure 27 shows that the 1-foot extents were progressively underestimated with increasing distance. Unfortunately, the procedure of obtaining judgments of increasingly distant extents, in ordered succcession, confounds the distance variable with a practice variable. Figure 27 also suggests that the rate of change (slope) with increasing distance was greater for the three younger groups as contrasted with the

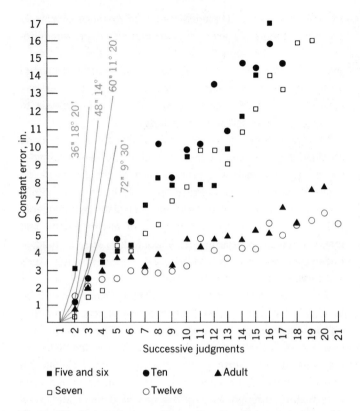

Figure 27. Constant error for successive distance judgments. The line curves at the left represent visual-angle functions for a hypothetical S whose eyes are 36, 48, 60, and 72 inches above the ground. (*From Harway*, 1963, p. 387.)

two older groups. An analysis of variance confirmed these observations and also showed that the height at which the judgments were made did not affect the judgments. The pattern of constant errors was the same for the normal-height and adjusted-height conditions. Further evidence on this point and on the influence of interpupillary distance was obtained by computing two correlations for each group: (1) between the distribution of normal heights and distance judgments and (2) between the distribution of interocular distances and distance judgments. No significant correlations were found. In other words, when age is held constant, distance judgments are not associated with height or interocular separation.

Harway's results reveal a developmental trend in the perception of distance. Underestimation of distance extents is greater and more closely correlated with visual-angle requirements for Ss between 5 and 10 years old than for Ss 12 years and older. Figure 27 indicates that a marked change in the magnitude of underestimation occurs between the ages of 10 and 12 years. Harway offers no hypothesis to account for the developmental results.

How general are Harway's findings? Will similar results be obtained for a variety of task variables and over a broader range of distances? A cursory review of the literature on space perception (Denis-Prinzhorn, 1960; Epstein, 1963) provides ample reason for believing that distance judgments will vary as a function of a number of environmental and task variables. An experiment by Wohlwill (1963) conducted under conditions which differed greatly from Harway's study will serve to demonstrate this fact.

The experimental setting and procedure were those used in Wohlwill's investigation (1964) of the effects of practice on distance judgments (see page 91). The experimental environment consisted of a large box, into which S looked monocularly. By inserting appropriately designed panels, the optical texture of the floor of the box could be varied from zero texture through varying degrees of density and regularity. The task required S to bisect a 90-centimeter extent of the floor. The extent was demarcated by two red arrows that touched the floor, the nearer one located 63 centimeters from the eyepiece. S was instructed to direct E to stop a moving pointer when it reached the objective midpoint between the two arrows. Ascending and descending judgments were obtained for each of the six floor panels. A practice session preceded the test judgments. This was done in order to guarantee that the children understood the task. The Ss were five groups of 24 Ss each, taken from grades 1 (mean ages 6 years 10 months), 2 (8 years 10 months), 5 (11 years), 8 (13 years 11 months), and 11 (16 years 10 months).

The results showed significant main effects of age and texture, as well as a significant interaction. The interaction effect was due mainly to a difference between the older and younger groups for only one texture (maximal density and regularity). Therefore, the texture variable will be disregarded, in order to exhibit the age function more clearly.

Figure 28 presents the mean errors for the bisection judgments for each age group, for all textures combined. The
kindergarten (K) data are from a supplementary study; the
adult data are from another study (Wohlwill, 1964). Positive errors indicate overconstancy: S judged the midpoint to
be back of its objective midpoint. Negative errors indicate
underconstancy: S judged the midpoint to be to the front of
the objective midpoint.

Figure 28 shows an overall trend from underconstancy
for the two younger groups to overconstancy for the older
groups. In contrast to Harway's findings of increasing accuracy with age, Wohlwill found decreasing accuracy with
age. An additional developmental trend was noted in the
differences between the intervals of uncertainty for the
groups. The interval decreased steadily with age. Older Ss
displayed greater precision in their judgments, as well as
greater error.

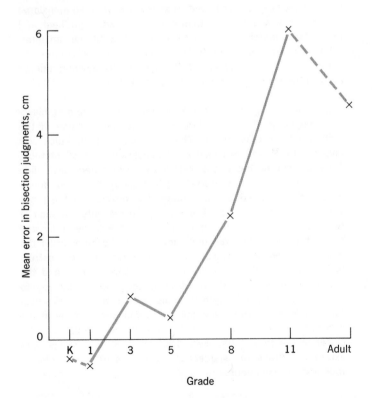

Figure 28. Age changes in errors for bisections of a 90-centi-
meter distance. (*From Wohlwill*, 1963, p. 298.)

A similar study, involving the perception of relative distance in photographic slides, has been reported by Wohlwill (1965). The experiment was conducted to confirm the findings of the earlier (Wohlwill, 1963) study, and in particular to reexplore the possibility of an age-texture interaction. The hypothesis was ". . . that age and texture would interact, with age differences being maximal under low-texture conditions and minimal under high-texture conditions" (Wohlwill, 1965, p. 164). The chief differences between this study and the one described in the preceding paragraph are the following:

1

The viewing-box scene was not exposed directly. Instead, S was shown a projected photographic slide of the scene. The textured panels of varying regularity and density were photographed under conditions that were designed to duplicate the optic array available to S's eye at the observation aperture of the viewing box. It was hoped, that the use of two-dimensional projections would force S to rely on the texture gradient and that this condition would be favorable for exhibiting an interaction between age and texture. Instead of the pointers to demarcate the standard extent, the figures of a cow and a horse marked the near and far boundary of the extent.

2

The second main difference was the method of obtaining bisection judgments. The procedure was a modified version of the method of constant stimuli. This modified method, which was invented by Piaget, is called the "clinical concentric" method. For each texture, two series of slides were prepared. Each slide showed the "cow" and "horse" against one of the backgrounds and a fence located between them. The position of the fence varied from slide to slide. The slides were presented in each of two orders: in one order the positions of the fence converged concentrically on the true midpoint, and in the other order the fence diverged concentrically from the midpoint. The instructions were as follows: "Do you see the cow in front and the horse way in back, and the fence in between? I want you to make believe that you were standing right in the field in which this picture was taken. Now tell me, if you were looking at the cow and the horse in that field, which do you think would be closer to the fence" (Wohlwill, 1965, p. 168). The slides were exposed in "rapid-fire sequence." Each S made judgments for four texture conditions.

There were 120 Ss, evenly distributed among five age groups: grade 1 (6 years 11 months), grade 4 (9 years 8 months), grade 8 (13 years 8 months), grade 11 (17 years), and adults. The results did not agree with the findings of the earlier study by Wohlwill (1963). All Ss exhibited undercon- stancy, i.e., displacement of the apparent midpoint toward the front. The constant error diminished as the texture be- came more determinate, e.g., high density and high regu- larity. The error also decreased as age increased, the great- est diminution occurring between grade 8 and grade 11. However, the changes correlated with age were not as pro- nounced as in the earlier study. These results seem to be in greater accord with Harway's findings than with Wohlwill's previous experiment.

These studies, and those (e.g., Denis-Prinzhorn, 1960) which have not been described, permit only a limited conclu- sion. The evidence suggests that changes in the accuracy of distance perception accompany changes in age. However, the direction and rate of change cannot be presently stated. It seems likely that the exact characteristics of the develop- mental trend which is observed will depend on features of the experimental situation. This remark certainly must rank as a scientific truism. Nevertheless, to the degree that these contingencies are not simply artifactual, they present prob- lems for the generalized developmental hypotheses. To be useful, these hypotheses must specify precisely those condi- tions under which a predicted shift will be observed. Stated somewhat differently, the developmental theory of distance perception must explain the interaction between age and the task and environmental variables.

Perception of size with distance variable If distance judgments vary as a function of age, so should size judg- ments (Epstein, Park, & Casey, 1961). Most of the studies of this question have only limited value. Their limitations stem from the restricted conditions that have been studied. For example, a great number of experiments purporting to study size constancy have not varied distance. Instead, the standard and variable are placed at two different distances, which remain the same throughout the experiment [see Wohlwill's (1963) review.] This procedure provides only minimal information about the pivotal relationship involved in size perception.

Two developmental studies which have investigated size

perception over a range of distance have been reported by Beyrl (1926) and Zeigler and Leibowitz (1957). Beyrl used the method of constant stimuli to obtain size judgments from seventy-five children between the ages of 2 and 10 years and from five adults. The experiment was conducted in a well-illuminated room. The standard was a disk or cube located at a distance of 1 meter from S. The comparison stimuli were presented at each of seven distances, ranging from 2 to 11 meters. Although the procedure involved a great number of comparisons, Beyrl found that the children remained motivated and attentive throughout. The results showed an overall tendency for size underestimation which decreased with age. More interesting is an apparent interaction between distance and age. The effects of increasing distance diminished as age increased. For example, the matches for a 10-centimeter standard disk ranged from 12.25 to 18 centimeters, 10.5 to 15 centimeters, 10.25 to 12 centimeters, and 10 to 10.5 centimeters for the 2-year, 5-year, 9-year, and adult groups, respectively.

Zeigler and Leibowitz (1957) obtained a similar pattern of results. The procedure was modeled after that used in the classic experiment by Holway and Boring (1941) on the determinants of perceived size. The S sat at the junction of an L-shaped arrangement of two alleys. The comparison alley contained a dowel located at a distance of 5 feet from S's eye. The length of this dowel could be varied continuously. In the standard alley, the standard dowels were presented at distances of 10, 30, 60, 80, and 100 feet. Following the procedure of the Holway-Boring study, the lengths of the standards were selected so that at the respective distances the standards subtended the same visual angle, 0.96°, at S's eye. Normal illumination prevailed, and S viewed the scene with unimpeded binocular vision. The instructions for both children and adults were as follows: "I am going to move this stick (comparison) up and down. I want you to tell me when it looks as high as the one out there (standard)" (Zeigler and Leibowitz, 1957, p. 106).

There were only thirteen Ss, one 7 years old, five 8 years, two 9 years, and five men ranging from 18 to 24 years. Needless to say, this is not an adequate sampling of Ss for the purpose of demonstrating a developmental function.

However, there was evidence of a marked difference between the children and the adults. The adults showed a high degree of constancy, although there was a small negative constant error at the three farthest distances. The children also exhibited constancy at the shortest distance. However, for the remaining distances, their matches were underestimations. The magnitude of these underestimations increased with distance. Thus, the same interaction between age and distance which was observed by Beyrl was also obtained in the Zeigler and Leibowitz study.

These two experiments have produced comparable results despite the procedural differences between them. One difference which should be noted concerns the relative distance of the standard and variable. In Beyrl's study, the standard was near and the variable was distant; in the study by Zeigler and Leibowitz, the positions of the standard and variable were the reverse. Therefore, the results are obtained even when the "error of the standard" (see Vurpillot, 1959) should produce overestimation of the standard.

We have considered experiments that examined perceived size and perceived distance separately. By comparing the results of the separate experiments, it may be possible to derive certain inferences about the development of the relationship between perceived size and perceived distance. However, the inconsistent results of the experiments which have examined the dependence of perceived distance on age prohibit ready inferences about the size-distance relationship. The only experiment to obtain both size and distance judgments is an investigation by Wohlwill (1962a) of the responses of children and adults to an illusion of perspective. However, since no significant developmental trends were noted, this experiment does not contribute to our question.

One type of experiment which could contribute significant information is an expanded Holway-Boring experiment. Like the original Holway-Boring (1941) study, the distance of the standard and the availability of distance cues should be varied. However, the proposed experiment would vary the age of the Ss and the attitudes of judgments, and obtain distance judgments. In addition to providing data for the assessment of the size-distance relationship, this study would enable us to examine the possibility that there are different developmental trends for the various distance cues, as well as differential trends for the various attitudes of judgments.

The perception of form   There have been a variety of emphases in the developmental investigations of form perception. One type of study has focused on developmental differences in part-whole or figure-ground perception (e.g., Elkind, Koegler, & Go, 1964; Ghent, 1956). Unfortunately, many of the studies have used meaningful, representative materials as stimuli. For example, overlapping outline drawings of a violin, drum, and clarinet were used in one study. The use of meaningful forms introduces an obvious confounding of differential perceptual organization with differential availability of verbal designations of the various alternatives. Using nonrepresentative forms enables E to minimize this problem. A number of studies that have used nonrepresentative forms (e.g., Ghent, 1956, Exp. II) have followed a procedure that is poorly suited to the study of form perception. The procedure was that of Gottschaldt's embedded-figures test. The Ss were told to trace the part of the complex figure which looked exactly like the simple figure. This task is too complex for the intended purpose of determining differences in the capacity for form discrimination. It probably would be useful to begin by studying this question at a more primitive level. Thus, the rules of figure-ground articulation (Koffka, 1935, pp. 190–196) might be individually investigated to determine the presence of developmental trends. The studies (e.g., Rush, 1937) of age-correlated changes in the effectiveness of various grouping principles should be reexamined for their relevance to this question.

A second group of experiments has been concerned with the role of spatial orientation in the discrimination of forms. Several different questions have been examined:

1
Are unfamiliar, nonrepresentative geometric forms seen as having a "right side up" by Ss of all ages?
2
Do changes in the orientation of a form affect its recognizability in the same way for children and adults?
3
Are children able to discriminate between forms which differ only in orientation?

Although these questions have a long history, no conclusive answers are available. A number of studies by Ghent (Ghent, 1960; Ghent, 1961; Ghent, 1964; Ghent and Bernstein, 1961) illustrate the experimental approaches to these questions.

The experiment which has been selected for detailed examination is a study of the development of the ability to discriminate letterlike forms. This study by E. J. Gibson, J. J. Gibson, Pick, and Osser (1962) is notable for its careful attention to the properties of the stimulus forms, as well as a general thoroughness of analysis not often matched in the developmental literature. Another point of special interest is the writers' interpretation of their results in terms of the differentiation theory of perceptual earning [J. J. Gibson and E. J. Gibson (1955); see the description on page 124 of this book].

The experiment was designed to obtain form matches on a recognition test in which the alternatives were four main types of transformations. The critical data were the "confusion errors" and their distribution among the transformation types. A confusion error is an incorrect selection, i.e., identification of a variable as a standard. Developmental trends were determined for the various transformations.

The standard forms are shown in the left-hand column of Figure 29. The standards were constructed according to rules of construction derived from an analysis of the structural features of English letters. They may be considered to be artificial graphic forms. Each row in Figure 29 pictures the twelve alternatives for the standard in the first cell of the row. The alternatives represent four types of transformation:

1
Columns 1 to 3: transformation of line to curve or curve to line
2
Columns 4 to 8: transformations of rotation or reversal
3
Columns 9 and 10: perspective transformations, a 45° slant left and a 45° backward tilt
4
Columns 11 and 12: topological transformations, a break and a close

As Figure 29 shows, each array of alternatives had from one to three copies of the standard.

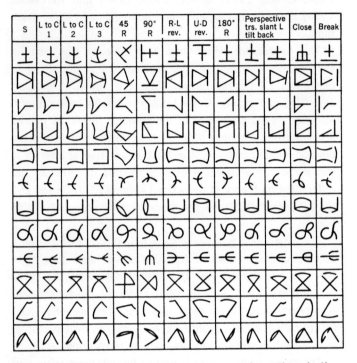

Figure 29. The standard forms and their transformations in the study by E. J. Gibson et al. of the development of the ability to discriminate letter-like forms. (*From E. J. Gibson et al., 1962, p. 898.*)

Figure 30 shows the display apparatus for the discrimination test. E put a standard in the center of the upper row of the display. Then E indicated the appropriate row and S scanned the row, searching for any form which was "exactly like the standard." No correction was provided. In order to ensure that the task was understood by all Ss, several demonstration tests were administered. The Ss were 167 children, distributed among five groups, ages 4 to 8 years (see Table 23 for the number in each group.)

Two kinds of errors were recorded: (1) omission errors— failure to select the true match—and (2) confusion errors— selection of a variable as a match for a standard. The S was free to make several selections for each standard on a single test trial. Therefore, on a given test trial, S's responses could

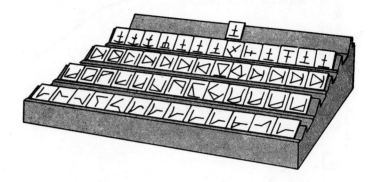

Figure 30. Apparatus for displaying forms in the matching task. (*From E. J. Gibson et al.,* 1962, p. 899).

include a number of confusion errors, in addition to the correct match. In fact, the mean total number of omission errors for the 4-year group was only 1.31, while the mean number of confusion errors was 58.12 for the same group. Since omission errors were very infrequent, they were disregarded in favor of an analysis of the confusion errors.

The mean number of confusion errors decreased steadily with increasing age. The greatest decrease occurred between 4 and 5 years, and the smallest decrease between 5 and 6 years. Thus, a developmental trend is evident. However, this undifferentiated analysis is not very instructive. More informative is an analysis of errors by transformation, over the age scale. The results of this analysis are presented in two ways: in Table 23 and in Figure 31. Table 23 shows the age trends for each of the twelve transformations separately. Figure 31 shows the age trends for the twelve transformations consolidated into four curves, each representing one of the four main transformation types.[20]

It is obvious, on inspection, that the confusion errors were not distributed equally among the transformations. Furthermore, the rates of decrease were different for the various transformations. In other words, the different transformations were not equally discriminable from the standard. Nor

[20] For justifications of this procedure, the reader should see the original source. This matter, as well as other details of statistical nature, have been omitted from our description.

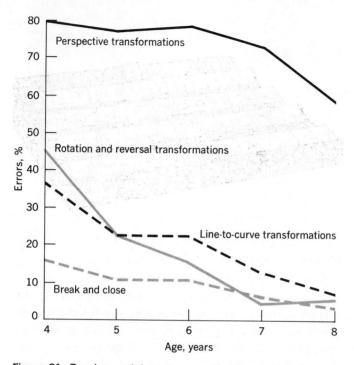

Figure 31. Developmental error curves for four types of transformation. (*From E. J. Gibson et al., 1962, p. 901.*)

Table 23
Mean errors made for each transformation by age groups*

Transformation	Age groups				
	4 (N = 25)	5 (N = 35)	6 (N = 29)	7 (N = 30)	8 (N = 32)
Curve to line (1)	5.85	4.06	4.00	2.53	1.28
Curve to line (2)	4.42	2.60	2.69	1.33	0.53
Curve to line (3)	3.04	1.46	1.76	0.60	0.31
45° rotation	5.19	2.14	1.79	0.53	0.78
90° rotation	4.31	1.48	1.28	0.03	0.34
Right-left reversal†	6.56	3.96	2.07	0.97	0.59
Up-down reversal†	6.47	3.55	2.44	1.56	1.08
180° rotation†	5.24	2.74	1.10	0.14	0.38
Perspective, hor.	9.88	9.20	9.69	9.27	7.34
Perspective, vert.	9.23	8.97	9.31	8.20	6.81
Close	1.19	0.69	0.83	0.43	0.31
Break	2.62	1.86	1.86	1.07	0.59

* From E. J. Gibson et al., 1962, p. 901.
† These figures have been corrected to allow for the fact that oppor-
tunities for error were less than for the other transformations.
NOTE: N = number of children in each group.

did increasing age result in equivalent improvements for all transformations. For example, perspective transformations were most difficult to distinguish from the standard. Confusion errors of this type were very frequent, even for 8-year-old children. In contrast, errors involving line-to-curve transformations were never more than half as frequent as the errors involving perspective, and they occurred only infrequently for the oldest Ss. A similar ranking of the relative frequency of errors for the four transformations was obtained in a supplementary study, which used real letters as standards.

E. J. Gibson et al. (1962) attribute the developmental differences to a learning process of the sort proposed in an earlier analysis of perceptual learning (J. J. Gibson & E. J. Gibson, 1955). "It is our hypothesis that it is the distinctive features of grapheme patterns which are responded to in discrimination of letter-like forms. The improvement in such discrimination from four to eight is the result of learning to detect these invariants and of becoming more sensitive to them" (E. J. Gibson et al., 1962, p. 904).

This is a plausible description of the process which is responsible for the decreasing number of confusion errors as age increases, but an additional assumption is required to explain the distribution of errors among the transformation types and their different rates of decrease. The assumption is made that in addition to learning to abstract and respond to the invariants, S also learns that certain variations can be tolerated, with no consequences for shape identity. Examples of tolerable variations are the perspective transformation and the right-left reversal. On the other hand, a topological transformation is significant and will often alter the identity of the object, e.g., C and O.

To account for their findings, E. J. Gibson et al. suggest that confusion errors are frequent for those transformations which are usually tolerated in the identification of nongraphic, solid forms. Nor will these errors drop out with increasing age. The data for the perspective transformation fit this interpretation. Confusion errors will be infrequent for transformations that involve distinctive features and will decrease with increasing age. The results for the topological (break and close) transformations illustrate this trend.

A general question may be raised concerning the conditions that are necessary for the type of perceptual learning which is hypothesized. E. J. Gibson et al. (1962) deal with this question in a manner consistent with their general view: "It may be that the child learns which varying dimensions . . . are significant and which are not by simply looking repeatedly at many samples containing both varying and invariant features. The distinctive features . . . are not taught but they are nevertheless learned" (p. 905). The results of the investigations of the hypothesis of acquired distinctiveness do indeed suggest that sheer repeated observation may facilitate discrimination, but one can legitimately wonder whether unreinforced observation is a sufficient condition for the improvement with age. The fact that the normally extended developmental period can be compressed into a relative brief period by the application of operant conditioning procedures suggests that differential reinforcement may be a factor.

A good example is the success of Bijou and Baer (1963) in training young children to discriminate mirror images. Cross-sectional comparisons show a developmental trend. Vernon (1957, p. 25) reports that 5-year-old children are simply unable to distinguish between mirror reversals. Yet, using operant conditioning procedures, Bijou was able to train 5-year-olds to the level of flawless performance. Thus, two interpretations of the development of form discrimination can be contrasted:

1
The extended developmental period is necessary in order to expose S to a sufficient number and variety of forms.
2
The period is extended because fortuitous reinforcement schedules and uncontrolled stimulus settings are inefficient for the purpose of establishing discrimination.

Apparent movement   Brenner's investigation (1957) of the developmental changes in the threshold for apparent simultaneity and apparent movement will be our final illustration. The stimulus was an inverted V. Under optimal exposure frequency the V appears to perform a pendulumlike movement. With more rapid frequencies a report of simultaneity is obtained, while slower frequencies result in reports of succession. Brenner's procedure was to start with a very high frequency (descending trials) or a very low frequency (ascending trials) and to continue altering the frequency until S reported the two changes in the appearance of the display, e.g., descending: simultaneity $\longrightarrow$ pendulum move-ment $\longrightarrow$ succession. The data were used to determine the lower and upper thresholds for apparent movement. There were 111 Ss, distributed among fourteen groups, ranging in age from 3 to 19 years. With the exception of the youngest group ($N = 3$), each group had from seven to ten Ss.

Figure 32 shows the mean lower and upper thresholds as a function of age. The thresholds are expressed in terms of frequencies per second. It is obvious that the thresholds change with age. With increasing age, there is a gradual increase in the optimal frequency for the perception of apparent movement. The young children report apparent movement at frequencies which yield succession reports for

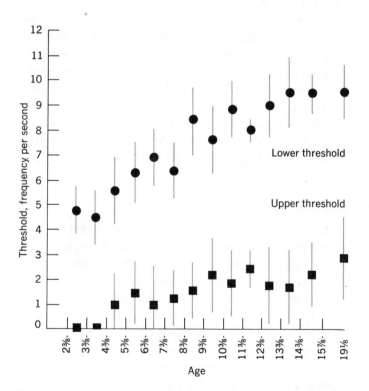

Figure 32. Changes in thresholds of apparent movement with age. Filled squares are the mean upper thresholds for each age group; filled circles are the mean lower thresholds for each age group. The bars represent 1 SD on either side of the mean. (*From Brenner,* 1957, *p.* 171.)

older Ss, and the young children tend to report simultaneity at frequencies which yield apparent motion in older Ss.

Brenner suggests two hypotheses to account for her findings. Neither of these hypotheses is convincing. The first hypothesis, originally proposed by Meili and Tobler (1931), states that ". . . both apparent simultaneity and apparent movement are gestalt processes, and that children had greater facility in forming a gestalt. . . . Strength and speed of closure might be related to the ability to see apparent movement" (Brenner, 1957, p. 172). Why this relationship is to be expected is not intuitively clear. In any event, Brenner (Exp. II) subsequently found that, contrary to expectation, the time required to achieve closure on a test similar to the Street completion test decreased steadily with age. Therefore, Brenner concluded that the hypothesis of Meili and Tobler is not tenable.

The second hypothesis proposed by Brenner is that "the discriminative ability" increases with age and experience and for this reason higher frequencies are required for the illusory appearances. Brenner does not elaborate this hypothesis. One possible construction is that the illusions of movement and simultaneity may be construed as failures to discriminate temporal succession—a discriminative ability which grows with age and practice. Brenner's hypothesis, however it is interpreted, has not been tested.

Evaluation and proposals

In the introduction to this chapter, we observed that developmental studies can make important contributions to an understanding of perceptual learning. That this promise has not been realized does not alter our assessment. But to fulfill their potential these studies must broaden their scope to include more than the establishment of age functions for various phenomena. The demonstration that one may write a statement of the form $R = f(Age)$ only sets the problem for investigation. The crucial problem is one of identifying the processes responsible for the change. Of course, these processes require time, and so the process variable and the age variable are confounded. Nevertheless, it is generally accepted, in the logic of science, that the passage of time per se is never a sufficient condition. Time is only the necessary

condition for the occurrence of the critical process. Therefore, the significant analysis of any time-correlated phenomenon will focus on these critical processes. Until the developmental studies complement their current emphasis by a
focus on process, their contribution to an understanding of
perception will not be significant.

Stated most simply, the argument of the previous paragraph is that once a developmental trend is discovered, the
next step should be the formulation of experimentally testable hypotheses to account for these age-correlated changes.
There are at least two acceptable procedures for testing
these hypotheses: One is to manipulate the variables (task,
environmental, or subject) which are implicated by the hypothesis and observe how these manipulations affect the
developmental trends. For example, E might hypothesize that
the developmental trend in size judgment is due to the fact
that with increasing age increasingly greater proportions of
the Ss at each age level shift from an analytic to a perspective attitude (Epstein, 1963). This hypothesis can be tested
by varying the instructions so as to emphasize various attitudes. Needless to say, the postulated difference in attitude
preference will also require explanation. This example will
alert the reader to a potential limitation of this general
approach. The underlying difference, which is presumed to
be responsible for the age-correlated changes, *itself* may be
the result of time-related changes. Thus, in our example, the
perspective attitude may be a by-product of a mature level
of intellectual conceptualization and therefore may be beyond
the grasp of young children. A judgment about the severity
of generality of this limitation should be reserved until the
approach has been given a more extensive trial.

Another approach to the testing of developmental hypotheses was alluded to in the earlier reference to Bijou's experiment on the discrimination of mirror images. Bijou and Baer
(1963) have introduced the term "constructed history" to
refer to this approach. The following is a general summary
statement of the constructed-history approach:

1
Formulate a hypothesis which refers to process variables which
can be controlled by E.
2
Select Ss who cannot perform the perceptual task in question.

3
On the basis of the hypothesis, prepare a program of training aimed at enabling the Ss to perform the task.
4
When the program is successful, E will have enhanced the plausibility of his hypothesis. His hypothesis describes *one* of the ways in which the differences between age groups could have developed.

The current interest in this approach is tied to the entry of the operant conditioning specialists into the field of developmental psychology. However, the approach is not a contemporary innovation. The widely known study by Watson and Rayner (1920) on the development of fear reactions is an early illustration of this approach. For a variety of reasons, the constructed-history approach has not been prominent in developmental analyses. One of the principal reasons has been a recognition that experiments like Bijou's cannot establish that normally extended extralaboratory development actually does proceed on the basis of the processes implied by the experimental program. However, it has already been noted that the advocates of the constructed-history approach do not claim this accomplishment. "Such an experimental history would not be expected to coincide with the way children of comparable age learn the same task in their everyday experiences. . . . It would, however, provide *one* account of the variables of which such behavior is a function" (Bijou & Baer, 1963, p. 203). Any conclusions about naturally occurring development will always involve extrapolations from a narrower or more restricted set of observations. Therefore, the risks involved in extrapolating from the data of a constructed-history experiment are not peculiar to this procedure.

Two procedures for testing developmental hypotheses have been described. Other approaches could be described, but, instead, let us consider the hypotheses themselves. The most appropriate source of hypotheses is the viable body of theory concerned with perception. Advocacy of a given theoretical formulation will usually require a specific view of the nature of perceptual development. This view is likely to have testable hypotheses. To illustrate these remarks about the origins of hypotheses, we will consider briefly three of the contemporary theoretical alternatives: (1) J. J. Gibson's psychophysical theory (1959), (2) Brunswik's probabilistic functionalism (1956), and (3) the operant conditioning model (Bijou & Baer, 1965).[21]

Psychophysical theory   The hallmark of J. J. Gibson's theory is his generalized psychophysical hypothesis. Simply stated, this hypothesis asserts that visual perception is a function of optical stimulation. To maintain the integrity of this proposition, in the face of evidence of changes in perception without physical changes of stimulation, the differentiation hypothesis of perceptual learning was proposed [J. J. Gibson & E. J. Gibson (1955); also see Chapter 6]. As was noted in our description of the experiment by E. J. Gibson, J. J. Gibson, Pick, and Osser (1962), the same hypothesis can be applied to age-correlated changes. Perceptual development is a process of learning to respond to aspects of stimulation which were not responded to previously. Perceptual development is the learning of new stimuli, not the learning of new responses.

Probabilistic functionalism   For Brunswik (1956), perception is a ". . . ratiomorphic subsystem of cognition" (p. 146) involving three relationships, all of which are probabilistic. The relationship are ones of ". . . probable partial causes and probably partial effects." The three relationships are the correlations between the distal source and the proximal stimulation, between the proximal stimulation and perception, and between perception and the distal source. These three types of covariation are called "ecological validity," "criterial validity," and "functional validity," respectively. Information about these relationships is acquired by a form of generalized probability learning. Brunswik finds the existence of developmental changes in perception entirely compatible with his theoretical views. In fact,

---

[21] Obviously this selection is not exhaustive. Other alternatives could be considered. Piaget's formulations immediately come to mind. Piaget has been principally interested in the processes which underly the qualitative development of intellectual structures, but he has maintained an active interest in perceptual theory and experimentation. An excellent summary of Piaget's thinking has been presented by Flavell (1963, pp. 226–236, 350–356). Additional discussion of several details of Piaget's views on perception is available in articles by Vurpillot (1959) and Wohlwill (1962b). There are other theoretical approaches which deserve attention, notably those advocated by Wapner and Werner (1957) and by Witkin, Dyk, Faterson, Goddenough, and Karp (1962).

Brunswik (1928) performed an early developmental study of brightness constancy, and Beyrl's investigation (1926) of size constancy was performed under Brunswik's direction.

Brunswik's account of Beyrl's results stresses acquired differences in attitude of observation. But alternative hypotheses can be formulated, stressing changes in the amount and accuracy of information about ecological validities, as well as acquired, age-correlated changes in criterial validity. As we grow from infancy to adulthood, we learn more about the objective relationships between variations of proximal (optical) stimulation and variations of the distal (external) source. In addition, we develop tendencies to repose different degrees of confidence in the various proximal cues. These confidences, which are referred to as criterial validities, are not simply reflections of ecological validities. Other variables affect criterial validity, so that criterial validity will, most often, be correlated with ecological validity only partially. To be of significant value, these speculations need to be transformed into explicit and testable hypotheses. The study of thinking by Bruner, Goodnow, and Austin (1956), which is based on Brunswik's conceptual framework, may provide useful leads.

Operant conditioning   Perception may be analyzed within the system of principles advocated by the proponents of the operant conditioning model of behavior change. The most important principle is that differentiated responses which are not part of the genetic endowment are established by the deliberate or adventitious administration of selective reinforcement. The developmental changes of perception are simply instances of the general class of behavior modification. A clear exposition of this theoretical view is found in the discussion by Bijou and Baer (1965) of ". . . perceiving behavior to physical stimuli" (Ch. 9). The following excerpt might serve as a hypothesis to account for the developmental changes in form discrimination: "Through selective reinforcement . . . reactions come under the control of one or a combination of several dimensions or components of a complex stimulus. For this kind of discriminative behavior which is often called abstracting behavior to come into existence, it is necessary for the mother, father, and other members of the family to arrange antecedent and consequent stimuli so that responses to the critical dimension of a stimulus (e.g., its triangularity feature) are systematically reinforced and responses to all other dimensions (e.g., its size, color, location, and spatial orientation) are regularly followed by neutral or aversive consequences" (Bijou & Baer, 1965, pp. 154–155). Bijou and Baer (1963, p. 210) contend that the general form of this hypotheses could be similarly applied to the developmental changes in other perceptual tasks, e.g., depth perception and motion perception.

Three hypotheses concerning developmental change have been presented. No effort will be made to assess their relative merits. In a field of investigation which has provided only infrequent instances of hypothesis testing, every plausible hypothesis should be treated kindly. An occasion for evaluation will be on hand after appropriate experimentation has been completed. Again, a distinction must be maintained between demonstrating an age-correlated change and explaining the change. All too often the argument has taken the form "My theoretical formulation leads to the prediction of an age-correlated change in perceptual function X. The change is observed, so the formulation is confirmed." This argument is unconvincing, because the gross prediction of change can be derived, with equal plausibility, from other theoretical formulations. The hypotheses, and the studies which are designed to test them, need to be more analytic.

References

Baldwin, A. L. *Behavior and development in childhood.* New York: Dryden Press, 1955.

Beyrl, F. Über die Grossenauffassung bei Kindern. *Z. Psychol.,* 1926, **100**, 344–371.

Bijou, S. W., & Baer, D. M. Some methodological contributions from a functional analysis of child development. *Adv. Child Devlpm. Behav.,* 1963, **1**, 197–231.

Bijou, S. W., & Baer, D. M. *Child development. Vol. 2. Universal stage of infancy.* New York: Appleton-Century-Crofts, 1965. Ch. 9.

Brenner, M. W. The developmental study of apparent movement. *Quart. J. Exp. Psychol.,* 1957, **9**, 169–174.

Bruner, J. S., Goodnow, J., & Austin, G. S. *A study of thinking.* New York: Wiley, 1956.

Brunswik, E. *Perception and the representative design of psychological experiments.* Berkeley, Calif.: Univer. of California Press, 1956.

Denis-Prinzhorn, M. Perception des distances et constance des grandeurs (étude génétique). *Arch. Psychol., Genève,* 1960, **37,** 181–309.

Elkind, D., Koegler, R. R., & Go, E. Studies in perceptual development: part-whole perception. *Child Develpm.,* 1964, **35,** 81–90.

Epstein, W. Attitudes of judgment and the size-distance invariance hypothesis. *J. Exp. Psychol.,* 1963, **66,** 78–83.

Epstein, W. Experimental investigations of the genesis of visual space perception. *Psychol. Bull.,* 1964, **61,** 115–128.

Epstein, W., Park, J., & Casey, A. The current status of the size-distance hypotheses. *Psychol. Bull.,* 1961, **58,** 491–514.

Fantz, R. L. The origin of form perception. *Sci. Amer.,* 1961, **204,** 66–72.

Fantz, R. L. Ontogeny of perception. In A. M. Schrier, H. F. Harlow, & F. Stollnitz (Eds.), *Behavior of nonhuman primates.* Vol. 2. New York: Academic, 1965.

Flavell, J. H. *The developmental psychology of Jean Piaget.* New York: Van Nostrand, 1963.

Ghent, Lila. Perception of overlapping and embedded figures by children of different ages. *Amer. J. Psychol.,* 1956, **69,** 575–587.

Ghent, Lila. Recognition by children of realistic figures presented in various orientations. *Canad. J. Psychol.,* 1960, **14,** 249–256.

Ghent, Lila. Form and its orientation: a child's eye view. *Amer. J. Psychol.,* 1961, **74,** 177–190.

Ghent, Lila. Effect of orientation on recognition of geometric forms by retarded children. *Child Develpm.,* 1964, **35,** 1127–1136.

Ghent, Lila, & Bernstein, L. Influence of the orientation of geometric forms on their recognition by children. *Percept. Mot. Skills,* 1961, **12,** 95–101.

Gibson, Eleanor J. Perceptual development. In H. W. Stevenson (Ed.), Child psychology. *Yearb. Nat. Soc. Stud. Educ.,* 1963, **62,** Part I.

Gibson, Eleanor J., & Olum, Vivian. Experimental methods of studying perception in children. In P. H. Mussen (Ed.), *Handbook of research methods in child development.* New York: Wiley, 1960. Pp. 311–373.

Gibson, E. J., Gibson, J. J., Pick, A. D., & Osser, H. A developmental study of the discrimination of letter-like forms. *J. Comp. Physiol. Psychol.,* 1962, **55,** 897–906.

Gibson, J. J. Perception as a function of stimulation. In S. Koch (Ed.) Psychology: *a study of a science.* Vol. 1. New York: McGraw-Hill, 1958. Pp. 457–501.

Gibson, J. J., & Gibson, E. J. Perceptual learning: differentiation or enrichment? *Psychol. Rev.,* 1955, **62,** 32–41.

Gilinsky, Alberta S. Perceived size and distance in visual space. *Psychol. Rev.*, 1951, **58**, 460–482.

Gilinsky, Alberta S. The effect of growth on the perception of visual space. Paper read at East. Psychol. Ass., New York, April, 1960.

Harway, N. I. Judgment of distance in children and adults. *J. Exp. Psychol.*, 1963, **65**, 385–390.

Hershenson, M. Visual discrimination in the human newborn. *J. Comp. Physiol. Psychol.*, 1964, **58**, 270–276.

Hess, E. H. Development of the chick's responses to light and shade cues of depth. *J. Comp. Physiol. Psychol.*, 1950, **43**, 112–122.

Holway, A. H., & Boring, E. G. Determinants of apparent visual size with distance variant. *Amer. J. Psychol.*, 1941, **54**, 21–37.

Kessen, W. Research design in the study of developmental problems. In P. H. Mussen (Ed.), *Handbook of research methods in child development*. New York: Wiley, 1960. Pp. 36–70.

Koffka, K. *Principles of Gestalt psychology.* New York: Harcourt, Brace & World, 1935.

Lambercier, M. La Constance des grandeurs en comparaisons sériales. *Arch. Psychol., Genève*, 1946, **31**, 79–282.

Meili, R., & Tobler, E. Stroboscopic movement in children. *Arch. Psychol., Genève*, 1931, **23**, 131–156.

Munn, N. L. *The evolution and growth of human behavior.* Boston; Houghton Mifflin, 1955.

Rush, Grace P. Visual grouping in relation to age. *Arch. Psychol.*, 1937, **31**, No. 217.

Staples, Ruth. The response of infants to color. *J. Exp. Psychol.*, 1932, **15**, 119–141.

Vernon, Margaret D. *Backwardness in reading.* New York: Cambridge Univer. Press, 1957.

Vurpillot, Elaine. Piaget's law of relative concentration. *Acta. Psychol., Amsterdam*, 1959, **16**, 403–430.

Walk, R. D., & Gibson, E. J. A comparative and analytical study of visual depth perception. *Psychol. Monogr.*, 1961, **75**, No. 519.

Wapner, S., & Werner, H. *Perceptual development.* Worcester, Mass.: Clark Univer. Press, 1957.

Watson, J. B., & Rayner, R. A. Conditioned emotional reactions. *J. Exp. Psychol.*, 1920, **3**, 1–4.

Witkin H. A., Dyk, R. B., Faterson, H. F., Goddenough, D. R., & Karp, S. A. *Psychological differentiation: studies of development.* New York: Wiley, 1962.

Wohlwill, J. F. Developmental studies of perception. *Psychol. Bull.*, 1960, **57**, 249–288.

Wohlwill, J. F. The perspective illusion: perceived size and distance in fields varying in suggested depth, in children and adults. *J. Exp. Psychol.*, 1962, **64**, 300–310. (a)

Wohlwill, J. F. From perception to inference: a dimension of cognitive development. In W. Kessen and Clementina Kuhlman

(Eds.), Thought in the young child: report of a conference on intellective development with particular attention to the work of Jean Piaget. *Monogr. Soc. Res. Child Develpm.*, 1962, **27**, (2), 87–112. (b)

Wohlwill, J. F. The development of "overconstancy" in space perception. In L. P. Lipsit and C. C. Spiker (Eds.), *Advances in child development and behavior.* New York: Academic, 1963.

Wohlwill, J. F. Changes in distance judgments as a function of corrected and noncorrected practice. *Percept. Mot. Skills,* 1964, (2), 87–112. (b)

Wohlwill, J. F. Texture of the stimulus field and age as variables in the perception of relative distance in photographic slides. *J. Exp. Child Psychol.,* 1965, **2**, 163–177.

Zeigler, H. P., & Leibowitz, H. Apparent visual size as a function of distance for children and adults. *Amer. J. Psychol.,* 1957, **70**, 106–109.

Chapter eleven
General conclusions and
proposals

The preceding chapters have reviewed the literature dealing with the varieties of perceptual learning. The reader who has progressed to this point, after reading each chapter in order, probably has experienced some irritation with the disconnected state of the field. The investigators in this field do not share a common theoretical orientation; their constructs are derived from different theories invented to account for descriptively different phenomena. The principal link between their separate endeavors is definitional. In each case, it is possible to define the subject of their investigations as the modification of perception in the absence of changes in the physical properties of optical stimulation.

A degree of skepticism is certain to exist regarding the possibility of formulating any general statements about perceptual learning that are not merely analytic. An attempt to propose a general theory of perceptual learning may be greeted, justifiably, with even greater incredulity. Yet, we should refuse to succumb completely to this discouraging summarization. Much empirical work has been done, and while many of the findings are equivocal, there has emerged a finer appreciation of the methodological requirements of research in perceptual learning. In addition, although no general theory is possible, there is reason to be hopeful that viable miniature theories are being developed to account for specific types of perceptual learning.

Having eschewed integration and broad-theory construction, this chapter will have a number of lesser objectives. The evidence for perceptual learning will be summarized, and outstanding unanswered questions will be reviewed. In addition, the general question of perceptual learning will be considered in relation to contemporary theoretical formulations of perception.

The nature of the evidence

The examination of perceptual learning has involved the evaluation of five main propositions:

1
Assumptions that are learned through everyday experience are important determinants of perception.
2
Practice, in the form of prior exposure, controlled rehearsal, or differential reinforcement of selective perceiving, can modify perception.
3
Extended exposure to conditions of conflict leads to a gradual modification of perception.
4
When visual stimulation is transformed or distorted the perceiver adapts to the distortion.
5
A variety of perceptual functions exhibit developmental changes.

The assumptive context

The contention is that perceptual experience is determined, at least partially, by the assumptive context, i.e., the assumptions about the environment and its relationship to stimulation. The proposition is plausible. Yet, the evidence (Chapters 2 to 4) is not sufficiently compelling to persuade the skeptic.

What accounts for the equivocal status of the evidence? And can experiments be designed that will increase our confidence in the validity of the proposition? To answer these questions, let us reexamine the experimental procedures. Two general procedures have been employed:

1
In the procedure that has been followed most frequently, the S is shown a familiar, representative standard which has characteristic properties. The E presumes that S's identification of the standard, e.g., "playing-card," is accompanied by a set of assumptions about the properties of the standard and its appearance under variable conditions of observation. The experiment is designed to exhibit the influence of these assumptions.

2

The alternative procedure seeks to establish assumptions in association with a standard that is nonrepresentative and unlikely to have preexperimental associations with specific assumptions. For example, S may be trained to associate size and color, with the expectation that color identification will lead to assumptions about the size of the target when S is asked to judge its distance.

The principal feature of the first procedure is the remote control of the critical variable, i.e., the S's assumptions. Rarely is independent evidence provided to show that the S's assumptions do in fact correspond to the assumptions that are imputed to him by the experimenter. This is not to argue that the inferences made by E have been implausible; but they may be inaccurate in some important detail. The degree to which this discrepancy has confounded the objectives of the experiment cannot be assessed without additional information about S's assumptive network. An experiment by Carlson and Tassone (1962) illustrates one procedure for obtaining such information.

The study proposed to obtain information regarding S's assumptions about the size-distance and brightness-distance relationships. Carlson and Tassone (1962) were primarily interested in the ". . . perspective attitude—defined as the implicit assumption on the part of O that the visual appearance of the magnitude of an object diminishes with increasing distance of the object" (p. 644). Independent evidence of this assumption was sought by examining S's attitudes about the size-distance relationship on a test that contained no references to actual objects and distances.

There were two stages in the experiment: In the first stage, a verbal test was administered. The test consisted of a series of twelve items. Each of the items was a set of three words. The following were four critical items: large–far away–small; nearby–large–far away; small–nearby–large; far away–nearby–bright. The S's task was to decide whether the center word had a connotative association with either of the adjacent words, and to indicate the degree of association by checking one of several underlined spaces.[22] In the second stage of the experiment, S made size judgments under phe-

---

[22] This procedure is a version of the *semantic differential* invented by Osgood, Suci, and Tannenbaum (1957).

nomenal, perspective, and objective instructions. (These instructions are summarized in Chapter 2, page 25. Full-cue
conditions prevailed, and the method of adjustment was
used. The variable and standard were at distances of 10 and
40 feet, respectively.

The first stage of the experiment was designed to examine
the size-distance and brightness-distance associations. The
results showed that "small" and "dim" were highly associated with "far away," or "distant"; "large" and "bright,"
with "nearby." These results provide independent information about S's assumptions. The evidence is consistent
with the typical inferences that investigators have made in
this connection. The second stage was included to determine
the degree of correlation between the verbal measures and
size judgment. Carlson and Tassone expected significant
correlations only for the perspective and objective instructions. Phenomenal instructions are designed to counteract
the perspective attitude; therefore, a significant correlation
was not expected. Correlations computed between the size-
distance association and size judgments agreed with these
expectations. Correlations were not computed for the brightness-distance assumption.

The investigation by Carlson and Tassone illustrates one
procedure for examining the assumptive context, independently of perceptual performance. Such investigations can
supply more reliable information about assumptions, and
this information may provide a basis for formulating more
precise experimental hypotheses. For example, in experimental tests of the Known Size—Apparent Distance Hypothesis, the predictions should be sharpened by determining
the degree of assumptive association between size and
distance.

The acquisition of sufficient information about the assumptive context will not settle all the difficulties with the
"remote control" approach. Another problem, which will be
recognized by those who have actually conducted such
experiments, is to guarantee that the relevant assumptions
are indeed operative in the specific experimental setting. One
often has the impression that the conditions of the experiment have induced competing assumptions, which tend to
modify or diminish the relevance of the preexperimental
assumptions. Sometimes, the effect seems to be a weakening

of the degree of assumptive association and, on occasion, a suspension of assumptions—"All bets are off." An independent measure of the assumption, obtained before and after the experiment, would be instructive. This experiment effect is not particularly surprising, but it is troublesome, and no obvious remedy is available.

The second procedure involves the experimental establishment of assumptions. This procedure avoids some of the difficulties described above. It is important to recognize that often more than the introduction of new learning is involved. Frequently, unlearning of preexperimental assumptions also may be involved. Thus, if S is required to learn a color-size assumption, he must also unlearn the preexperimental tendency to disregard color in judging size. Therefore, the training procedure may have to be extended to ensure a high degree of overlearning of the prescribed assumption. Otherwise, S may revert to the preexperimental tendency when the critical perceptual tests are administered.

The second procedure may be usefully applied to determine the special consequences of differences between assumptions. Two differences that can be discerned in many of the experimental examples are specificity and precision. "Specificity" (generality) refers to the size of the class of stimuli or conditions with which the assumption is associated. An example of a very general assumption is the assumption of "wholeness" (Ames, 1955, pp. 25–27). This is the assumption that an object or a visual form is whole and has continuous contours even when it cannot be directly perceived in entirety. This assumption, which applies to *all* objects, is presumed to be operative in determining the effects of interposition on perceived relative distance (see Figure 13). The "wholeness" assumption can be contrasted with a highly specific assumption which is restricted to a particularly designated stimulus. An example of the latter is the color-shape assumption tested in the studies of memory color.

"Precision" refers to the degree of constraint or determination imposed by the assumption. Thus, an assumption may be imprecise in the sense that it only specifies the range of compatible variations of the perceptual property, e.g., the range of perceived distances or sizes. An assumption may also be highly precise; it may specify exactly what value the object may assume. Differences in precision may be traced to a variety of conditions. One obvious basis for the difference is that some stimuli, e.g., a coin, are consistently associated with a single value of an attribute, e.g., size, while other stimuli, e.g., a ball, are routinely associated with a range of attribute values. Thus, the size assumption induced by identification of a standard as a specific coin will precisely specify the size of the coin. However, the size assumption induced by the identification of the standard as a ball will specify only the range of permissible sizes.

These variations, as well as others, have been recognized in the literature, but they have not been investigated systematically. Investigations of this question which follow the remote-control approach are unlikely to succeed. However, the alternative procedure of experimental control should allow *E* to introduce these variations and examine their effects. This procedure also makes feasible detailed investigations of the development of assumptions, and most importantly the manner in which their relative weights are established.

The evidence that has been reviewed in Chapters 2 to 4 is derived almost entirely from experimental settings that have been specially contrived to reduce drastically the amount and specificity of the information. Long-term students of the psychology of perception have adapted to this particular research strategy, and perpetuation of this strategy is not likely to be very disturbing to them; but others probably will not share their equanimity. The chief reservation concerns the generality of the conclusions derived from studies of this type. Are these conclusions that contribute to a *general* theory of perception or to a limited theory that is restricted to perception under impoverished stimulus conditions?

This question cannot be ignored. But the force of the question derives from a particular view about the extent of psychophysical correspondence that is present under normal conditions of observation. According to this view (e.g., Gibson, 1959), under normal conditions of stimulation, perception is characterized by a high degree of stimulus-response specificity. There are stimulus-correlates of perception which account for all the variance in the *S*'s response. It follows that past-experience variables are not assigned great significance, *except* when *E* strives to make the conditions of stimulation ambiguous or uninformative. Principles of perception derived from impoverished situations apply only to those situations.

Many investigators of the assumptive context would not accept the generalized psychophysical hypothesis. The Transactionalists, who have stimulated much of the work reported in Chapters 2 to 4, would reject the hypothesis entirely. In fact, it is one of their contentions that retinal stimulation is *always* equivocal; any given retinal situation is compatible with a number of different perceptual consequences. Therefore, they would argue that the impoverishment that characterizes the experimental conditions merely serves to exaggerate an ambiguity that characterizes all conditions of stimulation. The purpose of the experimental procedure is to allow *E* to exhibit the factors which enable the perceiver to resolve the fundamental optical ambiguity. The principles uncovered in experiments like those reviewed in Chapters 2 to 4 are general principles of perception.

In this argument, the disagreement is concerned only secondarily with the bare question of whether extrapolation from an artificial laboratory situation is permissible. The critical issue seems to involve questions of representativeness. Do the conditions of the reduction or omission experiments alter or distort the situation so essentially as to produce a qualitative as well as a quantitative difference? When the conditions of perceptual judgments are so drastically altered, is the nature of the judgment altered as well? Viewed in this manner, it becomes clear that the question is not an empirical one. Without a preliminary theoretical consensus about the nature of perception, it is not possible to propose an empirical investigation that could settle the matter. What are reflected in the alternative assessments of the value of the reduced-cue experiments are theoretical or definitional disagreements that cannot be resolved by experiment.[23]

The effects of practice
Chapters 5 to 7 were concerned with the effects of practice. Four principal conditions of practice were examined:

[23] An excellent discussion of this question is provided by Gibson (1951).

1

Rehearsal. S engaged in a series of practice trials on the criterial discrimination task or on one closely related to the criterial task.

2

Exposure. Prior to the test, S was exposed to the relevant stimuli, but no practice on the criterial test was given.

3

Distinctiveness training. S was preexposed to the test stimuli and was required to learn verbal labels for the stimuli.

4

Reinforced practice. In the preliminary (practice) trials, certain percepts were differentially reinforced.

Three kinds of effects have been examined:

1

Increased accuracy or psychophysical correspondence. Thus, practice was expected to enhance the accuracy of distance judgments or to increase the probability of discriminating between different forms.

2

Decreased accuracy or decreased psychophysical correspondence. For example, associating common labels to discriminable forms was expected to diminish their discriminability and increase the probability of "same" reports. Or selective reinforcement was administered to produce overestimation of size.

3

Selective perception. Differential reinforcement of a specific percept was expected to increase the probability of occurrence of that response to the test stimulus. For example, the reinforced profile in the Schafer-Murphy ambiguous composite should be reported most frequently.

Although the literature dealing with the various practice effects is extensive, there are relatively few convincing experiments. The evidence of figural persistence is good, but little has been done to explore the parameters of the effect. The "enrichment" studies seem to be in general agreement in showing that unreinforced prior exposure can facilitate subsequent discrimination. In both these cases, the experiments have been largely demonstrational. Explicit hypotheses to account for these practice effects are not conspicuous, and so there is little in the way of hypothesis testing. The evidence regarding the two remaining types of practice effects is not impressive. The many experiments that have studied the effects of labeling have been incon-

sistent; the tests of the ADC hypothesis have yielded negative results as frequently as positive results. The influence
of reward and punishment has also not been impressively
established. Although most of the evidence is consistent
with the hypothesis of "autism," there are grounds for
doubting the generality of the findings.

The practice paradigms are the most direct experimental
approaches to perceptual learning, and it may seem curious
that they have not yielded more clear-cut results. But it is
not difficult to diagnose the nature of the problem with these
experiments. Apart from specific methodological flaws that
may be present, the most disturbing aspect of many of the
experiments is their failure to translate the hypotheses into
meaningful operations. Apparently, the opinion is prevalent
among investigators that all operations are valid if they have
the formal characteristics implied by the hypothesis. Thus,
the association of any verbal label with any visual form is expected to enhance the distinctiveness of the form, regardless
of the manner in which the association is established, the
sense of the association, and S's motivation to use labels to
help him distinguish between visual stimuli. The administration of small monetary "rewards" and "punishments" is
expected to condition perception, without evidence of relevant motivation and information regarding the incentive value
of these "reinforcers."

Plainly, the chief justification of these operations is that
they fit the formal requirements of the ADC model and the
instrumental conditioning model. Needless to say, any experiment that is designed to test these models of perceptual
learning must satisfy these requirements. But this does not
mean that all such operations are equally good. Obviously,
this will be a matter of judgment, and it is always easier to
make such judgments after the fact. In any event, the
implication of the foregoing remarks is that new experimental operations and procedures should be explored.

An analysis of perceptual learning outside the laboratory
may provide valuable leads. For example, an examination of
acquired distinctiveness in everyday life points to training
conditions that are very different from the labeling practice
of the typical ADC experiment. As one illustration, consider
the acquired distinctiveness of two very similar door keys.
When the keys are first received, they are very difficult to

distinguish, as evidenced by our inability to select the correct key confidently. Gradually, the confusion errors drop out, and correct selection becomes the rule. It seems likely that one of the factors that is responsible for the enhanced discriminability of the keys is that they are associated with distinctive specific functions or objectives.

As another example, consider the urban apartment dweller who moves to a rural campus town. On a trip to the local tree nursery, he complains that many of the different shrubs look alike. There follows a period of informal education, which may take the form of having the different shrubs on the grounds of various houses pointed out for his attention. Eventually, the ability to distinguish the different variations is acquired. Repeated naming of the different shrubs is certainly involved, but another important factor may be the association of the different shrubs with different environmental contexts. Both these examples have involved James's "adhesion of distinctive associates." But the associates have not been abstract labels, nor is it certain that the process of association is like that represented in paired-associates learning. Experiments that originate from observations of this nature may be better suited to an evaluation of the hypothesis of acquired distinctiveness. Similar benefits might accrue from an analysis of extralaboratory examples of the other types of practice effects.

Perceptual conflict
The experiments on perceptual conflict and the experiments on adaptation to transformed stimulation were treated in separate chapters. This segregation seemed useful for expository purposes, and it also reflected the fact that the original sources do not contain references to the possibility of relating these studies. However, there are grounds for subsuming the adaptation studies under the general rubric of perceptual conflict. In each of the major experiments described in Chapters 8 and 9, conditions have been arranged to produce a discrepancy or an incongruity. The studies in Chapter 8 were concerned with discrepancies that arise when competing cues or competing contents are simultaneously operative and also with the discrepancy between perception and actions contingent on perception. The adaptation experiments involve all these discrepancies, as well as an intermodal or intersensory discrepancy.

In considering these conditions of conflict as experimental arrangements for studying perceptual learning, it should be recognized that to serve this purpose, the experiment has to be designed to provide measures of change over time. It is this temporal feature which makes it plausible to interpret the experiments as designs for the study of learning.

Of the various conflict situations, the most significant are the cue conflicts studied by Wallach and the optically induced conflicts reviewed in Chapter 9. In both these cases, there is clear evidence of perceptual modification. In Wallach's experiments, the effects of binocular disparity are modified; after exposure to rotation, a given disparity produces different amounts of perceived depth. In the adaption experiments, exposure to discrepancy resulted in modifications in the visual and proprioceptive systems.

The study of conflict as an occasion of perceptual learning is a recent development. Therefore, it is not surprising that many important questions are still unexplored. To answer these questions, two kinds of effort are required: parametric studies are needed to establish a set of functional relationships between perceptual change and the environmental and task variables that seem relevant; second, an effort should be made to explicate the motivational basis for the perceptual learning that has been observed.

The lack of quantitative determination of important functional relationship is especially disappointing in the case of the adaptation phenomenon. The investigations in this field have been devoted primarily to demonstrations of adaptation and to testing the validity of the reafference principle. This preoccupation with the question of reafference reflects the fact that Von Holst's model generated predictions concerning movement but had nothing explicit to say about other variables. However, Von Holst was not concerned directly with the adaptation problem, and there was no reason to expect that he would treat the specific variables that might regulate adaptation. In taking over the Von Holst model, many investigators have also taken over his emphasis on the importance of reafference.

This interest in reafference has led to important findings, but it has also had the unfortunate effect of diverting attention from the task of identifying the other controlling variables. Such determinations are necessary for the development of hypotheses about the learning processes that result

in adaptation. Knowledge about the specific functional relationships will also allow us to assess the degree to which
adaptation is analogous to other learning phenomena.

Concurrent with these empirical investigations, it will be
important to consider the question of motivation. Jones
(1955, p. vii) has described the problem of motivation as
one of determining ". . . how behavior gets started, is ener-
gized, is sustained, is directed, is stopped, and what kind
of subjective reaction is present in the organism while all
this is going on." This question may be legitimately introduced in discussions of all types of learning. The question
is especially intriguing in the case of perceptual conflict,
because many of the standard answers cannot be readily
applied. We have suggested that a beginning can be made
by assuming that the presence of discrepancy or incon-
gruence sets into motion a tendency to eliminate the discrepancy. This assumption is founded on the premise that
perceptual conflict is an unstable state like the more general
states of conflict. It is obvious that this hypothesis is
addressed primarily to the question of the initiation or
energizing of perceptual modification. The hypothesis does
not specify the precise nature or magnitude of the modification. It seems reasonable to assume that these characteristics are related to the intensity of the conflict and the
relative strength of the competing cues. Unfortunately, there
are presently no coordinating, operational definitions for
intensity of conflict and potency of cues.

The results of the search for the controlling variables will
bear importantly on the evaluation of the conflict model of
motivation. Many of the functional relationships that are
determined may help specify the properties of the conflict
model. For example, as a rule, modification or adaptation is
incomplete. This suggests that some notion of capacity or
tolerance threshold may have to be incorporated in the
model. Further information about this possibility can be
derived from studies of the relationship between the amount
of change and the magnitude of the original discrepancy.
The prediction would be that the modification will be asymp-
totic at the point at which the same absolute discrepancy
remains. Thus, in an experiment on adaptation to optical
tilt, the absolute shift should be linearly related to the
amount of optical tilt that is introduced. On the other hand,
if the amount of adaptation is a constant proportion of the

optical tilt, then the capacity or threshold notion would have to be reconsidered.

In summary, two general lines of research have been suggested: the first would identify the stimulus variables that regulate learning in conflict situations; the second line of investigation would identify the motivational basis for this type of learning. In addition to enhancing our understanding of perceptual conflict, these investigations will enable us to relate these effects to more general principles of learning.

Perceptual development

The evidence considered in Chapter 10 is sufficient to allow the conclusion that there are changes in perception as a function of age. We have insisted on divorcing the question of development from the nativism-empiricism issue. Evidence of developmental change neither entails an empiristic inter- pretation of the origins of perception nor precludes a nativistic account.

The experiments have been concerned largely with estab- lishing age functions and only secondarily concerned with identifying the variables that account for the age-correlated changes. Further studies of this nature are still required. Many of the early developmental studies have not sampled the age variable satisfactorily. In addition, the specification of the dependent variable has frequently been open to ques- tion. It is uncertain whether the observed changes reflect changes in perceptual functioning or only changes in the utilization of perceptual information and in the availability of a differentiated terminology for describing experience. Additional experimentation which satisfies the sampling and response-specification requirements would be useful.

Assuming that age-correlated perceptual functions are reliably established, the question arises regarding an ex- planation of these changes. This question can be approached in a variety of ways. A theory of development may be formu- lated that is largely independent of general theories of learn- ing and perception. In other words, developmental changes can be viewed as peculiar growth-specific changes which require special hypotheses. Another approach is to consider the developmental changes as resultants of the same learn- ing and perceptual processes that are observed more generally. According to this view, instead of seeking to formulate hypotheses about unique learning processes, we should attempt to determine whether the developmental changes may be attributed to already identified forms of learning.

There is no point in denying in advance that there may be principles of learning that apply uniquely to the growing child. But it seems more prudent to reserve that possibility until we have determined whether accounts of development can be formulated in terms of known forms of perceptual learning. With this admonition in mind, the investigator of perceptual learning who studies developmental changes will want to assess the role of the variables discussed in Chapters 2 to 9 in modifying perception in the growing child.

Postscript

In concluding this summary of the data, we may take passing notice of an approach to the study of perceptual learning that has been insufficiently exploited. This approach involves the use of laboratory-reared animals, e.g., primates who have visual systems that are similar to those of human beings. With such Ss, the total exposure history can be controlled and varied systematically to test specific hypotheses. This capability is especially crucial in the context of the problems discussed in this book. Much of the ambiguity that characterizes the current status of many of the problems can be attributed to the absence of direct and specific knowledge of the S's exposure history, his commerce with the environment, and the nature of the reinforcement contingencies that have been part of his experience. This deficiency can be remedied by using laboratory-reared animals whose histories are known in detail.

Although animal research may prove to be generally fruitful, the possibilities are especially promising in the case of the adaptation phenomena discussed in Chapter 9. In this case, the precise control of the distal-proximal stimulus relationship, in interaction with the broad range of movements of the observer, does not seem feasible with human Ss. Certainly, precise control is out of the question for long periods such as those studied by I. Kohler. However, a high degree of control, over extended periods, can be achieved with animals. The results of such studies can contribute significantly to an understanding of adaptation and perceptual learning.

The significance of perceptual
learning for general theories
of perception

In his introduction to the psychology of perception, Koffka (1935) stated the problem of perception in the following succinct question: "Why does the world appear as it does?" The variety of alternative answers which have been proposed testifies to the difficulty of the question. The major alternatives are the proposals of Gestalt psychology, J. J. Gibson's psychophysical theory, and a variety of empiristic positions, e.g., transactionalism, Brunswik's probabilistic functionalism, and conditioning theory.

The attitude of these theories toward the question of the role of learning in perception has been varied. The Gestalt psychologists are inclined to minimize the influence of learning. Despite the historical fact that several impressive demonstrations of learning in perception have been produced by investigators sympathetic to Gestalt psychology, the general attitude is one of reticent recognition of the possible effects of learning.

J. J. Gibson, who shares some of the views of Gestalt psychology, has handled the question of perceptual learning differently. He suggests that the principles that govern perception are not the same under all conditions. The conditions of unrestricted stimulation require one set of principles, while the conditions of restricted, impoverished stimulation require another. In the former case, perception is a function of stimulation; learning effects are confined to the possibility of increasing differentiation of higher-order variables of stimulation. In the latter case, psychophysical correspondence and stimulus determination are precluded, thus forcing the observer to rely on assumptions, learned associations, and probabilistic cues. In summary, Gibson contends that, except in one restricted sense, learning is not involved in the way the world normally appears, but he readily admits that under subnormal, marginal conditions, past experience and learning may be important.

The variety of empiristically oriented theories are obviously most hospitable to the evidence of perceptual learning. Nevertheless, they may be challenged by the diversity of the findings. As a rule, the various approaches have tended to emphasize one type of learning to the neglect of others. Thus, one formulation may stress the influence of subjective assumptions, while another stresses reinforcement history. It is doubtful that any of the versions of empiristic theory could claim that the variety of perceptual learning phenomena was anticipated in their theoretical statements.

Regardless of theoretical persuasion, the research reviewed in this book has provided a body of findings that cannot be disregarded. Perception is influenced by learning and exposure history. The influence is not as pervasive as a generation of uncritical empiricists would wish. Nor are the effects as minimal and restricted as the more tenacious among the antiempiricists repeatedly claim. But this assessment is no cause for an expression of relief. The middle ground is an especially demanding position. It requires that one specify the conditions and limits of the effectiveness of many diverse variables. The risks of internal inconsistency are particularly great, because the variables are extractions from theoretical contexts that often have incompatible premises. Nevertheless, it seems inevitable that in order to be an adequate account of perception, a theory is required that will integrate the facts of perceptual learning with the facts of psychophysical correspondence.

References

Ames, A., Jr. *An interpretative manual.* Princeton, N.J.: Princeton Univer. Press, 1955.

Carlson, V. R., & Tassone, E. P. A verbal measure of the perspective attitude. *Amer. J. Psychol.*, 1962, **75**, 644–647.

Gibson, J. J. Theories of perception. In W. Dennis (Ed.), *Current trends in psychological theory.* Pittsburgh, Pa.: Univer. of Pittsburgh Press, 1951.

Gibson, J. J. Perception as a function of stimulation. In S. Koch (Ed.), *Psychology: a study of a science.* Vol. 1. New York: McGraw-Hill, 1958. Pp. 457–501.

Jones, M. R. (Ed.) *Nebraska symposium on motivation.* Lincoln, Nebr.: Univer. of Nebraska Press, 1955.

Koffka, K. *Principles of Gestalt psychology.* New York: Harcourt, Brace & World, 1935.

Osgood, C. E., Suci, G. J., & Tannebaum, P. H. *The measurement of meaning.* Urbana, Ill.: Univer. of Illinois Press, 1957.

Glossary

The following glossary of terms is selective and not exhaustive. Terms are not included if their introduction in the text is followed by a definition or explanation. Definitions of such terms may be located by consulting the subject index.

Achromatic color. A color lacking a distinguishable hue. Achromatic colors vary in brightness, ranging from white to black.

Adjustment (method). A psychophysical method in which S is instructed to adjust a comparison or variable stimulus until it appears equal to the standard.

Aperture vision. An experimental arrangement for eliminating the accommodation reflex of the eye, which is normally correlated with changes in the distance of the target. The target is viewed through a tiny aperture (2 to 4 mm.) which restricts vision to the central foveal area. This arrangement is also useful in experiments which are designed to investigate perception of targets isolated from their background.

Autochthonous cues. A term sometimes used to refer to determinants of perception that have been considered to be independent of subject variables.

Autokinetic movement. The illusory movements of stationary point(s) that are viewed without an accompanying stable visual framework, e.g., in a completely dark room.

Binocular rivalry. The phenomenon whereby if very different colors or figures are stereoscopically presented to corresponding areas of the two eyes, they are not combined but, instead, are perceived alternately, in a state of rivalry.

Constant error. A systematic occurrence of errors in one direction. For example, the method of *adjustment* may reveal a consistent tendency to overestimate or underestimate the standard. The former case would be an example of a positive constant error; the latter, of a negative constant error.

Constant stimuli (method). A psychophysical method of determining thresholds in which preselected intensities, or values, of a stimulus are presented to the S for comparison with a standard stimulus.

Diacritical experiment (design). A term introduced by Egon Brunswik to refer to experimental designs which pit two alternative determinants of behavior against each other.

Difference limen (threshold). The smallest difference between two stimuli that can be perceived as different. The specification of the threshold is based on a statistical analysis of data obtained through the application of psychophysical methods.

Differential angular velocity. See *motion parallax.*

Differential reinforcement. The term "reinforcement" has been defined in many ways. A relatively atheoretical definition is that reinforcement is a procedure for altering the probability and rate of responding. Reinforcement is differential when it is administered selectively, e.g., following one response and not following another response, or associated with one stimulus setting and not another. This is the typical procedure that is followed in discrimination training.

Diopter (prism diopter; pd). The deviation power of a prism defined as 100 times the tangent of the angle through which the light rays are bent by the prism.

Egocentric localization. Localization with respect to the position of the body. Thus, if S is asked to point straight ahead, egocentric localization is being tested.

Fovea. A central region of the retina where cones are closely packed together and visual acuity is best. When S "fixates," or looks directly at, an object, the image will be on the fovea.

Fractionation judgment. A task which requires that the S estimate specified fractions of a standard.

Frontoparallel. In a plane perpendicular to the observer's line of sight.

Full-cue viewing conditions. Test conditions that provide the variety of cues which are available in a typical real-life setting. No attempt is made to reduce the number of cues, e.g., by requiring monocular vision or by presenting the standard in isolation.

Galvanic skin response (GSR). A change in the electric resistance of the skin. This change can be measured by appropriate instrumentation. The GSR is frequently observed upon the introduction of affective or aversive stimuli.

Ganzfeld. A term introduced by W. Metzger to refer to a field of perfectly homogeneous stimulation. A satisfactory, albeit imperfect, Ganzfeld can be produced by exposing S to a carefully whitewashed wall that fills the entire visual scene. If S is at a suitable distance from the wall, the unavoidable inhomogeneities in the painted surface will not disturb the effect. A perfectly uniform Ganzfeld requires precise control of the conditions of illumination and the characteristics of the reflecting surface, as well as provisions for eliminating facial shadows.

Homunculus. A term (literally, a diminutive man) used to characterize hypotheses which seem to assign critical functions to an unobservable operator inside the organism.

Incidental learning. Learning that occurs in the absence of instructions to learn the particular task. It also usually implies that a postexperimental interview will not provide evidence of self-instructed intention to learn.

Induced color. The color appearance of a restricted region of the visual field, not produced solely by the stimulation correlated with this region but dependent on the concomitant stimulation from neighboring regions.

Interaction effect (statistical). The interdependence of factors in determining the values of the dependent measure. Factors A and B interact when the effect of A differs according to the level of B, or vice versa.

Intermanual transfer. Transfer of training from the hand which is used in the original practice to the hand not used previously.

Introspection. A term with several prominent meanings, used in the text in two ways: as *analytic* introspection, referring to the procedure associated with Wundt and Titchener, a type of introspection that is a detailed analysis of experience in terms of certain descriptive categories, e.g., sensation and feeling, and as *phenomenological* introspection, a method in which S is instructed to report on his immediate experience without analysis—an approach advocated by the Gestalt psychologists as a preliminary to experimentation.

Kinesthetic. Pertaining to the sense of kinesthesis, which provides information about the movements and position of the body.

Kinetic depth effect. The perceived depth or solidity of objects resulting from the continuous transformations of the image of the object when either the object is turned or S moves in a path around the object.

Labile. Literally, liable to change, unstable. A labile stimulus configuration is one which seems to alternate between mutually exclusive appearances. The Necker cube is an example.

Limits (method of). A psychophysical method of determining thresholds in which a series of stimuli of increasing (ascending trial) or decreasing (descending trial) is presented. The S typically responds "yes" or "no" to each presentation. This allows E to determine the transition points.

Monochromatic. When referring to stimulation, this term indicates that the light is in a single wavelength.

Motion (movement) parallax. A cue consisting of the differential angular velocity between the line of sight to the fixated object and any other object in the visual field and serving as an indication of the relative distance of points in the visual field when a S moves with respect to the environment or when the environment moves with respect to the S.

Normalization. A perceptual shift that occurs when a stimulus that deviates from its normative values is continuously inspected. The shift is such as to make the stimulus assume its normative appearance. For example, a bowed line will begin to appear straight.

Ontogenetic. Pertaining to development in the individual organism.

Operant conditioning. A term introduced by Skinner to refer to a type of conditioning paradigm in which S operates on the environment with consequences that affect the probability and rate of future responding. The Skinner-box, bar-pressing situation is the best known example.

Optical texture. A term introduced by J. J. Gibson to describe the retinal correlate of an environmental surface that normally is textured. The gradient of optical texture is a determinant of the perceived orientation of surfaces.

Optomotor reflex. A response whereby if a striped cylinder is turned around a stationary insect, the insect turns itself in the same direction.

Orthogonal design. An experiment that follows an orthogonal design explores the influence of at least two variables simultaneously. At least two values of each variable are studied.

Paced anticipation. A procedure, widely employed in studies of paired-associates learning, in which stimulus items and complete S-R pairs are presented alternately (i.e., A, A-B; C, C-D) at a constant rate and the subject is required to anticipate the response during the interval when the stimulus is presented alone.

Perceptual constancy. The phenomenon whereby under certain conditions perception will remain constant and objectively accurate despite local retinal variations.

Physiognomic (properties). The expressive properties perceived in an object, e.g., aesthetic or affective qualities.

Prägnanz. A term introduced by the Gestalt psychologists to refer to the hypothesized tendency of the visual system to organize perception in favor of the most simple or stable organization.

Predifferentiation. A pretraining procedure that consists of practice with elements of the criterial task prior to its initiation. Thus, stimulus predifferentiation would consist of preliminary exposure to the stimulus members of S-R combinations followed by learning of the S-R combinations.

Prism diopter. See *diopter.*

Projective. In geometry, pertaining to the projection of one surface onto another. If the two surfaces are not parallel, the projection will result in a projective transformation. Thus, a circle that is projected onto a surface, e.g., the retina, that is not parallel to the plane of the circle will result in an elliptical projective shape.

Proprioceptive. Pertaining to the position sense, or the sense by which we know the relative locations of various parts of our body even without the aid of vision. Changes in the position sense may be called proprioceptive changes.

Retinal disparity. The difference between the images on the retinas when viewing a solid object. The disparity between the two images is due to the fact that the eyes are separated by an interocular distance and, consequently, each eye views the object from a slightly different angle. The same disparity can be obtained with properly designed pictures viewed in a stereoscope. Retinal disparity is a depth cue.

Retinal subtense. The area of the retina that is occluded by an object in the visual field.

Reversible figure. A stimulus pattern that yields spontaneous alternations between two or more perceptual organizations. The Necker cube is a well-known example.

Saturation. A dimension of color that refers to the richness of the color, or the degree to which the color differs from an achromatic color of the same brightness. When in everyday description we refer to one red sample as "deeper" than another, we are responding to the dimension of saturation.

Spearman rank order correlation. A statistical measure of the correlation between the rank orders of values or scores for two dependent variables or tests.

Stereogram. A drawing prepared for presentation in a stereoscope.

Stereoscope. An instrument devised for the study of depth perception. The principal purpose of the stereoscope is to present disparate stereograms individually to the two eyes. Usually, stereoscopes will also permit the investigator to vary convergence and accommodation. The term "stereoscopic perception" refers to perception in a stereoscope.

Subliminal stimulation. Stimulation at a level below S's threshold for detecting the presence of a stimulus.

Tachistoscope. An instrument designed to permit the investigator to expose stimuli for very brief intervals.

Threshold (absolute). The minimum value of the stimulus which can be detected by an observer. See *difference limen (threshold).*

Transfer. The effect of learning or practicing a task on performance of a succeeding task. If the prior practice facilitates later performance, the effect is labeled *positive* transfer; if the prior practice inhibits subsequent learning, the effect is labeled *negative* transfer.

Transformation. A term that figures prominently in J. J. Gibson's analysis of the stimuli that are important for perception. When an object's position is altered with respect to an observer, its retinal image undergoes lawful transformation. Gibson contends that these transformations are specific to the object and are therefore a very important source of visual information about the environment.

Trigram. A unit in a verbal learning task, consisting of three letters. The typical nonsense syllable is one example of a trigram.

Veridical. A term for which several different definitions may be presented. The most common usage is in reference to perceptual reports which agree with the properties of the environment as determined by conventional physicalistic measurement. Such perceptual reports are labeled as "veridical perception."

Visual angle. The angle subtended by an object in the visual field at the nodal point of the eye. (Actually, the front surface of the cornea is the most frequently used point.) Visual angle is directly proportional to the size (e) of the object (e.g., length, diameter) and inversely proportional to the distance (R) of the object along the line of regard. It is expressed in the form of a simple equation: $\theta = e/R$ in radians or $\theta = 57.3e/R$ in degrees.

Name Index

Page numbers in italics are reference citations

Subject Index

Acquired distinctiveness,
amount of practice, 126–127, 129–131
correction for chance, 131–132
in everyday life, 297–298
implicit labeling, 135–137
and meaningfulness of stimuli, 130
model of, 122
number of labels, 128
and observation effects, 139
paired-associates pretraining, 127–129, 137–138
stimulus complexity, 130
summary of findings, 133–134
Adaptation, classic studies, 5, 187
ADC (acquired distinctiveness of cues), 121
Age, as an independent variable, 258
methodological considerations, 261–263
Association between depth cues, strength of, 174
Assumed size, effect, on perceived distance, 33–40
formula for prediction of, 36
Attention, behavioristic analysis of, 157
conditioning of, 157–160
Auditory localization following exposure to prisms, 240, 244–246
Autism, hypothesis of, 144

Autokinetic motion, definition, 69
determinants of, 69
effect of movement connotation, 69–71

Balloon demonstration, 167
Binocular rivalry, definition, 181
determinants of, 181
involving rivalrous contents, 181–184
Body height and distance perception, 263–265

Centration factor, 158
decentration, 158
Clinical concentric method of obtaining judgments, 268
Conceptual scale of distance, 90
training of, 90–92
Conflict and adaptation, 250–251, 298–301
Confusion errors in recognition of form, 273–277
as a function of age, 276
as a function of transformation, 275–277
Conscious correction as account of adaptation, 235
Constructed-history approach to study of development, 281–282
Converging operations, definition, 11
illustrations of, 12–13
need for, 106, 161–162